WHEN RULES CHANGE

STUDIES IN LAW AND ECONOMICS

A series edited by William M. Landes and J. Mark Ramseyer

PREVIOUSLY PUBLISHED

Politics and Property Rights: The Closing of the Open Range in the Postbellum South, by Shawn Everett Kantor

More Guns, Less Crime: Understanding Crime and Gun Control Laws, by John R. Lott, Jr.

Japanese Law: An Economic Approach, by J. Mark Ramseyer and Minoru Nakazato

Are Predatory Commitments Credible?: Who Should the Courts Believe? by John R. Lott, Jr.

When Rules Change

An Economic and Political Analysis of Transition Relief and Retroactivity

Daniel Shaviro

THE UNIVERSITY OF CHICAGO PRESS

CHICAGO AND LONDON

DANIEL SHAVIRO is professor of law at New York University and author of *Do Deficits Matter?*

The University of Chicago Press, Chicago 60637
The University of Chicago Press, Ltd., London
© 2000 by The University of Chicago
All rights reserved. Published 2000
Printed in the United States of America

09 08 07 06 05 04 03 02 01 00   1 2 3 4 5
ISBN: 0-226-75114-7 (cloth)

Library of Congress Cataloging-in-Publication Data

Shaviro, Daniel N.
    When rules change : an economic and political analysis of transition relief and retroactivity /
Daniel Shaviro.
        p.   cm.
    ISBN 0-226-75114-7 (cloth : alk. paper)
    1. Taxation—Law and legislation—Economic aspects—United States. 2. Law
reform—Economic aspects—United States. 3. Retroactive law—Economic aspects—
United States. 4. Law reform—Economic aspects. 5. Retroactive laws—Economic
aspects. I. Title.
KF6219.S53   2000
336.2'00973—dc21   99-29116
                                                                                    CIP

⊗ The paper used in this publication meets the minimum requirements of the American National
Standard for Information Sciences—Permanence of Paper for Printed Library Materials, ANSI
Z39.48-1992.

For Pat, Peter, and Charles

ACKNOWLEDGMENTS

For their comments on earlier drafts or portions thereof, I am grateful to
Joseph Bankman, David Bradford, Barry Friedman, William Gentry, Louis
Kaplow, Andrew B. Lyon, Richard Posner, and David Weisbach.

I also received valuable comments upon discussing this book at work-
shops sponsored by the American Enterprise Institute, Georgetown Law
School, Harvard Law School, Law and Society Association, National Bu-
reau of Economic Research, New York University School of Law, Princeton
Tax Club of New York, State University of New York at Buffalo School of
Law, and University of Chicago Law School.

ONE

INTRODUCTION

Suppose Congress repealed the income tax deduction for home mortgage interest. Should owners of existing homes be granted transition relief, such as a grandfather rule permitting them to continue deducting interest for the life of their outstanding mortgages or homes? Would the analysis be any different if the deduction were newly enacted rather than repealed, thus potentially giving homeowners a transition gain rather than loss?

Similarly, if Congress "privatized" Social Security by creating a system of mandatory individual retirement accounts in lieu of existing payroll taxes and benefit formulas, to what extent should current workers' and retirees' expectations under the rules now in place be protected? When Congress amended the Clean Air Act to create tradeable permits for the emission of sulfur dioxide, should it have imposed a transition loss on existing polluters by conducting an auction or otherwise charging for the permits, rather than distributing the permits for free?

These questions provide but a few illustrations of a broader policy issue. A change in government rules often has retroactive effects, in that its impact on particular individuals depends on decisions that they made before its adoption—decisions they might have altered had they correctly anticipated the change. Or the rule change can have transition winners and losers wholly without regard to past decisions, as when it alters the tax consequences of an immutable characteristic such as gender or year of birth. These retroactive and other transition effects can be mitigated through a variety of devices, such as compensating losers and taxing winners, delaying full implementation, and adopting "grandfather" rules that exempt particular persons, assets, or transactions from the new rule. Or transition effects can simply be allowed to stand, through full immediate implementation of the new rule. How does one decide which transition policy is best?

This book seeks to reframe the scholarly transition debate, and possibly even influence political practice, through two distinct contributions. The first is to advance economic understanding of the transition issues posed by rule changes generally, albeit with particular reference to issues in the federal income tax. The second is to integrate the economics with a political science analysis that is distinctive to the present federal income tax system, in order to propose norms that should generally guide transition practice in this area. Ultimately, it is perhaps an aesthetic question which aspect is more important. The first contributes more to basic theoretical understanding of transition issues, but the second offers a concrete policy payoff for those who accept certain controversial premises that underlie my tax policy views.

A. ECONOMICS

Retroactive effects are often unavoidable. When taxes increased in 1942 to help pay for World War II, this was bound to affect people who had chosen high-wage careers. What is more, retroactive effects are often clearly desirable because they encourage useful anticipation. If American steel companies began increasing their capacity in 1940, hoping for increased public demand if we entered World War II, that would have been all to the good. At other times, however, retroactivity may simply yield undesirable uncertainty or penalize past decisions that are best not discouraged. At the limit, an inability to commit to the retention of current policy would prevent the government from credibly promising to honor its contracts or refrain from expropriating all wealth within its reach.

If one thing is certain, it is that our intuitions and practices regarding transition problems vary with the context. In some cases, such as Congress's annually changing discretionary spending or the Federal Reserve Board's changing monetary policy and thereby affecting the value of various financial assets, we take it for granted that no transition relief is necessary. In other cases, such as enacting *ex post facto* legislation to criminalize someone's past acts or repudiating an explicit government contract, we take it for granted that retroactivity is undesirable. A wide range of cases are intermediate, and transition policy is therefore controversial.

Writing about tax transitions, however, has tended to suggest that the answer is close to unitary. In the legal literature, scholarly debate has had three discernible stages. An initially prevailing "old view" held that when income tax rules favoring a particular investment are repealed, transitional relief in the form of grandfathering should generally be provided. This ostensibly was both fair, because it protected investors' reliance interests based on expecting legal continuity, and efficient, because it reduced the need for costly precautions against the risk of tax law change. Then, celebrated articles by Michael Graetz (1977) and Louis Kaplow (1986) partly displaced the old view in legal academe—if not tax practice (Green 1997)—in favor of a "new view" that transitional relief and, in particular, grandfathering protection upon the repeal of tax preferences generally should not be provided. Graetz argued that investors ought to be encouraged to anticipate policy changes that were socially desirable (as he assumed most were). Those who, in effect, bet against change could not rightly complain if they happened to lose. Kaplow made a similar argument that was expressly limited to certain cases of desirable policy change but that was widely interpreted more broadly. Recent years, however, have seen movement back towards the old view, through renewed advocacy of transitional relief upon the repeal of income tax preferences (Shachar 1984; Ramseyer and Nakazato 1989; Goldberg 1994; Logue 1996).

The economic literature concerning retroactive tax law changes has been similarly inconclusive. Two main traditions loosely resembling the legal literature's old and new views have predominated, but they have largely ignored each other, as well as the intuition that the value of reliance may vary with the context. The tradition that parallels the old view posits a normative requirement of "horizontal equity" that is violated by surprise changes in the tax rules, creating a ground for compensation that needs to be traded off against the welfare gains from immediate full implementation of a desirable reform (Feldstein 1976; Zodrow 1981). The tradition that parallels the new view treats surprise as affirmatively desirable, as a means of imposing taxes that are conditioned on people's past decisions (such as whether to work and save) yet that ostensibly prompt zero behavioral response in the future as well as the past (Auerbach and Kotlikoff 1983; 1987).[1]

The unresolved gap between old and new views reflects the ineluctable nature of the underlying dilemma: choosing between the competing virtues of policy stability on the one hand and policy flexibility on the other. Reducing retroactivity promotes stability; increasing it promotes flexibility. The case for stability dates back at least to Adam Smith's maxim that the only good tax is an old tax; the case for flexibility is made anew each time anyone argues for a particular change in the law.

The literature's tendency towards "corner solutions," in which tax rule change ostensibly justifies transitional adjustment either almost always or almost never, should excite skepticism. While arguing for the value of stability or flexibility (whichever one happens to prefer) is easy enough, one should recognize that both have value, and that transition issues turn not so much on *which* of them is important as on *when* each is more important.

One cannot sensibly base arguments for a particular tax transition practice on unsupported analogies to other settings where most people would agree that protection against rule change either is (as with government contracts) or is not (as with monetary policy) justified. Rather, one needs to define the generic transition problem and then evaluate it in different settings based on an explicit normative framework.

This book's framework is utilitarianism. However, one need not be a utilitarian to accept most of the analysis, so long as one agrees that people's well-being is important. Methodologically, the key assumption, drawn from neoclassical economics, is rational expectations. That is, I generally assume that people anticipate future government policy with approximate accuracy. However, the claim is not that people predict future government policy with any precision (which would be absurd) but, rather, that one should not assume their expectations to reflect systematic error in any particular direction unless one has a good explanation for the prevalence of that kind of error.

Thus, on the occasions when incentives for new investment are increased (or, equivalently, reduced), one's benchmark prediction would be that investors, on average, expect just about the amount of change that actually occurs, even if each time they collectively err on either the "high" or the "low" side. Or suppose that the government's preannounced policy is one of taxing capital lightly, but that every now and then it enacts an overnight capital levy. Over time, we should expect people to observe the real level of capital taxation with approximate accuracy—sometimes being caught by surprise, but other times anticipating a capital levy that does not materialize—unless we can explain why, on balance, either under- or overestimation should prevail. Systematic error is not ruled out; it simply needs to be explained.

Most prior work concerning tax transitions assumes at least implicitly, but generally without explanation, that people systematically err in the direction of assuming the perpetual retention of current law. It also assumes without sufficient explanation that capital levies, if not fully anticipated in advance, provide the tax collector with a "free lunch"—even though this requires investors to ignore the levies' evidentiary value concerning the government's true long-term tax policy, and thus to be permanently fooled by events that occur in broad daylight. Unexplained departures from the rational expectations benchmark prevail even more in economic than in legal scholarship, as we will see in examining the influential work of Alan Auerbach and Laurence Kotlikoff (1983; 1987).[2]

Applying rational expectations to transition problems makes clear the usefulness of considering the incentive effects that a retroactive outcome would have had if preannounced. This approach generally has not been tried, based on the mistaken view that any behavior receiving a retroactive burden or benefit is fixed, since it took place in the past. Retroactivity has been treated as raising a one-shot distributional problem, perhaps constrained by horizontal equity concerns but otherwise in the realm of the free lunch. The inadequacy of such a view becomes clear once one considers how often tax or other rules change and transition issues therefore arise. In standard game-theoretic terms, retroactive policy self-evidently presents a repeated rather than a one-shot game.

The expanded use of rational expectations is one of this book's three main contributions to the economic analysis of transition problems.[3] Second, I decompose the issues proposed by retroactivity into two distinct elements: what I call the "transition risk" and the "retroactive tax." Each element has unique implications, but I argue that the latter is the crucial one in situations where people can, with sufficient ease, achieve preferred risk positions through their own efforts.

In the legal literature, it is a commonplace that potential retroactivity exposes taxpayers and other investors to a risk concerning the future tax consequences of their current decisions. When I make an investment, I may know its tax treatment today, but I can only surmise what its tax treatment will be tomorrow. Thus, discussion is often in terms of whether or not this transition risk ought to be mitigated and, if ineluctable, who ought to bear it. Yet one must distinguish between the element of pure *variance* if future policy is uncertain, and that of *bias* or *asymmetry* if the expected value of relevant possible changes has a particular direction. A risk of change that is biased or asymmetric implies not only variance but also an expected value of positive or negative change in long-term tax burdens that should affect distribution and resource allocation today, even though nothing has yet been enacted, in the absence of expected transitional adjustment that would prevent it from having retroactive consequences.

A useful illustration is provided by municipal bonds, the interest on which is currently tax exempt. Suppose that all taxpayers have marginal tax rates of 20 percent that people believe will remain fixed forever, and that grandfathering or other transitional adjustment for old assets definitely will not be offered if the tax law changes. The only possible changes in the taxation of the bonds, each of which is equally likely, involve making them either fully taxable or doubly exempt (such that, for each $1 of bond interest that one received, one would actually *reduce* one's taxable income by a dollar).

For analytical convenience, suppose the following time sequence: at time 0 (T_0), people believe that the taxation of municipal bonds will never change. At T_1, they learn that a coin will be tossed at T_2 to determine whether the bonds should be made fully taxable or doubly exempt. After the coin toss, the tax treatment of the bonds will again be expected to remain fixed forever—except insofar as investors draw broader lessons after T_2 about the society's general steady state and transition policies.

Under these circumstances, an investor who holds a perpetual municipal bond paying $10 per year learns at T_1 that he faces a considerable transition risk, since after T_2 the bond's annual after-tax yield will be either $8 or $12. Risk aside, however, the prospect of the coin toss has no effect at T_1 on the value of the bond to him or anyone else. Despite the creation of new uncertainty, the mean expected future tax rate on the bond, like the known current tax rate, is still zero. (The outcome of the coin toss will, however, provide new information that has a direction or bias, if only as one datum concerning the long-term "honesty" of the coins that Congress tosses to decide on rule changes.)

Now suppose instead that the coin toss at T_2 will determine whether the interest exemption should be repealed or retained (rather than expanded). Now, at T_1 the taxpayer faces not only a new transition risk but also a retroactive tax—more precisely, an expected future tax on the bond income that differs from the current tax, in this case by being 10 percent higher (given the one-half chance of imposing a 20 percent tax on the interest). Even though nothing concrete has yet happened, the change in information between T_0 and T_1 has reduced the bond's value by 10 percent (ignoring time value considerations), thus affecting investment decisions even by risk-neutral taxpayers. Accordingly, no matter what ultimately happens at T_2, behavior will be different between T_1 and T_2 than between T_0 and T_1 by reason of the changed information and the practice of not granting transition relief. Perhaps most pertinently, new bond issues will have to offer a higher pretax yield relative to their issue prices between T_1 and T_2 than previously, even though no new rule has yet been enacted and perhaps none will ever be. In addition, the actual outcome may again affect expectations after T_2.

Presumably, when people observe a significant possibility of a rule change and have any particular information about the factors bearing on it, the case of pure symmetry, where the prospects in each direction have precisely equal expected value, is only a rare coincidence, akin to tossing a coin such that it lands poised on its edge. Thus, bias or asymmetry is of central importance to the analysis of rule changes. This concern roughly generalizes to determining what one thinks about the retroactive taxes that will ultimately be imposed in the absence of transitional adjustment. From a rational expectations standpoint, actual outcomes provide the best initial benchmark for determining what taxes people will anticipate beforehand, as well as remember afterwards.

Some clarifications about the term *retroactive taxes* may be in order. Retroactive taxes can be either positive or negative, both absolutely and in relation to the taxes that would have been imposed had the rules remain unchanged. A transfer or subsidy is a negative tax, rather than something belonging to a different realm. Moreover, retroactive taxes should be thought of in terms of economic benefit and burden, rather than just with reference to the amounts shown as due on various tax returns. They thus are equally posed by rule changes that are not classified as belonging to the "tax system." Burden includes the excess burden that results from people's costly tax avoidance behavior. Price changes may cause economic incidence to differ from nominal incidence. Indeed, some of the retroactive burden imposed by price shifts has little to do with tax payments as such. Consider the retroactive tax (in my usage) on individuals who first acquire the knowledge and experience needed to practice tax law and then lose the economic value of their expertise due to the repeal of the income tax.

This brings us to this book's third main contribution to the economic analysis of transition problems. In evaluating the merits of imposing retroactive taxes, legal scholarship in particular often either assumes (Graetz 1977) or mainly emphasizes (Kaplow 1986) cases where the desirability of the retroactive tax turns directly on that of the policy change that gave rise to it. Thus, upon ungrandfathered repeal of the municipal bond preference, the desirability of the retroactive tax on bondholders may depend on that of the new policy. After all, if one dislikes subsidies for borrowing by state and local governments, then inducing people to anticipate repeal even before it occurs is presumably a good thing, risk aside, for the same reasons that repeal is desirable prospectively. Similarly, if one dislikes repeal of the bond preference prospectively, then one probably should dislike the retroactive tax. For cases like this, where the retroactive tax just extends the reach of the prospective or steady-state new policy, I use the term *policy change retroactive taxes*. Despite its relative prominence in the literature, however, this turns out to be merely a special case of retroactive taxation. In other cases, the desirability of a retroactive tax turns on factors wholly distinct from the steady-state merits of the new rule that gives rise to it. The distinction between policy change and other retroactive taxes turns out to be crucial to the lucid evaluation of tax (and other) transitions.

For an example of a non–policy change retroactive tax, consider the example where repeal of the income tax destroyed the value of tax lawyers' specialized expertise. In that case, at least from an incentive standpoint, anticipation was desirable whether or not repeal of the income tax was good policy. After all, even if the income tax ought to have been kept, once it was repealed the tax lawyers' practice skills lost economic value. If prospective income tax lawyers were promised transition relief (such as full compensation for their lost earnings) in the event of repeal, they would have an incentive to disregard the prospect of repeal when choosing their careers, thus potentially inducing wasteful overinvestment in this area of specialization. More generally, the societal costs of reallocating resources in the economy in response to a new rule may tend to be reduced if people must bear the consequences of any bets regarding future rules that are implicit in their allocative choices regarding the investment of their human or other capital.

In practice, there is little prospect that income tax lawyers would be offered such compensation.[4] Yet income tax changes frequently give rise to a very different type of non–policy change retroactive tax, relief from which has a greater prospect of being politically feasible and perhaps even desirable. Tax law changes often create a prospect of imposing what I call *accounting change retroactive taxes.*

Any given tax rule can conveniently be described as having two types of attributes: those that are policy relevant and those that are merely accounting conventions. By policy relevant, I mean the features that decide how tax burdens actually are distributed between taxpayers and allocated between economic activities at equilibrium. For example, the municipal bond preference favors municipal bonds relative to various other financial instruments. By accounting conventions, I mean the details of exactly how, when, and from whom the taxes that give rise to these relative burdens are collected, given (and holding constant) the taxes' real allocative and distributive features. Thus, the municipal bond preference happens to be provided to bondholders rather than to issuers—a point that likely would have no effect on economic incidence if all bondholders were in the same marginal rate bracket. It also happens to be provided in annual increments throughout the life of the bond. In principle, tax benefits of equal present value at the time of issuance could instead be provided up front, as by permitting bondholders to expense the cost of the bonds and then include the interest income,[5] or at the back end, through a tax refund with interest at the time of bond redemption by the issuer. Thus, the current tax rule for municipal bonds can be decomposed into (1) its policy content of favoring the bonds relative to privately issued, but otherwise comparable, financial instruments, and (2) its mere accounting content of accomplishing this policy via a tax benefit for bondholders (rather than issuers or anyone else) with a particular time sequence (dictated by the bond's stream of interest payments and the bondholder's marginal tax rate during the years when these payments are received).

Tax enactments often involve mere accounting changes in addition to any real policy change—often without the distinction being clearly understood. The retroactive tax that would result in the absence of transitional adjustment often turns, at least in substantial part, on the mere accounting change. The desirability of taxpayer anticipation of an accounting change is unrelated to that of any accompanying policy change.

Thus, suppose we shift from an income tax in which capital outlays, such as the cost of purchasing a rental building, are deducted over a series of years, to a consumption tax in which they are expensed (that is, deducted in the year when they were incurred). The real difference between the systems goes to the present value of deductions, which is greater under the consumption tax because the same total dollar amount is deducted sooner. Yet the different timing, as distinct from the time value, of deductions under the two steady-state systems is a mere administrative detail. There is nothing inherent to consumption taxation about placing all cost recovery in the first year, or to income taxation about spreading cost recovery over a period of years. One would still have a consumption tax if one provided deductions with the present value of expensing across the time period indicated by economic depreciation, such as by providing interest compensation for deferral relative to expensing (Bradford 1998). Likewise, one would still have an income tax if cost recovery, in an amount that had the same present value as economic depreciation, was provided in the year when an investment outlay was made (Auerbach and Jorgenson 1980).

The fact that the current income tax is paid "early" (because deductions are taken late) while a conventional cash-flow consumption tax is paid "late" (because deductions are taken early) is merely a matter of accounting convenience, serving to simplify the needed computations under each system. While the choice between "early" and "late" cost recovery with the same present value matters little in a steady-state world where all tax rules remain the same over time, it suddenly becomes important if Congress, while making a policy change between income and consumption taxation, simultaneously makes the associated accounting change.

The one-time disappearance of the income tax basis (the tax system's record of outlays that qualify for eventual cost recovery but have not yet been deducted) from a "cold turkey" or untransitioned shift from income to consumption taxation has nothing to do with the policy difference between these two systems, and everything to do with the accounting change from early to late payment. If one liked the resulting capital levy, one could impose it within the income tax by simply wiping out all of the existing basis, with or without a prospective shift in the accounting rule. If one disliked it, one could avoid it in the shift to a consumption tax, either through explicit transition relief or by adopting an early-paid system, where deductions are deferred as under the income tax but with interest.

Nominal timing is only one example of a mere accounting detail of income tax rules that can have retroactive consequences when altered. Consider nominal liability, or how the parties to a transaction are required to allocate among themselves its net tax consequences. This detail is economically irrelevant so long as nominal prices adjust to reflect who is paying what. For example, suppose that wine initially sells for $10 a bottle, taxes aside, but is subject to a $5 excise tax that is due from the buyer upon leaving the store. Changing the law so that the seller now pays the tax upon ringing up the sale would presumably change the nominal price to $15 per bottle, but without making any allocative or distributional difference at equilibrium. It might, however, result in an accounting change retroactive tax in the fanciful case where the tax law changed just as a buyer was heading for the door.

The distinction between policy changes and accounting changes is particularly easy to make in the tax law because a rule's policy content is relatively easy to define, in terms of the present value of long-term tax burdens. However, the distinction between policy and accounting content can be made in other areas as well. For example, suppose that a country changes its currency, say, from green to red dollar bills. To cancel the old currency without permitting it to be exchanged for new currency would impose an accounting change retroactive tax, the desirability of which is unrelated to that of the currency change itself. Anyone holding green money at the moment of transition would lose, simply because of a change in which pieces of paper happened to be serving the fixed purpose of facilitating exchange transactions.

Or suppose that rules of environmental law governing the emission of a pollutant are revised (as for sulfur dioxide under 1990 amendments to the Clean Air Act) so as to provide for the issuance of tradeable permits. To the extent that a given company's right to emit pollutants remains unchanged, merely being newly evidenced by a permit, this is just an accounting change. Tradeability is a policy change, however—just as, under the income tax law, the present value of expected tax burdens would change if deductions were made tradeable (for example, to taxpayers in a higher marginal rate bracket than one's own).

From the standpoint of economic analysis of transition issues, one should keep in mind that the distinction between policy and accounting change retroactive taxes is just a means to the end of more clearly identifying and understanding the causation and incentive effects of particular retroactive taxes. Thus, returning to the tax law, when Auerbach and Kotlikoff (1987, 124) discuss what they call the steady-state welfare effects of switching from income to consumption taxation, it is worth knowing that their conclusions are conditioned on assuming an accounting change, from early to late payment, that has no analytic connection to the economics of either tax base, and that could be imposed or not without regard to whether the steady-state tax base changed (in addition to reflecting their "free lunch" view of capital levies). Sorting out the steady-state policy choice from the transition issue enables us to analyze each more rigorously. The debate concerning the choice between income and consumption taxation can focus on the actual difference between the two systems, which pertains to the tax treatment of the return to waiting, rather than emphasizing issues that have nothing to do with this. And the debate concerning the retroactive tax from wiping out the income tax basis can focus on the incentive effects of doing this periodically, with or without an accompanying policy change.

This book will show by repeated example just how significantly the distinction between policy change and other retroactive taxes can advance our understanding of transition issues. Nonetheless, there is something frustratingly incomplete about the analysis thus far. Consider the policy change retroactive tax that would be imposed by ungrandfathered repeal of the municipal bond preference. The understanding that supporters of the repeal should like, and opponents dislike, the incentive effects of the retroactive tax that would result without grandfathering, helps only so much. It offers them no common ground to resolve this dispute even if there are important things about which they agree. Such concerns may be eased, however, once economic analysis is supplemented by political science analysis, as I discuss next.

B. POLITICS

A descriptive theory of politics can aid transition policy in two main respects: by illuminating the forces that guide decision making in different areas, with possible implications for how much retroactive discretion is desirable; and by showing how transition practice may influence substantive political outcomes. As an example of the former, consider the "new view" claim that political decisions are generally for the good because they reflect new information or changes in public taste, suggesting that policy change retroactive taxes ought generally to be imposed (Graetz 1977). As an example of the latter, consider the claim in the literature on government takings that requiring, say, the highway authority to compensate me when it takes my land will improve its cost-benefit analysis of highway construction by requiring it to internalize the full resource costs of what it does (Blume, Rubinfeld, and Shapiro 1984; Fischel and Shapiro 1988).

The theory of politics deployed in this book emphasizes what I call problems of organization (such as interest group politics), information (such as fiscal illusion), and aggregation (such as random cycling between competing outcomes). The scope of these problems in different areas helps determine how well the political process works and what biases can be expected. One learns, for example, that Congress may be less prone to impose transition losses than administrative agencies are to impose uncompensated takings, because of differences in how interest group politics and fiscal illusion operate in the legislative and administrative arenas.

Problems of organization, information, and aggregation undermine any new view-type assumption that policy decisions are systematically for the good. Legislative tax politics suffers from unusually severe defects, owing to the combined effect of interest group politics, characterized by logrolling between concentrated interests, and fiscal illusion. The main source of fiscal illusion is what decision researchers call the "endowment effect," under which people systematically underweight opportunity costs relative to equivalent out-of-pocket costs. Due to the endowment effect, voters commonly draw an erroneous distinction (from the standpoint of their own material self-interest) between money that is never paid in to the Treasury, and money that is first paid in and then taken back out. This makes tax subsidies politically more popular than substantively identical programs that take the form of proposed direct spending. The fiscal illusion problem in tax politics leads to bad policy driven by both interest group politics and politicians' quest for appealing soundbites; and I argue that overall policy might improve if subsidies via the income tax were discouraged.

Awareness of the defects of legislative tax politics helps motivate the widespread scholarly consensus that a fixed and relatively comprehensive tax bas (CTB), under which same-period consumption or investment choices are treated as uniformly as possible, is preferable to a tax base that reflects political choices to favor some resource uses over others. (No similar consensus holds that, say, the allocation of federal spending between health care and national defense should remain fixed.) A CTB can be of either the income tax or the consumption tax genre, and recent research indicates that the real difference between these bases is surprisingly small (Bradford 1996; Gentry and Hubbard 1998). I conclude, therefore, that changes towards more uniform treatment of same-period consumption or investment choices are generally good; that changes away from such uniformity are generally bad; and that Congress's tax base changes generally, if equally likely to go in either direction, tend to be of random merit rather than systematically either good or bad.

This argument of political economy for a CTB norm matters to tax transition policy because of its implications for policy change retroactive taxes. One may want good but not bad changes to influence preenactment behavior. Thus, in the municipal bonds case, an advocate of the CTB norm might want expansion but not curtailment of the preference to be accompanied by grandfathering. Given, however, that Congress is unlikely to accept a transition regime that distinguishes between its "good" and "bad" changes (decided in light of a norm that it rejects), one needs to ask the "constitutional" question of what simple, general rules for tax transition, if sufficiently accepted as appealing norms to influence political behavior at the margin, would have good effects overall, even if not in each case. By "constitutional," I refer to a stable long-term rule or at least aspiration that constrains or at least influences political behavior, without necessarily being part of our formal constitutional law. The CTB norm is an example, since it clearly does not provide the right answer all of the time, yet it may improve Congress's decisions at the margin.

In this book, I argue that the main transition norms communicated by tax policy thinkers should be twofold. First, generally deny transitional adjustment in the case of policy change retroactive taxes. Second, generally provide transitional adjustment in the case of accounting change retroactive taxes. (These conclusions are not, however, generalizable, as I show with regard to the Clean Air Act and Social Security reform.)

The first of the two proposed norms would need little explanation under a "new view" belief that policy changes are generally for the good. Since I reject that belief, I would actually reverse this norm and propose instead that policy change retroactive taxes generally be eliminated through transition relief, if the norm were in fact a binding legal constraint, applied uniformly or at least consistently. After all, imposing even moderate transition risk seems pointless if anticipated tax changes have no systematically good effect on incentives or distribution. The crucial point, however, is that no norm for policy change retroactive taxes will in fact be applied with rigorous uniformity. The most that one can hope is to affect Congress's transition decisions at the margin, by influencing what has the prestige of being considered good policy (much as the CTB norm has helped define "tax reform"). From this perspective, I argue that the main effect of the new view-type norm I propose would be to reduce the asymmetric provision of transition relief mainly to those who lose when an income tax preference is repealed, rather than win when it is expanded. The norm might therefore slightly reduce over time the actual scope of preferences' application— assuming, as I argue in chapter 3, that Congress does not fully respond by simply "scaling" preferences to be nominally larger or more prepaid.

My argument for the second transition norm, favoring transitional adjustment to eliminate accounting change retroactive taxes, is more straightforward. Whereas a policy change may have a mean desirability of zero if it is equally likely to move towards or away from the CTB, the sheer randomness of accounting change retroactive taxes makes them undesirable on balance. In illustration, consider Kaplow's (1986, 613) hypothetical example of a change between calendar-year tax filing to the use of a June 30 fiscal year. Suppose that, in the absence of transitional adjustment, a change from calendar-year to fiscal-year filing would cause six months of income to be taxed twice, while the opposite change would cause six months of income to go tax free. Here, in contrast to a case of back-and-forth change to the municipal bond preference, anticipation of *both* directions of retroactive tax is undesirable, since they induce inefficient behavioral responses designed to move income or deductions into or out of the specially taxed six-month period.

The argument for each of my proposed transition norms can reasonably be challenged. Yet I will feel I have succeeded if readers accept the basic structure of my transition analysis and use it to argue for their own transition norms. Again, my aims are twofold—both to establish a basic framework for people with serious tax policy interests to use in thinking about transition issues; and to provide a concrete policy payoff in the form of specific transition norms concerning the income tax.

The book's structure is as follows. Chapter 2 sets forth my normative and methodological framework and describes the generic transition problem with its risk and tax elements. Chapter 3 provides the basic risk and tax analysis. Chapter 4 discusses problems of political choice, illustrating the analysis through two nontax examples (compensation for takings and pollution permits) before turning to tax politics. Chapter 5 discusses constitutional norms for tax policy in light of the defects of legislative tax politics, with brief reference as well to tax law changes that are imposed by a court or administrative agency. Chapters 6 through 9 evaluate a broad range of particular tax transition issues, such as changing income tax rates or preferences, adopting corporate integration, and shifting from income to consumption taxation. Chapter 10 looks at the transition issues raised by Social Security reform. Chapter 11 considers alternative transition relief mechanisms, such as compensation, grandfathering, and delaying full implementation. Chapter 12 provides a brief conclusion.

TWO

The Generic Problem of Transition between Government Rules

A. Establishing a Normative and Methodological Framework

1. Utilitarianism

Transition policy requires a framework for making normative judgments. I use the social welfare norm of utilitarianism, which seeks to maximize social welfare, defined as an additive function of everyone's subjective well-being. While intensely controversial, utilitarianism contains a widely accepted core, which is that people's subjective well-being matters. If I want to be as happy as possible and accept a certain type of moral equivalence between myself and others, then what I want (or at least one thing I want) should be for everyone collectively to be as happy as possible.

The step of going further to say that subjective well-being is all that matters makes one a welfarist (Sen 1982, 248). Some welfarists reject utilitarianism based on an egalitarian principle that assigns greater weight to the well-being of worse-off than better-off individuals. Yet this distinction, while important, can recede to the background when limited information prevents precise social welfare calculations under the alternative views. Even a pure utilitarian can have a strong preference for helping the worse-off at the expense of the better-off under certain empirical beliefs, such as that wealth has declining marginal utility and that people generally have similar utility functions (including rates of converting wealth into utility at different wealth levels). In contemporary terms, a utilitarian will likely conclude that Bill Gates should pay more tax than his housekeeper, who should pay more tax than a homeless person.

In this book, I expect neither my restricting morally relevant concerns to effects on subjective well-being nor my preferring utilitarianism to other welfarism to prevent the analysis from being pertinent to readers whose normative frameworks differ, so long as they agree that subjective well-being is important. Also tangential are the vast array of philosophical objections to utilitarianism (so long as one agrees that subjective well-being matters) and the rich welter of disputes about how to interpret it—for example, concerning whether utility should be defined hedonically or in terms of preference satisfaction. However, three nonwelfarist principles that have often been advanced in the transition setting deserve brief mention.

The first is the view that only Pareto improvements (which leave someone better off and no one worse off) should be adopted, thus making unanimous consent a requirement for new political decisions. This view requires more than that one simply be skeptical about the feasibility of making interpersonal utility comparisons when some people gain and others lose. Mere epistemic uncertainty should not imply *status quo* bias, since it makes the superiority of an existing state of affairs to a prospective one no clearer than the reverse. One possible basis for demanding Pareto improvement is a theory of Lockean (or other) entitlement, such as that of Robert Nozick (1974), under which respect for individual rights, held to extend to protecting all legal expectations, largely forecloses redistribution. My own view is that such a stance would be question begging, given the collective political framework that was necessary for current expectations to come into being, even if it were otherwise normatively appealing (as it is not to a utilitarian).

Alternatively, one could argue, along with the economists James Buchanan and Gordon Tullock, that a Pareto or unanimity rule is best in practice because it addresses defects in collective decision making by requiring all societal costs to be internalized by the decision makers (1962, 89–90). Here, the decision to permit only Pareto improvements (as even Buchanan and Tullock decline to do) could be a prudentially grounded application of utilitarianism, based on concerns of a sort that this book considers.

The second nonwelfarist principle that often arises in transition policy is horizontal equity, or the view that people who are relevantly equal should be treated equally. In tax-transfer policy, where vertical distributional concerns provide the reason for not simply levying a uniform head tax, this principle is generally not thought to be violated by progressive redistribution. Bill Gates is better off than his housekeeper, who in turn is better off than a homeless person; thus, the three of them are not relevantly equal. Suppose, however, that one further posits that other distinctions between individuals are generally irrelevant to the proper distribution of tax burdens. This may suggest that rule changes that yield unexpected winners and losers are offensive from the standpoint of horizontal equity (Feldstein 1976). Why should two people who would otherwise be equally well-off end up at different wealth levels just because, say, one happened to buy tax-exempt bonds that subsequently, and wholly unexpectedly, became taxable? (The argument assumes that the tax exemption is fully capitalized under the assumption that repeal is impossible, and thus that, ignoring the prospect of a rule change, tax-exempt bonds offer the same after-tax return as otherwise similar but taxable bonds.)

I reject horizontal equity because it imports concerns distinct from the well-being of individuals. Thus, at the limit, it can suggest making some people worse off and no one better off (Kaplow 1990 152 n. 13, 153 n. 26). Even short of that point, it puts a thumb on the scales of measuring welfare effects that is inappropriate if people's welfare is what one cares about. Note, however, that utilitarianism shares the implication against moving apart in wealth two people with similar utility functions featuring declining marginal utility, since the person who becomes wealthier will enjoy the gain less than the one who becomes poorer minds the loss. Utilitarians simply do not give the "equal treatment" principle separate, nonwelfarist weight, however inclined they may be to follow it in practice.

Even if one accepted horizontal equity as a nonwelfarist principle, its applicability to retroactive rule changes would be question begging without consideration of people's deliberate risk bearing. Suppose, for example, that a municipal bondholder purchased the bonds as a deliberate bet against a well-known possibility of repeal. Since "[n]o principle of ethics requires that Monte Carlo produce only winners" (Ramseyer and Nakazato 1989, 1160), and any decision with long-term consequences is at least an implicit bet about the future, this point can come close to eliminating the horizontal equity objection as such to retroactivity. What survives in its place is concern either about unsuccessful bettors—raising broader issues about the return to betting skill or luck in private markets without limitation to transition problems (Graetz 1977, 65)—or about forcing people to bet where they are risk averse. Yet utilitarians share these concerns, assimilating the former to distribution and giving the latter the rubric of undesired risk bearing.

While horizontal equity is often introduced as a fundamental tax principle with little explanation other than that it is "widely accepted" (Musgrave 1959, 160), its roots may lie in concern about the proper exercise of government power, which ought to reflect all people's interests (not just those of dominant political actors) and yet which involves coercion, thus preventing consent or revealed preferences from playing the same role as in a voluntary market transaction. These collective and coercive elements give rise to an abhorrence of invidious distinctions, or those in which one person's interests are preferred to another's for no good reason. Reliance on normatively irrelevant characteristics to allocate benefits and burdens may indicate that something unsavory is going on, thus in practice helping to make horizontal equity a useful metric for welfarists (Kaplow 1990, 149–50) on grounds that lie within my normative framework.

A final nonwelfarist argument in the tax transition area treats pre-existing tax rules, at least when they benefit the taxpayers who make a particular investment, as involving a government promise that the rules will remain in place. Repeal is thus analogized to breaking one's word after inducing detrimental reliance. The key assumption here, however, is that current tax rules actually are and should be viewed as promises. One could argue both that investors do not actually view tax rules this way given observed political practice, and that encouraging them to take such a view is undesirable (Graetz 1977, 74–79). After all, tax rules do not—perhaps for good reason—take the legal form of an express contractual commitment. In this book, I ignore nonwelfarist moral arguments that one should keep one's word as an end in itself, but consider the instrumental value of being able to generate reliance through firm promises. Chapter 3 discusses "transactional flexibility," or the ability to fine-tune risk allocations between parties, and argues that, while it supports making full reliance possible by having a class of definite commitments (mainly explicit contracts), it also supports maintaining a range of instruments that induce lesser reliance.

2. Rational Expectations Subject to the Possibility of Systematic Error

A second key element of this book's framework is merely methodological, in the sense of involving a baseline empirical assumption. This is the view that "the rationality assumption, applied routinely in microeconomics to explain the utility maximization of households and the profit maximization of firms, also applies to the formation of expectations" (Auerbach and Kotlikoff 1995, 358). Thus, when people have reason to care about future government policy, I generally assume that they make reasonably good use of available information that sheds light on it, including what the government has done in the past, its leaders' incentives or apparent beliefs, and the balance of political forces. Making such use implies educability and a capacity to avoid making the same error repeatedly.

A sophisticated rational expectations view recognizes that people have only limited information, to which they give only limited attention. It also accepts that they can err or be fooled in particular cases and that they have sufficiently limited foresight to be surprised frequently by new information. It holds only that people's use of the information available at any time should not too readily be presumed to involve systematic error in any predictable direction. One can make a systematic error claim that departs from assuming rational expectations, but it requires a decent explanation of why the error should be expected to emerge and persist.

To a considerable extent, rational expectations rests on modesty about the analyst's or policymaker's abilities, rather than on exaggerating those of the average economic actor. Even if people are not smart enough to exhibit perfect rationality given their aims, one who tries to predict how they will err, or to exploit their errors by persistently fooling them, faces obstacles given his own limited powers and knowledge. All too often, analysts who dismiss the rationality assumption fail to extend the dismissal to themselves or the policymaking process, and imagine that once they have produced a few counterexamples they can treat expectations as nonexistent or utterly fixed, rather than facing any obligation to propound and defend an alternative theory. Rational expectations need not apply in full for the "Lucas critique"—which holds that policy analysis risks serious error if it ignores expectations and people's learning capacity—to be worth keeping in mind (Auerbach and Kotlikoff 1995, 451).

A thumbnail intellectual history may help to place rational expectations in perspective. It was first explicitly set forth by John Muth (1961) with regard to price movements in private markets. In this setting, it continues to underlie the efficient capital markets hypothesis, which holds that stock prices sufficiently reflect available information about publicly traded companies to prevent one using this information to reap abnormally high profits (Malkiel 1989, 127). Explicit application to people's responses to government policy began with the rational expectations revolution in macroeconomics in the early 1970s, emerging in response to the failure of 1960s Keynesian fiscal policy to maintain the stable Phillips curve tradeoff between unemployment and inflation that leading Keynesians had promised.

Keynesian models of the 1960s had "assumed that workers and firms did not exploit available information and thereby would commit the same mistakes time after time. For instance, higher inflation was assumed to raise the willingness to work because workers were continually fooled into thinking that their real wage was higher than it was" (Barro 1996, 168). Accordingly, rather than urging that macroeconomic policy merely be countercyclical, seeking to ease both inflationary booms and recessionary busts, Keynesians now "counseled running stimulative [budget] deficits all the time, pending achievement of the elusive state of full employment" (Shaviro 1997, 55). By the early 1970s, however, problems of stagflation, or combined inflation and recession inconsistent with the claim of a stable Phillips curve, suggested that economic actors were catching on. They now expected the government to attempt to use surprise inflation as a tool for stimulus, and each other to act on the basis of inflationary expectations. The resulting inflationary cycle could not be broken until the late 1970s and early 1980s, when the government demonstrated that it had abandoned perpetual stimulus by sticking to a contractionary monetary policy through the course of a significant recession.

The breakdown of 1960s Keynesianism inspired economists such as Robert Lucas and Thomas Sargent to argue that *no* government policy based on outsmarting people in a predictable fashion was likely to work for long, if at all. Thus, not just perpetual stimulus, but any macroeconomic policy that consistently pursued rational aims such as easing the business cycle, would quickly break down given its predictability. For example, firms would swiftly learn to discount a surge in market demand for their goods at a given nominal price that resulted from expansion of the money supply, even if they could not contemporaneously observe the expansion. All that would be required was observable economic conditions that, given the government's known aims and track record, made expansion the logical policy for it to pursue.

The full-fledged rational expectations approach to macroeconomics has not entirely carried the day. Indeed, while its critique of 1960s Keynesianism is widely accepted, the mainstream view today is that loosely Keynesian countercyclical policy can enjoy modest success for a long time, and perhaps even indefinitely. However, this reflects countercyclical policy's short-term scope. A lag of just a few months in adjusting to new information that bears on what the government is likely to do may be enough for countercyclical policy to work. Rational expectations still holds over a longer term, however. Today, people correctly observe the current policy of pursuing macroeconomic stability whether it calls for easing up or tightening monetary controls, just as they correctly observed the preceding policy of attempting perpetual stimulus.

Now consider applying rational expectations to retroactive rule changes. Here, while surprise on particular occasions is inevitable given limited foresight, the view suggests that people will tend to observe accurately the government's true policy over time, thereby relegating proposals for the systematic exploitation of *ex post* surprise to the category of "proposals for perpetual-motion machines or free lunches" (Barro 1996, 124). Thus, suppose policymakers sought to reduce the impact of wealth taxation on work and savings decisions by imposing such taxes retroactively, not just through preannouncement. Or equivalently, suppose retroactive wealth taxation was positive for reasons of political economy without reflecting any deliberate plan. In the long run, the retroactive component of wealth taxation should be no less observable than that which was preannounced— just as a macroeconomic policy of permanent stimulus cannot be long concealed by limiting its contemporaneous observability.

Rational expectations suggests that, if one is thinking about the long run, the incentive effects of retroactive rule changes can fruitfully be analyzed by ignoring their retroactivity and treating them instead as if they were preannounced or otherwise fully anticipated. While the full anticipation assumption may not be literally true (i.e., a given change may be a partial or complete surprise), it provides a simple metric for incorporating the observation effects that are likely to arise afterwards. The act of imposing a retroactive surprise is a new data point that permits people to update their estimates of the government's long-term policy. Indeed, the greater the surprise, the stronger the lesson that prior expectations were mistaken, and perhaps that the government is prone to attempt surprise. This is the fundamental problem of asymmetric information. If policymakers exploit surprise because they know the most about their own intentions, they may be unable to forswear it persuasively when they would like to do so (at least, absent a specific commitment device that is credible, such as a constitutional amendment that is hard to repeal or ignore). Today's "surprise party" may therefore prompt tomorrow's "surprise non-party," resulting in compensating errors in anticipation of retroactive change that prevent the government from using surprise to its advantage on balance.

The strongest objection to rational expectations—whether as applied to transition problems or anything else—goes to the basic rationality assumption that is common in economics work generally. The growing field of what Richard Thaler (1991) calls "quasi-rational economics" attests to the experimental evidence from contemporary decision research that people frequently and persistently violate principles of rational maximizing behavior in a number of respects. Prominent examples, along with their possible relevance to transition problems, include the following:

Availability heuristic: People tend to "assess the frequency of a class or the probability of an event by the ease with which instances or occurrences can be brought to mind" (Tversky and Kahneman 1974, 1127). Both recent personal experience and salience may affect availability. Thus, people's estimates of the probability of a given retroactive rule change may be biased by their recent experiences, perhaps inducing underestimation if they have not been recently affected by a similar change and overestimation if they have. Or two equivalent changes may have different observation effects because one is more transparent or, for reasons of form, more violative of intuitions about "fairness."

Endowment effect and transactional accounting: People tend to over-weight out-of-pocket costs relative to pure opportunity costs such as fore-gone gains. Similarly, they think about sequences of events in terms of discrete transactions, and apply loss aversion at the transaction level rather than based on their overall positions (Kahneman and Tversky 1979). Accordingly, out-of-pocket losses and those that result in a perceived transaction loss may tend to be more salient than others, with consequences for availability.

Optimism bias: In a wide range of settings, people are overly optimistic about their prospects and abilities (Weinstein 1980). This may induce overestimation of how they are likely to fare on deliberate bets about retroactive rule changes, along with broader underanticipation of potential retroactive losses.

Overreaction to new information: People tend to underweight prior or base rate information concerning the probability of an event, while overweighting new information that bears on the same issue (Kahneman and Tversky 1973). Thus, various studies suggest that stock market prices may be systematically over-volatile because investors overreact to new information, such as by exaggerating the predictive value of a company's recent profit or loss performance (Shiller 1981; Thaler 1991, 258–309). This suggests that people may overestimate the predictive value for the future of recently adopted retroactive changes, along with recent political events (such as an isolated election result) bearing on the likelihood that a given change will be enacted.

Anchoring: In some settings, people give new information too little rather than too much weight. This occurs when the starting point in an estimating process, despite having been selected arbitrarily or under limited information, sufficiently sets the range for further deliberation to end up biasing final estimates (Tversky and Kahneman 1974, 1128). While experimental demonstrations of anchoring typically involve a finite inquiry with an endpoint, the evidence for it may suggest that, in more dynamic and ongoing settings, people continue using obsolete rules of thumb and struggle for a while to reconcile new information with them. As a result, people's responses to new information may tend to be lagged, as well as lumpy or discontinuous, rather than reflecting continual seamless adjustment.

These various biases plainly rebut a pure rational expectations view in particular cases. However, their significance for evaluating transition problems at an abstract or general level that focuses on the long run is more limited. Often, they have offsetting effects in a given case. Thus, suppose that optimism suggests underestimating the likelihood of an adverse retroactive change while availability encourages overestimation. It may be difficult for the observer to tell which bias is more significant. Even when specific cases have a clear direction of bias, broad groupings of them may involve similar offset. Thus, consider the suggestion from availability that a first-time controversial retroactive loss in a given area would be underestimated as it approached but would induce subsequent overestimation of its likely recurrence (presumably subsiding back to underestimation with the passage of time). Over the entire cycle, it might be hard to say whether under- or overestimation prevailed on average.

I conclude that, even though rational expectations fails to provide a fully accurate descriptive account of how people anticipate *ex ante* and respond *ex post* to retroactive rule changes, it nonetheless provides a useful benchmark. The more that one is considering the long run, and evaluating broad groupings of cases in which offsetting biases may be found, the more satisfactory a rational expectations view is likely to prove, at least compared to any obvious alternatives. I therefore will generally use it in evaluating transition problems, supporting the use of a "full anticipation" view of retroactive changes as a simpler proxy for "anticipation plus observation," but subject to rebuttal or modification in particular cases.

One could certainly make a decent argument that behavioral or "quasi-rational" economics should play a larger role in transition analysis than I am giving it. For example, detailed analysis might show that certain types of retroactive taxes tend to be consistently underestimated over time, while others tend to be consistently overestimated. This would tend to support an argument from efficiency for utilizing the former and avoiding the latter. Nothing in this book should be taken to reject such possibilities. I generally ignore them on the partly expositional ground that rational expectations provides a sufficiently good benchmark to be used, for want of anything better, in a general survey of transition problems of the sort that this book aims to provide. The rational expectations benchmark might well need significant adjustment in a particular case study.

At the same time, however, I should not be taken to be claiming too little. Anyone who believes that, as a general matter, retroactive taxes are underestimated in a predictable (and, by the government, exploitable) fashion may have reason to reject some of the analysis in this book.

For example, if retroactive wealth taxation—and, at the limit, periodic confiscation—is indeed a tool that in general permits the government to induce stable underestimation of the extent to which it actually taxes wealth, then that tool has advantages that I will be overlooking. Yet those (such as Auerbach and Kotlikoff, 1987) who view retroactive wealth taxation as efficient have offered no arguments from behavioral economics in support of that view—as opposed to designing models in which people are simply assumed to expect that preannounced policies will henceforth prevail and that observed transition decisions will not be repeated. I will be proceeding on the assumption that, until such a case for systematic error is made, the rational expectations benchmark generally applies to retroactive taxation across the board.

This is hardly an eccentric or unusual way to proceed in basic economic analysis of general scope. Analysis of prospective taxation, no less than that of retroactive taxation, must ultimately deal with the possibility that the incentives people actually perceive differ from those a rational actor would detect. The difference is simply that, in the prospective arena, rational expectations has appeared sufficiently obvious as an initial benchmark for its general applicability to be assumed rather than stated, thus reducing the attention that it attracts. Retroactivity should be no different unless one can show, with specific reference to behavioral economics, why it is different.

B. Defining Rule Changes, Retroactivity, and Transition Gains and Losses

Transition becomes an issue when government (or other) authorities apply different rules to different periods, and people's current rights, opportunities, or obligations therefore change. For example, in one year I can keep 70 percent of my salary after paying income tax, but then the tax rate increases and the next year I can keep only 60 percent. Or one day I have the right to live in my house, but the next day I must leave because a highway is coming.

In an American-style political system, such rule changes can arise in various ways. The legislature may pass a new law. Administrative or judicial authorities may issue a new decision that does not merely restate settled law. A discretionary government practice may change, such as annual defense spending levels or the discount rate that the Federal Reserve Bank charges banks. Or a government authority can embark on a specific exercise of a general power, as when a local highway authority uses its preexisting takings power to requisition someone's property. Rule changes can also arise without a new decision, if the original decision specified that different rules would apply in different periods.

The frequent association between rule changes and new decisions creates an association between rule change and uncertainty. A rule that was fixed forever would presumably be well understood, at least once it had been observed for a while. Where new decisions are possible, however, it is hard to know what rule will apply in the future. People's future decisions, whether made in the government setting or anywhere else, resemble the weather in being hard to predict beyond the very short term.

Even without any uncertainty, people's behavior can be importantly influenced by differences in the rules applying to them in different periods. For example, I may be inclined to shift my labor to years when I can keep 70 percent, rather than 60 percent, of what I earn. Or my decisions regarding maintenance or improvement of a house may be affected by the expected duration of my right to stay there, and by what compensation or liability rule will apply to me upon my departure.

Likewise, even without the ultimate occurrence of any rule change, the existence of interim uncertainty can influence behavior. Since asset prices reflect expectations about future rules, municipal bond prices would presumably decline if imminent repeal of the tax preference (without transition relief) were considered a significant possibility. People may also may respond purely to the magnitude of a particular uncertainty—for example, through risk-avoiding or risk-preferring behavior, or adjustments designed to offset a particular risk that they would otherwise bear.

Absent a transition policy of compensating losses and taxing away gains, any nontrivial rule change—or even a mere change in expectations about future rules—has transition winners and/or losers. In practice, most rule changes result in both. Yet, even when the excess of gains over losses makes full compensation of the losers theoretically possible, any such course may face substantial or even insuperable transaction costs.

When the transition consequences of a rule change depend on people's past decisions that might have been different had they correctly predicted it—thus implying a government decision after they acted—one can describe the government decision as applying "retroactively." The rule change has, in effect, reached back into the past to alter the consequences of private decisions that preceded it. This commonly happens even when the change is nominally prospective rather than nominally retroactive—for example, when it only changes future years' tax rules, not past years', but thereby alters the value of assets acquired in the past (Graetz 1977, 49).

In two circumstances, a rule change has transition winners or losers but no retroactive effects. The first is that where it was known in advance, as in the case where an initial political decision that everyone knew would not be changed set tax rates at 30 percent for one year and 40 percent for the next year. The second is that of a rule change that affects people based purely on who they are, without regard to their past decisions. One example would be enacting a tax or transfer scheme that relied on immutable characteristics such as gender, year of birth, or innate ability (assuming that such a thing exists and can be observed). Often, a rule change has distributional effects that include but are not limited to retroactive effects. For example, the burden from raising the tax rate on earnings may fall both on high earners' ability and on their past decisions to develop this ability.

The distributional choices posed by a transition policy always lie between individuals. Sometimes, however, a choice is described as lying between imposing costs on individuals or on the government. Thus, it has been argued in support of takings compensation that "forcing the government to pay for the resources it gets promotes efficiency" (Fischel and Shapiro 1988, 269). And grandfathering upon the repeal of tax preferences has been urged, by analogy to the arguments for honoring explicit contracts, as a way of limiting "government opportunism," or the temptation to try to get things without paying for them (Logue 1996, 1145). However, given that a government, like a private corporation, is merely a legal entity that cannot itself experience benefit or burden, these statements are somewhat misleading. Having the government compensate resource owners merely changes the identity of the individuals who bear the resource costs. The claim that government payment as such independently matters can be meaningful only in the context of politics, where it may express a view about how different payment rules affect government decision makers' incentives (an issue that I address in chapter 4).

C. Decomposing Transition Consequences into a Risk and a Tax

In the transition literature, it is commonly recognized that the prospect of transition gain or loss, when uncertain, exposes taxpayers to a risk (Feldstein 1976; Graetz 1977; Kaplow 1986). This can be misleading, however. Without more, the word *risk* encourages one to think merely about variance in possible future outcomes, which matters *ex ante* to affected individuals only insofar as they have particular risk preferences, such as risk aversion at a given level of intensity. While variance can be important, what often matters even more is the systematic difference, if any, between a current rule and the mean anticipated future rule given the range of possible future decisions.

In some cases, the prospect of a rule change may be entirely symmetric. Suppose that I am considering a high-wage career such as law practice, and that the rate at which my earnings will be taxed in the future is important to my decision. The current tax rate for high earners is, say, 40 percent, but I know that it might change. If I have no particular reason to assume any difference in the expected value of possible rate increases as compared to rate reductions, then the mean anticipated future tax rate that I should take into account, like the present tax rate, is 40 percent. I face a problem of pure variance, which matters to me only insofar as I am risk preferring or risk averse.

Now suppose instead that I believe that the prospect of rate reduction has the greater expected value. While I still face variance, I also face an important asymmetry in the direction of expected rule change. I can now expect, on balance, to keep a higher percentage of my lifetime earnings than the current 40 percent rate suggests. At the margin, this asymmetry is likely to steer me towards choosing the high-wage career.

The extent of expectational asymmetries therefore has important allocative and distributional consequences that make it critical to transition analysis. Yet, before examining asymmetry's likely significance in practice, it is useful to start by noting a big-picture sense in which symmetry generally prevails.

In a sense that must be carefully delineated, the overall transition gains from a rule change inherently equal the overall transition losses. Merely changing the allocation of rights and obligations within the society does not, in a static sense (that is, ignoring behavioral responses to the change) alter total societal wealth. A society with three buildings yesterday will still have three today, even if the government seizes one and hands it to a new owner. Or in terms of taxes and government outlays, if a new political decision means that one person will henceforth get more or pay less than under the prior policy, then (all else equal) someone else must pay more or get less. This follows from simple arithmetic given the government's intertemporal budget constraint, under which the present value of all inflows must equal that of all outlays over the long run (Auerbach and Kotlikoff 1995, 232).

Several important qualifications to this principle are necessary, however. One is that dynamic or behavioral effects can cause transition gains to differ from losses, leading to an overall wealth change. Suppose that eliminating tariffs unlocks previously stifled gains from trade, thereby yielding gains in excess of losses and making a Pareto improvement theoretically possible. A second qualification is that a transferred right or power may go to someone whose subjective value for it differs from that of the prior owner. My house may go to someone who values it less than I do, although absent transaction costs, we can overcome this by his selling it back to me. Or a dollar may be transferred between individuals to whom it has different subjective value. A third qualification is that the rule change may actually involve altering society's stock of resources—for example, by converting the property that contained my house into a section of road that may be worth either more or less than my house was. Finally, even if overall gains equal losses, retroactive gains need not equal retroactive losses. Thus, suppose that current voters receive a tax cut, increasing the return from their past decisions to develop their income-earning abilities, in exchange for a tax increase on future generations, whose members have not yet made any decisions.

Retroactive symmetry matters, to the extent that it holds, because it indicates that *ex ante*, everyone collectively faces a symmetric risk of gain or loss from rule change. Until one has more information, rule changes are as likely to make things better as worse for any given individual. Transition therefore does not primarily involve loss problems, as the literature and politics—presumably reflecting the endowment effect—suggest. Still, that which holds globally (even insofar as it does) need not hold locally. For any person, asset, or activity, and indeed for any limited set of rule changes that one is considering, there may be not only variance but also systematic direction.

A fuller version of the municipal bond example from chapter 1 may help to explain this issue's parameters and significance. Suppose that in perpetuity the tax rate is a flat 20 percent and the interest rate (in perfectly competitive financial markets) is 10 percent. The after-tax return from taxable bonds is therefore 8 percent. At T_0, when the municipal bond interest exemption is expected to remain in place indefinitely, a state or local government that wishes to sell a municipal bond offering $10 per year can command an issue price of $125, since at that price the after-tax return equals the 8 percent offered by taxable bonds. By contrast, if municipal bond interest were taxable, the issuer would command an issue price of only $100.

At T_1, new information emerges suggesting that, at T_2 (the next day), a coin will be tossed to determine whether and, if so, how the taxation of municipal bonds should change. For computational simplicity, suppose for the moment that after T_2 there will be no further rule change pertaining to municipal bonds, that the bonds are perpetual (they have no maturity date but instead pay $10 per year forever), and that the market offers no risk premia. Assuming no grandfathering in the event of a rule change for municipal bonds, their value and issue price will remain $125 at T_1 if the expected T_2 coin toss will either double or repeal the preference. Here there is retroactive gain-loss symmetry with respect to the bonds, since their taxation is expected to change but in no systematic direction. Thus, ignoring questions of risk, the new information at T_1 has no impact on bond values or anyone's behavior between T_1 and T_2.

Now suppose instead that the expected T_2 coin toss will determine whether the preference should be repealed or retained (rather than repealed or doubled). This creates retroactive gain-loss asymmetry with respect to municipal bonds. The expected future tax rate on the bonds' interest is 10 percent (given the one-half chance of their being taxed at a 20 percent rate), whereas the current rate is 0 percent. Accordingly, assuming no grandfathering, the bonds' value and issue price declines at T_1 to $112.50, this being the price for taxable bonds that offer a $9 return after tax.[1] The presence of retroactive gain-loss asymmetry thereby alters bond values and incentives before any new rule is enacted, and wholly without regard to variance.

These results are based on assuming no transition relief in the event that a rule change is adopted at T_2. If we assume instead that bonds issued before T_2 will definitely be grandfathered in the event of a rule change at that time, then the bonds' value and issue price remains $125 at T_2 whether the coin toss offers a symmetric or asymmetric payoff to bondholders.

Here, then, is the reason why the degree of retroactive gain-loss symmetry for a given asset matters. Asymmetry in the direction of an expected rule change has anticipatory effects on incentives and asset values even before any rule change is actually adopted, wholly without regard to variance—but only in the absence of transition relief. In general, one would think that information about the rules that will apply at a given future moment tends to improve as that moment approaches. Thus, actual rule changes tend to be positively anticipated by an asymmetric shift in expectations, causing them systematically to affect preenactment behavior in the absence of expected transition relief.

Even without positive anticipation, the rule change actually adopted and its permitted transitional consequences may have subsequent observation effects. Thus, if the bond preference actually is repealed at T_2 and need not remain fixed thereafter, the T_2 outcome provides information about the coins that government decision makers are notionally tossing. (Twenty heads in a row, for example, might suggest that a coin was biased rather than honest, and one heads differs from this only in degree.) Accordingly, at any later T_3 where the possibility arises of a further rule change with retroactive application, people's estimates of the probabilities may be slightly different than they would have been had the T_2 coin toss never occurred or come out differently. This is why the government cannot rig the T_2 coin toss against the bondholders, reasoning that this will permit it to trick people who make decisions between T_1 and T_2, without potentially inducing future anticipatory responses through adjustments in prevailing estimates of the odds.

Retroactive gain-loss asymmetry as to a given asset can result not only from anticipating rule change as more likely in one direction than the other but also from anticipating an asymmetric transition regime. Thus, in the otherwise symmetric case where the interest exemption will either be doubled or repealed at T_2, suppose that bondholders at T1 expect to be grandfathered in the event of repeal, but to be allowed retroactive gain if the preference is expanded. Now, the new information at T_1 affects asset values and incentives despite the symmetry of the expected steady-state rule change. If the preference is repealed, existing municipal bonds will continue to be worth \$125 given grandfathering, but if it is doubled without grandfathering, their value will increase to \$150. Accordingly, due to the asymmetry in transition practice, the value and issue price for municipal bonds rises at T_1 from \$125 to \$137.50. The actual T_2 resolution then presumably continues to exert a subsequent influence on general expectations.

In sum, the extent of retroactive gain-loss symmetry for a given asset matters because it determines whether the prospective of a retroactive change implies more than general uncertainty. My behavior may differ when I merely expect a tax rule to change somehow—a problem of pure variance—than when I expect the change, on average, to have particular systematic effects at a given margin. Any asymmetry induces me to adjust now for the expected consequences of future rule changes, and would have this effect even absent variance or if I were risk neutral.

One way to generalize these points is that, depending on the extent of retroactive gain-loss symmetry, the prospect of rule change exposes people to a *risk* plus a positive or negative *tax* (broadly construed to include, say, the effect on one's bonds of a Fed-initiated change in interest rates). People face uncertainty about future rules, and in a relevant set of cases, the expected consequences of rule change are biased in a particular direction. Definitionally, the risk is the element of pure variance that results from uncertainty about what rules, including transition rules, will apply in the future. The tax is the actual change in outcomes given the rules that end up applying. Under rational expectations and improving information, the tax will tend to be positively anticipated as it approaches and also to be remembered afterwards. Thus, looking just at the tax without regard to the risk, it should have roughly the same long-run incentive effects as it would have had if preannounced.

While the risk and the tax are typically intermingled in practice—one may face both uncertainty and a likely direction of change—they are worth distinguishing because they have different analytical implications. Thus, the next chapter follows the strategy of examining first the risk and then the tax, under the artificial assumption that the other element is absent.

THREE

ANALYZING THE RISK AND THE TAX

A. TRANSITION RISK EFFECTS

Transition risk matters because people often have risk preferences that make them sensitive to variance even though (as such) it lacks any systematic direction. Some people in some situations are risk preferring, but the more usual case is risk aversion. Widespread risk aversion explains the facts that risky investments typically must offer risk premia to attract investors and that insurance is a feasible business.

Transition risk increases with the frequency and magnitude of rule change—thus providing a "constitutional" argument for impeding change when there is no reason to think that it involves systematic improvement, even in the sense of responding to new information. Holding constant the amount of change, a full-compensation policy, understood to tax away transition gains as well as compensate losses, could in principle eliminate transition risk except for the net societal gain or loss from a given rule change, which could at least be dispersed as broadly as possible.

Once we assume that risk aversion is the usual case, one might think that full compensation should be the aim of normative transition policy—at least so far as the risk analysis is concerned, although potentially subject to modification by the tax analysis. Matters are more complicated than this, however, for two reasons. First, people who differ either in their risk preferences or in their information and beliefs about particular risks may want distinct risk positions, rather than the single uniform position in which full compensation places them. Full compensation can be an unduly one-size-fits-all type of policy, differing markedly from how people often allocate risk through voluntary transactions. Second, people have some ability to achieve preferred risk positions through their own efforts. Hence, in some cases a full compensation policy may merely duplicate what they could have achieved, perhaps at equal or lower cost, on their own. In other cases, where they prefer distinctive risk positions, it may put them to the trouble of arranging extra transactions to get there (making it downright counterproductive).

1. Differences in Preferred Risk Position

Even if everyone is risk averse, maximum risk spreading need not be the result they prefer. After all, investors sometimes bet with each other concerning future states of the world, reflecting that they want their respective outcomes to vary depending on what happens in the future. A bet is inherently zero-sum rather than offering an overall risk premium, since it merely transfers wealth *ex post* from the loser to the winner, yet people frequently make bets, even outside the world of recreational gambling.

A simple example of a zero-sum bet is issuing versus holding long-term debt at a fixed interest rate. Such a transaction includes a bet on whether the interest rate will go up or down. If it goes up, the borrower wins, by virtue of having borrowed at what is now a below-market interest rate. If they go down, the lender wins, by virtue of having lent at what is now an above-market interest rate.[1] Perhaps in some cases this bet is accidental and the parties would just as soon avoid it (although they could simply use a floating interest rate that moves with the market rate). In other cases, however, the bet is clearly deliberate—indeed, so much so that modern "derivative" financial instruments have been developed to facilitate making it without the cash-flow requirements of the associated loan (Shaviro 1995, 652).

Another way to show that maximum risk spreading is not what people uniformly prefer is to note that a risk premium is merely the market price for a particular risk. At that price, some people enter the risk allocation market on the supply side and others enter on the demand side, with equilibrium emerging once everyone has the risk position he prefers, given prices. Risky investments attract those investors who assign less disutility to the underlying risk, or else have a higher estimate of the expected return. Such investments therefore do not end up being distributed proportionately to some metric such as expected future tax liability. (This point should not be overstated, however, because market prices suggest that riskiness is, in general, value reducing, and thus akin to a product defect.)

An identical analysis should apply to transition risk. For example, suppose there is a possibility that the tax preference for municipal bonds will be changed without grandfathering. This makes the decision of whether or not to purchase municipal bonds in part a bet about future tax rules that some investors may want to make at the market price, and others to avoid, depending on their risk aversion and political expectations. Mandatory transition relief amounts to preventing any bet by this means, and at least initially distributing the risk in a manner that is unlikely to match investors' preferences.

2. Attainability of Preferred Risk Positions through Private Arrangements

A second argument against too quickly assuming that risk aversion supports providing transition relief emphasizes people's ability to satisfy risk preferences through their own unaided efforts. Self-selection, as in the case where one's decision of whether or not to hold municipal bonds depends on how tolerant or sanguine one is about the risk of ungrandfathered repeal, is merely one device for selecting the level and type of risk exposure that one prefers. Other devices include the following:

1. *Explicit private insurance,* as in the case where the bonds' issuer, or perhaps a third-party insurance company, commits to make specified extra payments in the event of repeal, thus protecting the investor against transition risk. While purchasing the insurance permits one to avoid transition risk, agreeing to provide it permits one to take on more of the risk, if that is the position one prefers.

2. *Hedging or other implicit insurance,* as in the case where the investor has some sort of contract right that functions like an insurance agreement without bearing the name. An example might be a put option, entitling the investor to sell the affected municipal bonds for a specified price (reflecting expected value but for the repeal) if repeal occurs. Or the taxpayer may simply own other assets that are likely to appreciate if the municipal bond preference is repealed. Here again, while the hedger or implicit insurer lays off the transition risk, the other side to the hedging transaction deliberately takes it on (although, depending on his other assets and liabilities, he might be hedging as well).

3. *Diversification,* as in the case where the taxpayer's portfolio is spread so widely amongst different assets that a single rule change (such as repealing the municipal bond preference) is unlikely to have much effect. Insofar as the American tax regime for *all* business and investment assets might change dramatically, this could necessitate international diversification of one's holdings, and other steps to limit the reach of the American tax authorities. Here, the way to maximize bearing a given transition risk, rather than diffusing it, is to concentrate rather than diversify one's portfolio.

If these various devices for achieving preferred risk positions are available at zero cost, then the government's transition policy should be irrelevant, so far as the pure risk or variance component of transition problems is concerned. This is simply the Coase Theorem at work. Coase famously showed that the initial allocation of a particular right has no bearing on who will eventually end up holding it, if it is freely transferable and transaction costs are zero (Coase 1988, 13–15). Given, however, that (as Coase emphasized) transaction costs generally are not zero, transition risk analysis may matter after all. I therefore next ask where the risk analysis stands, given the nonuniformity of risk preferences and investors' ability, but perhaps only at a positive transaction cost, to select the risk positions they prefer.

3. What Is Left of the Risk Analysis?

a. The Gap-Filling Problem and Transactional Flexibility

Once the Coase Theorem has been invoked, the next step is fairly obvious; Coase emphasized that it is merely a preliminary to analyzing the real world of positive transaction costs (Coase 1988, 15). A straightforward example of this next analytical step relates to the question of how courts should fill in the gaps in incompletely specified contracts between two parties through "default" rules that apply if the parties have not stipulated to the contrary. This example is particularly pertinent here because, in significant part, what transition problems present is simply a gap-filling or incomplete contracting problem. After all, taxpayers and investors presumably would make complete agreements regarding how to allocate transition risk if contracting costs were zero.

What makes transition problems not just an application of incomplete contracting is the public choice element in government decisions. A crucial underlying assumption in the standard analysis of incomplete contracting is the principle of consumer sovereignty, which holds that people should generally be assumed to act in their own best interests. Consumer sovereignty suggests that the agreements people reach (or would have reached but for transaction costs) are Pareto optimal, absent negative externalities. Problems in collective choice (which I discuss in chapter 4) rebut applying this principle to the government's actual or implicit decisions on behalf of taxpayers or voters, and thus rebut any presumption that its actual or implicit agreements are Pareto optimal, or even good on balance. Nonetheless, the incomplete contracting approach has some relevance here.

Under a utilitarian approach to contractual gap filling, the general aim is to minimize the sum of the disutility from incurring transaction costs to opt out of a default rule, and from having the "wrong" rule apply to one's transaction where opting out is too costly. When we face a choice between alternative default rules, each of which would be correct in some cases but wrong in others, one approach, assuming limited information on which to base the decision, is to ask which rule most parties would have preferred (Goetz and Scott 1994, 56). This should yield the best available utilitarian result unless there is asymmetry between transaction costs or the average social cost of error in one direction versus the other (Ayres and Gertner 1994, 23). For example, the "majoritarian" approach to default rules would yield the wrong result from a utilitarian standpoint if the average error cost from imposing the default rule preferred by 60 percent of the contracting parties was only half the average error cost from imposing that preferred by the other 40 percent.

The treatment of transition risk need not, however, be restricted to selecting optimal default rules of broad application. To the extent that transaction costs permit, more promising still might be to advance what I call *transactional flexibility*, or people's ability to choose at low transaction cost between alternative risk-sharing arrangements. The underlying observation here is that the parties to a transaction may prefer to allocate different risks (or even the same risk) differently on one or more occasions, depending on the circumstances. Thus, consider the range of tools that the government uses to induce varying degrees of reliance on current rules. In some cases, it binds itself more or less irrevocably, by executing a contract. In other cases, such as the enactment of annual discretionary spending appropriations, it binds itself not at all. In still other cases, such as the enactment of tax rules or multiyear spending programs (such as Social Security) that automatically remain in force until amended, it creates no enforceable commitment, but it increases the perceived likelihood of rule continuity through its placement of the burden of inertia.

Transactional flexibility is furthered by having a range of handy "off-the-shelf" arrangements of understood import, so that the details of how transition risk is being allocated need not be hammered out explicitly each time. Once such a range of instruments exists, not only can the government choose between them in particular cases, but investors can decide what sort of guarantee they want at the relative prices that the government offers. Considerable case-by-case fine-tuning of transition risk is possible even assuming the choice of a given instrument. For example, given the fact that nominally retroactive changes (changing the tax treatment of items on past years' tax returns) generally are not made, the extent to which a tax rule is guaranteed against repeal can be fine-tuned through the choice of timing convention. An immediate $100 deduction may be more guaranteed than a deferred deduction with a present value of $100.

To similar effect, suppose that the government executes a contract with a defense company concerning the development of a bomber. The government's ultimate demand for the bomber might be zero, low, or high, depending on a variety of developments in foreign affairs, domestic politics, and military technology. One could imagine a wide range of allocations of the risk concerning how many bombers the government will ultimately want. Perhaps it will commit only that if it buys any bombers, it will buy them from this company. Perhaps it will commit to reimburse specified research expenses, or pay a penalty in the event of contract cancellation. Any such commitment might depend on the circumstances surrounding cancellation. Perhaps the government will commit to buy a specific number of bombers, either low or high, permitting wide variation in the extent to which the company's profit expectations depend on this commitment, rather than on the speculative hope of a larger ultimate sale. It would be absurd to assert that any one of these possibilities is always best—although this is the tenor of "old view" reliance arguments.

One way the government can increase transactional flexibility without negotiating separately with each investor is to offer the same rule in a variety of "flavors," which differ only in the details of their transitional guarantees. Consider United States bonds, which now can be purchased with or without indexing against inflation. To the extent that future inflation depends on government decisions, indexing provides a kind of transition relief. Not surprisingly, the United States government offers a lower nominal interest rate on indexed than unindexed bonds. While this reflects the presence of an expected inflation rate above zero, it also may reflect the elimination of any risk premium for symmetric inflation risk. Not only might the marginal investor demand such a premium, but a principled government might be willing to pay it—for example, if the discretion to vary the extent of implicit default through inflation, depending on subsequent events, has some value. Suppose, for example, that, in the event of a severe fiscal crunch, inflating away the value of unindexed United States bonds would be the least harmful among the politically feasible alternatives.

Equally unsurprisingly, some bondholders prefer the traditional, un-indexed United States bonds despite the government's opportunity to engage in a kind of implicit default by increasing inflation *ex post*. This presumably reflects such bondholders' understanding that implicit default, while in the government's short-term fiscal interest, would face a number of political impediments. These include the government's long-term reputational interest, the bondholders' political power, and the presence of "hostages," in that the government cannot reduce the real value of United States bonds without imposing inflation on the entire society.

In principle, this practice of offering the same rule in multiple "flavors" could be extended to other contexts. Thus, present law might make the tax preference for municipal bonds nominally larger for those who agreed to do without grandfathering in the event of a rule change than for those who asked that it be promised. One could even imagine further alternatives, such as grandfathering solely for preference expansion or preference curtailment, or transitional protection against the effect of income tax rate changes on the value of the preference.

Obviously, problems of transaction cost would prevent this practice of offering policies in multiple transitional "flavors" from going very far. Moreover, even insofar as it could be extended, public choice problems would reduce its normative value. For example, one might lack confidence that the price differentials at which the government would offer a rule in alternative transitional "flavors" would properly represent the collective interest of taxpayers or voters, as distinct from those of the political decision makers. Or one might want, in some settings, to limit the government's discretion to make (or forego making) long-term commitments for "constitutional" reasons relating either to government power generally or to the relative power of present versus future governments.

Nonetheless, we surely should welcome *some* government flexibility to offer firm guarantees in some cases but not others. One who disagreed would presumably want to locate completely at either pole—either barring the government from making enforceable contracts, or else requiring that all of its rules for different periods (including, say, international troop siting) be fully and unalterably set in advance. The absurdity of either result helps to show that transactional flexibility has value up to a point and could conceivably be extended to new settings where the transaction cost and public choice problems seem relatively minor.

Even given transactional flexibility's practical limits, it helps to underscore the difficulty of solving the gap-filling or incomplete contracting problem when a rule is offered in but a single transitional "flavor." Plainly, the diversity of our practices cautions against too readily assuming that investors and/or taxpayers generally prefer a particular transition regime, such as wanting to minimize transition risk for reasons of risk aversion. Any general conclusions must be more cautious, nuanced, and conditional.

b. Cases Where Government Insurance May Be Desirable

Despite people's varying risk preferences and ability to achieve preferred risk positions through their own efforts, a case can sometimes be made for mandatory government insurance on either of two grounds. First, people may fail to take the needed steps to achieve the levels of risk protection that they actually prefer. Suppose that "bounded rationality" (Simon 1957, 198) in a complex world induces them to ignore, and thus underestimate, certain low-probability risks, such as that of a future rule change that is not being prominently discussed. If a realistic estimate of such a risk would have prompted some response, such as increased asset diversification, transition relief may increase the extent to which people achieve their desired risk positions. This may have utilitarian benefits even if people do not suffer subjectively from facing future risks of which they are blissfully unaware. The fact that one is risk averse suggests that one's average satisfaction across the range of possible future states of the world, reflecting varying resolutions of the risk, is lower without transitional protection than with it.

This claim departs from rational expectations by suggesting error with a systematic direction. Thus, one could question whether it follows from bounded rationality. Do people start by assuming *no* transition risk, and thus on average underinsure until they specifically focus on the prospect of a given rule change? Or do they at least implicitly make risk adjustments that reflect, among other things, their general experience and intuitions about the political system? The latter scenario would weaken any inference that people are systematically underinsured against transition risks about which they do not specifically reflect.

In support of the underinsurance prediction, contemporary decision research establishes that people have systematic shortcomings in valuing various types of risk (Sunstein 1997, 128–36), in some cases involving underestimation of low-probability risk. The problem, however, is that the diversity of cognitive biases to which people are subject can lead to over- as well as underestimation (Noll and Krier 1990, 767–71). For example, saliency, as in the case of an airline disaster that receives extensive media coverage, can lead people to think that particular risks are statistically higher than is in fact the case. Thus, the finding of persistent error does not necessarily support a prediction of systematic underinsurance. In some cases, people might be overinsured against the risk of a rule change (given their preferences with accurate information) even without government protection, and mandatory protection would only make things worse.

The second ground for thinking that mandatory government insurance can improve on private risk-allocating transactions is that, in some settings, the former may provide cheaper or more effective protection. Possible reasons include the following:

1. Systematic transition risk that is common to most or all assets cannot be diversified in the same manner as, say, risk relating to the tax treatment of municipal bonds. Thus, absent transition relief, investors may ineluctably bear undesired risk that the United States tax treatment of investment generally (or some large category thereof) will change significantly. The government may be well situated to insure against such risk by promising transition relief.

2. Similar problems may arise with respect to assets that are costly or inconvenient to diversify. One example is human capital, since people typically need to specialize in specific occupations that may be sensitive to rule changes. Thus, there is a risk argument for insuring tax lawyers against the loss of their livelihoods upon repeal of the income tax, despite the adverse incentive effects of providing such insurance. Or consider home ownership, if homeowners with limited gross assets other than their homes have difficulty in achieving desired diversification (Sansing and VanDoren 1994, 569).[2]

3. Risk-shifting transactions may be illegal. Consider the constitutional ban on *ex post facto* criminal legislation, or that which newly makes an act criminal after it has already been performed. No such ban applies to imposing retroactive economic loss through civil legislation. Presumably, the reason for an antiretroactivity rule in the criminal law alone is that criminal sanctions are potentially more severe than economic losses, since they can involve the loss of liberty or even life (Munzer 1982, 443). One element of their greater severity, however, is that they are uninsurable. I cannot validly contract with someone to go to jail in my place if I am convicted.

4. Market failure may restrict the availability of private insurance or its equivalent. Thus, in defense of the constitutional requirement that the government pay compensation when it takes private property, some have argued that private firms would be unable to offer effective takings insurance, even if the government had not preempted the field, due to problems of moral hazard and adverse selection (Blume and Rubinfeld 1984, 596;

Fischel and Shapiro 1988, 586). Moral hazard arises when insured parties can unobservably reduce their efforts to mitigate a given cost because the insurer is bearing it. Adverse selection arises when prospective insureds have better information than the insurer about their own risk levels, causing the insurance to be purchased disproportionately by those to whom it is offered at too low a price given their actual risk levels.

However, for these market failure problems to make the case for government insurance, the government must be able to address them more effectively than can private insurers. In general, there is little reason to think that it has advantages in addressing moral hazard. It may face the same difficulties of observing the insured's behavior, and it lacks the pricing discipline that may result from a private insurer's profit motive (Kaplow 1986, 540–42). By contrast, the government sometimes is uniquely situated to respond to adverse selection. Given its power to issue commands rather than simply offer voluntary transactions, it can make everyone subscribe to a given insurance policy, thus preventing consumers from exploiting their superior information about their own risk levels. The classic example is progressive redistribution through the tax-transfer system—arguably a response to adverse selection if people who, behind the veil of ignorance, would voluntarily insure against the risk of drawing a low wage rate in life, disproportionately decline to do so when they find that they have drawn a high wage rate.

Yet the government's potential advantage in dealing with adverse selection appears inapplicable to transition risk. Here, in contrast to the wage rate example, it is unclear why prospective insureds would have better information than insurers about their own transition risks, which depend on generally observable political probabilities rather than their own private circumstances. Thus, market failure arguments for mandatory government insurance against transition risk may have little general force.

Accordingly, only when transition risk is systematic, hard to diversify, or illegal to insure against can one make especially strong arguments for mandatory government insurance. This suggests that the transition risk analysis often lacks significant policy implications. It is most pertinent in special cases, such as human capital and perhaps home ownership, where we have a particular reason to suspect that the risk averse will be left underprotected by their own best efforts. Admittedly, risk is never entirely irrelevant if people are generally risk averse and prone to be underinsured. I will mainly ignore it, however, both to simplify the exposition and because, heretofore, its significance has mainly been exaggerated.

B. Retroactive Tax Effects

1. Defining Retroactive Taxes

If people always assumed that future policy would be identical on average to current policy plus or minus the element of pure variance, then the preceding transition risk analysis would leave little more to say. We would not have such cases as the individual in 1940 who anticipates a probable income tax rate increase, or the prospective municipal bond investor who anticipates that any changes to the bonds' tax treatment will likely be for the worse. Once there is expected asymmetry, however, we need to consider its import for transition policy. Do we want a future rule change that is to some extent predictable to influence preenactment behavior, through the prospect of its retroactive application to preenactment decisions? What do we think of the allocative and distributional effects of the transition gains and losses that end up being imposed?

While the risk versus tax distinction has not been previously enunciated in the tax transitions literature, recognition of it has sometimes been implicit. Consider how Michael Graetz, in expounding the "new view" that transition relief such as grandfathering should generally be denied upon the repeal of a tax preference, responded to Martin Feldstein's (1976, 93) complaint that the risk of change induced "inefficient precautionary behavior." Graetz noted that tastes and societal conditions change all the time, leading to risk that is all to the good given its incentive effects on investors. Thus, we are glad that investment declines in a technology that may be approaching obsolescence, or in ice cream parlors if consumers' taste for ice cream may be about to decline. "Why should efficiency demand a different result when losses occur because a change in tastes or societal conditions is reflected through the political process, rather than in the market?" (Graetz 1977, 65).

Chapter 4 takes a closer look at Graetz's suggested analogy between private consumer and public political choice. For now, however, it is worth noting that while he frames the discussion in terms of allocating a "risk," he is really concerned with a "tax." Nothing of value is accomplished by reason of ice cream investors' being uncertain about future consumer demand. If someone knew this information with certainty, investors would pay for it in a Pareto-improving transaction. What is valuable is the fact that if the investors succeed to some extent in correctly predicting future consumer demand, they will adjust productive capacity to meet it. A positive or negative "tax" that causes their future wealth to depend on their success in predicting demand has desirable incentive effects, at least if one believes that market mechanisms tend to advance the satisfaction of consumer preferences.

Similarly, consider the "tax" on an uninsured (but deep-pocket) driver who rams his car into someone's house and is required to bear his own losses and compensate the homeowner. Here, as in the ice cream case, we have an efficient tax, variance aside. If drivers bear the full accident costs that their driving imposes on the society, their incentives regarding how much and how safely to drive are correctly aligned, at least in this respect. The existence of variance, in the sense that increasing one's driving or reducing one's care merely increases the likelihood of an accident rather than having an inexorable fixed cost, is a brute physical fact that society must deal with, but it adds nothing to the tax's efficiency. Indeed, we are glad to let drivers convert the variable cost into a fixed cost by purchasing insurance. To the extent insurance companies provide coverage—which is limited by moral hazard problems—what they charge in a competitive market is simply the expected accident cost plus a service fee.

As a formal legal matter, ice cream investors and car drivers bear these "taxes" due not to the tax system as such, but to a set of property and liability rules. The investors need to excite demand because they cannot simply seize money from consumers. If their receipts decline, they generally cannot sue anyone or count on the government to make up the shortfall (leaving aside the general insurance features of the income tax). Likewise, the reckless driver whose car is destroyed cannot sue for the damage done to it by the inconveniently situated house, and can be sued for damaging the house.

To some readers, calling these "tax" results may seem odd, since they are not formally associated with government revenue raising. Yet formal classification has only limited significance. Not only may all of these government rule systems serve the same utilitarian ends, but in principle they are interchangeable. Thus, suppose that all existing tort rules creating private causes of action were repealed, but that Congress and the various state legislatures enacted in their place a set of new taxes on tortfeasors, along with transfer programs to compensate tort victims. If the rules for determining tax liability and transfer entitlement were identical to those under the present law, then the old and new systems would differ only in their administrative details. Such details might be important but would not support considering the systems conceptually different.

There is one sense, however, in which the formal denomination of something as a tax, though not inherently significant, may correlate with something significant. The taxes that I have described thus far are "Pigovian" (named for the economist Arthur Pigou), in that they serve allocative purposes by responding to externalities. Any government revenue-raising or distributional purposes that they also serve may be secondary. Some taxes, however, and particularly those that commonly bear the name, serve primarily revenue-raising and distributional purposes. In particular, consider the income tax, which would be indefensible if its only significant attribute was to levy a fine on those who are crass enough to earn income. As we will see, distributional policy and government revenue-raising needs complicate the efficiency analysis of taxes, although without fundamentally modifying it.

2. The General Characteristics of Good and Bad Taxes

What makes a tax (whether Pigovian or revenue raising) a good one? A utilitarian or other welfarist view typically identifies two chief aims, efficiency and distribution, that often must be traded off against each other. Efficiency is a matter of making all possible Pareto improvements, such as by requiring an individual to bear costs that he would otherwise ignore as externalities. Thus, suppose that Smith, by operating a factory for one hour, would cause pollution that makes the rest of society $100 worse off. Efficiency may be advanced by requiring him to pay a Pigovian pollution tax of $100 (or forego a $100 subsidy) if he operates the factory for that hour. Absent transaction costs, this is the amount that others would demand as the price of permitting him to operate the factory, or offer to pay him to keep it closed, depending on who had the initial entitlement. Failure to levy the tax (or reduce the subsidy) results in foregoing a Pareto improvement that the parties could not accomplish through their own dealings due to transaction costs.[3]

From the standpoint of efficiency, non-Pigovian taxes should be lump sum, or invariant to taxpayer decisions. A uniform head tax is one such tax, but any tax on an unalterable personal characteristic would qualify. However, once one has embarked on non-lump-sum taxation for distributional reasons, efficiency concerns take the more defensive form of trying to minimize deadweight loss to taxpayers from foregoing Pareto improvements (as when people forego market work because of the income tax liability that it would trigger). This aim may involve such strategies as seeking to tax relatively inelastic decisions, or seeking to arrange offsetting tax distortions as a "second-best" substitute for imposing no distortions at all (Lipsey and Lancaster 1956).

The main utilitarian distributional concern reflects the default assumption that people generally have identical utility functions characterized by declining marginal utility. Thus, if all else is equal, transferring a dollar from a better-off to a worse-off individual increases the latter's well-being more than it reduces that of the former. This, however, is subject both to incentive and consequent efficiency issues and to other utility information.

Among the difficult theoretical problems that this view of distribution poses is how to rank people by relative well-being, so that we know from whom to whom we want to redistribute. When two people have the same opportunities but make different choices (for example, one chooses more work compared to leisure, or more saving compared to current consumption), it is hard to know who is better off, even if the worker or saver has greater material wealth at some point down the road. The worker's or saver's revealed preferences suggest that he values later market consumption more, thus countering the inference that, once he has more wealth, each dollar is worth less to him. Accordingly, absent further utility information of a sort that is hard to come by, one might prefer to base the vertical rankings that are used in distributional policy on relative endowments, ability, or opportunities (posing further knotty problems that are beyond my present scope).[4] In practice, however, since endowment cannot be measured and taxes must be paid in the form of material wealth, the tax system must rely on some proxy measure, typically income or consumption, that depends in part on endowment and in part on work or savings decisions. Hence, the often ineluctable tradeoff between efficiency and distribution, resulting from the unavailability of lump-sum endowment taxation.

Absent further utility information, a belief in declining marginal utility seemingly supports any and all transfers from better-off to worse-off individuals. Nonetheless, there is a strong case for preferring to pursue distributional objectives exclusively through the rate structure of the basic tax-transfer system that uses income, consumption, or wealth—rather than, say, through the "tax" element in transition policy or the tort law. The argument is twofold. First, from an efficiency standpoint, we will likely burden work or savings decisions no matter how we pursue redistribution. However, using a system of narrower scope than the basic tax-transfer system—say, by overcompensating poor pedestrians who are hit by rich car drivers—adds a further distortion of choice (such as how much to drive and walk) on top of the unmitigated work distortion (Kaplow and Shavell 1994). Second, holding constant the amount redistributed, the tax-transfer system will likely target it best—having, after all, been designed to measure well-offness in a comprehensive, if flawed, way. If a million dollars is to be transferred from rich to poor individuals, why merely shift it between, say, the rich and poor individuals who happen to have been involved in accidents (through transfers in excess of the usual damages), rather than between all rich and poor people?[5]

Thus, the case for considering distributional concerns other than in the general tax-transfer setting requires showing one of two things. The first is the presence of a special case raising distinctive efficiency or distributional issues. Thus, suppose that a particular transfer through the tort system or transition rules happens to offset the basic distortion and mismeasurement that result from taxing work effort. It might on balance offset, rather than augment, the tax-transfer system's shortcomings. The second is an argument of political economy. Suppose that, due to some attribute of the political system, one cannot trade in the worse for the better redistributive policy. Redistribution by inferior means may conceivably be better than doing nothing at all.

Obviously, one could say much more about the features of good and bad taxes—in particular, concerning the income or consumption tax that I argue should be the basic vehicle for distributional policy, and discuss further in chapter 5. Enough has already been said, however, to permit preliminary examination of the light that general tax policy considerations shed on the "tax" element of transition problems.

3. Evaluating Retroactive Taxes

In the transition setting, just like any other, the aim of tax policy is tautologically to impose good, and not bad, positive and negative taxes. Thus, when anticipation of a rule change has good incentive effects, its retroactive application is desirable from an efficiency standpoint. Likewise, distributional considerations support imposing transition losses on better-off individuals and conferring transition gains on worse-off ones, subject to the case for confining redistribution to the general tax-transfer system through its rate structure.

Since nothing about this is distinctive to the transition setting, one might think that it deprives transition issues of any distinctive character (their risk element aside). Where the question is just one of unchanging incentive effects, we may want desirable rule changes to be anticipated before enactment, just as we hope that they will influence behavior afterwards. Likewise, we may want undesirable changes not to be anticipated before enactment, and hope against hope that they are underobserved afterwards.

It turns out, however, that this relationship between transitional and steady-state policy is merely a special case and does not hold generally. Often, the merits of the retroactive tax are wholly independent from those of the rule change. Indeed, the two variables—good versus bad retroactive tax, and good versus bad rule change—yield at least three basic types of cases. The retroactive tax can be good only if the rule change is good, or good even if the rule change is bad, or bad even if the rule change is good.[6] This can be illustrated through a series of examples in which, to simplify the exposition, I mainly emphasize efficiency issues.

a. Case 1: Retroactive Tax Good if and Only if the Rule Change Is Good

Sometimes, the desirability of inducing people to anticipate a rule change does indeed depend on the change being a good one. Suppose that if a product turns out to be hazardous, it will be newly banned, or the tort law will be modified if necessary so that unusual causation does not prevent victims from being able to recover (Kaplow 1986, 529, 598). Producer anticipation of such retroactive changes is desirable precisely because it improves their incentive to take user hazard into account (a central aim of product liability law). By contrast, producers anticipating rule changes that retroactively worsened the fit between hazard and legal liability would have bad incentive effects.

Similarly, the desirability of investors anticipating repeal of the municipal bond preference mainly depends on whether repeal is good policy. As noted in chapter 2, the prospect of ungrandfathered repeal tends to drive the issue price for the bonds towards that of a taxable bond. This is good if the preference has been misallocating investment towards the state and local government sector, and bad if the preference has been improving resource allocation.

More precisely, the desirability of the retroactive tax is identical to that of the new rule as steady-state policy (ignoring transition risk) under two conditions. First, good policy must be the same in different periods. This condition would not be met if, say, a subsidy was desirable for municipal bonds issued in 2003 but not for those issued in 2004. In that instance of time-inconsistent good policy, repeal in 2004 would be desirable, but its retroactive application to bonds issued in 2003 would not be.

Second, adding retroactive to steady-state application must not result in "too much" of an otherwise good thing. Thus, suppose that the optimal municipal bond preference was greater than zero but less than under present law, that the only politically feasible change was to repeal the preference outright in 2003, and that this was better than doing nothing. Under these circumstances, it is conceivable that one would come closer to the optimal level of municipal bond investment over time by applying the rule change only prospectively.

All this talk of rule changes being "good" or "bad" may strike some readers as raising the wrong issue—one that goes to the merits of enactment, rather than the preferred transition policy assuming enactment. When one has views about rule changes, however, they are inescapably relevant to one's view of transition policy in this set of cases, where the incentive effects generally are the same retroactively as prospectively. There is, to be sure, a practical problem if one wishes to persuade those who reject one's substantive belief about a rule change to accept one's view about transition to it (Kaplow 1986, 566). Moreover, any proposal to design a general transition regime aimed at mitigating inherent defects in political decision making obviously cannot rest on the principle that "bad" changes, unlike "good" ones, should be limited, since few, if any, rule changes are admitted to be bad by their advocates.

Yet these persuasion and political economy problems should not stand in the way of clearly thinking through the logical consequences of one's own beliefs about good policy. And the challenge of designing a general transition regime that will improve political decisions overall (even if it gets some cases wrong) is one that I will defer until chapter 5.

b. Case 2: Retroactive Tax Good Even if the Rule Change Is Bad

In a second set of cases, the tendency of the retroactive tax to induce anticipation of a rule change is desirable wholly without regard to the change's steady-state merits. Suppose that I am considering building a house on a site where the government may at some point exercise its power of eminent domain in order to extend a highway. When and if the highway comes, should I be compensated for the value of my improvements? Here, my incentives will be better if the answer is no. The house will go to waste when and if the wrecking crew arrives, and it is best, all else equal, that I take this prospect into account. Yet I may be tempted to ignore it if I will be compensated for the extra value that results from my construction. For this purpose, it is irrelevant whether the highway ought to be built, treating the political decision whether to build it as fixed (Kaplow 1986, 529–30).[7]

Similarly, suppose that the government may, at some point in the future, decide either to ban all imports of foreign cars or to eliminate existing "voluntary" import quotas. Either change would significantly affect

American consumers' demand for domestically produced cars. Ignoring political incentive effects and assuming positive adjustment costs, it is efficient for American producers to anticipate any rule change by adjusting productive capacity in advance. The fact that the import ban might be bad policy has no bearing on the fact that, taking its imposition as given, it affects consumer demand for the American producers' cars.

Finally, suppose that it is 1965 and that I am considering opening a grocery store that only I can make a success. My investment will go to waste if massive escalation of our involvement in the Vietnam War leads to my being drafted and sent overseas. Whether or not we ought to fight the Vietnam War, my incentives are improved if I would bear this loss. My 1965 investment decision would be distorted by the prospect of my either being compensated for the destruction of the business if I am drafted, or allowed a draft deferment that is conditioned on my operating a business that needs my services.

The common feature of these examples is that the rule change, whether good or bad, changes the consequences of prior decisions. For example, my home construction will go to waste if the government, however misguidedly, levels it. Similarly, the import ban converts overinvestment by American car producers into a suitable level of investment.

c. Case 3: Retroactive Tax Bad Even if the Rule Change Is Good

In a third set of cases, the anticipation induced by the retroactive tax is undesirable without regard to the change's steady-state merits—generally because transition gains and losses are a kind of side effect, conceptually distinct from whatever makes the rule good or bad, and not independently desirable. Louis Kaplow (1986, 613) gives the example of a mere accounting rule change under the income tax, such as from calendar year accounting to the use of a fiscal year that ended on June 30. Absent deliberate transition relief, the result might be to tax six months of income either twice or not at all at the time when the change was made. Yet, whether or not the accounting year change is good policy, a double-or-nothing effect on tax liability in the year of the change would encourage inefficiency, such as shifting business activities into or out of the transition period.

Similarly, consider the Endangered Species Act (ESA), under which landowners may be enjoined from clearing or developing their property— say, to protect the habitat of a rare species of owl. Landowners are not compensated for what is often a substantial decline in property value, but can sometimes head off any restriction by "cutting down trees, repeatedly plowing their fields, or otherwise altering their land's ecology to make it unappealing to listed species in the region" (Thompson 1997, 349–50). Taking as given the difficulty of detecting and penalizing such behavior, private incentives might be improved by the prospect of compensation for the loss imposed by regulatory restrictions—whether or not the restrictions ought to be issued.[8]

Finally, suppose that the federal government decides to change the currency—perhaps to save printing costs, use nicer colors, honor new national heroes, or impede counterfeiting. A no-transition policy might involve a surprise announcement declaring the old currency worthless overnight and a distribution of the new currency on some basis distinct from holdings of the old. A policy of granting transition relief might involve allowing the old money to be traded in for its exchange rate equivalent in new money for a fixed period. Under these circumstances, unless pollution of the old currency by counterfeiting had reached massive proportions, few would disagree that the government ought to grant transition relief by allowing trade-in. The basic efficiency point is that, whether or not the currency ought to have been changed, there is no reason to give people an ex ante incentive to anticipate currency cancellation, and thus to avoid holding cash or relying on the currency's continued value.[9]

Perhaps the distributional element should be noted here, although ignored in prior examples, because it is potentially significant. The retroactive tax imposed by currency cancellation might result in progressive redistribution if the rich hold sufficiently more cash than the poor. Yet the incidence of the redistribution would likely be haphazard given the crudity of the relationship between cash holdings and how well-off one is. Thus, it ought not to be considered, even if the distributional benefits exceed the efficiency costs, unless political economy constraints prevent better-targeted (and less inefficient) redistribution.

This taxonomy decisively contradicts both the old view (as in Feldstein 1976) that retroactive taxes are generally inefficient, and the new view (as in Graetz 1977) that they are generally efficient. Nor can one generalize from the desirability of a particular rule change to that of the retroactive tax that it would impose absent transition relief. Only case 1 presents what I call *policy change retroactive taxes*—those that do the same thing as the steady-state new rule, and thus tend to be desirable if and only if it is. Cases 2 and 3 present issues distinct from the desirability of the rule change itself. Given the multiple categories, one's conclusions need to be context specific and to focus on exactly what the retroactive tax (as distinct from the steady-state new rule) actually does.

Despite the multiplicity of patterns presented by even the small number of cases described above, one can discern several recurring themes. In particular:

1. Retroactive taxes can provide incentives that affect adjustment costs, or the costs of reallocating resources in the economy in response to a rule change. Examples include the loss to tax lawyers from repeal of the income tax, the response of domestic automobile manufacturers to enactment of an import ban, the loss to one's personal grocery store business if one is drafted to fight in Vietnam, and the taking by the highway authority of property on which one has built a house. In general, the productive use of society's resources may be enhanced by requiring people to bear the consequences of the bets regarding future rules (or more precisely, future demand for competing resource uses given future rules) that they implicitly make through their allocative decisions.

2. Where the adoption or applicability of a new rule that would have retroactive tax consequences is conditioned on an individual's behavior before its adoption, he can have an incentive to take steps (otherwise undesirable) to bring on or avoid the retroactive tax. Examples include forestalling the imposition of loss under the Endangered Species Act by clearing one's property before the regulators arrive, or opening a grocery store just before one receives a Vietnam-era draft notice because this will enable one to stay home.[10] Here, the simple answer would be that (at least from an incentive standpoint) the new rule's application should not be thus conditioned on pre-adoption behavior, but eliminating the retroactive tax may have similar effects at this decisional margin.

3. Rule changes can cause problems of intertemporal distortion, simply because different rules apply at different times. An Endangered Species Act example would be clearing land more swiftly, rather than more completely, than one would have in the absence of the threat that the regulators would arrive and require one to stop.

4. Some retroactive taxes reflect the mere happenstance of a change in the mechanics of how a rule happens to be enforced, as in the earlier example of an uncompensated currency change. For a second example, suppose that, to facilitate inspections, the Clean Air Act is amended to provide that entitlement to discharge pollutants under its terms must henceforth be evidenced by a physical document called a permit. (Who can pollute and in what quantity otherwise remains unchanged.) Charging polluters for the permit, although economically similar to newly imposing a pollution tax

that has the same present value as the price charged for the permits, could be called a mere byproduct of the change in documentation requirements.

C. Transition Problems in the Tax Law Setting

So far, I have addressed retroactive taxes without particular attention to the "tax laws"—that is, the existing income tax and other formal taxes that serve revenue-raising and distributional purposes. Moving to this category of rule changes does not change the fundamental analysis. However, as a consequence of how the tax laws are administered, it turns out that, in this setting, the "happenstance" case described above—resulting in what I call *accounting change retroactive taxes*—arises with particular frequency. I therefore describe this category of non–policy change retroactive taxes next.

1. The Policy Content and Accounting Content of Steady-State Tax Rules

Any tax rule can be described as having both a policy content and an accounting content. The policy content describes its allocative and distributional character. Consider a tax on economic income. Allocatively, it burdens work (and market consumption) compared to leisure, and saving compared to immediate consumption. Distributionally, it burdens income-earning ability, along with those tastes—such as for work, market consumption, and saving—that induce people to direct their efforts towards generating income. Or consider the municipal bond preference within the present income tax. It favors borrowing and thus expenditure by state and local governments relative to other borrowing and expenditure. Distributionally, it favors net beneficiaries of the marginal state and local government spending and taxes that it induces, and high-bracket investors whose implicit tax from the bonds' reduced pretax yield in response to the preference is less than the tax liability they would have incurred absent the preference.

For convenience, I define "policy" as necessarily time consistent. Thus, to change the degree to which municipal bonds are tax favored is to enact a policy change, even if a consistent set of normative views could lead one to believe that both the old and new policies were optimal for their times. Changed circumstances or information may alter what constitutes good policy, but there is still a policy change, in my usage, if one alters the tax rules' steady-state allocative and distributional content.

The accounting content of a tax rule consists of details in its implementation that could in principle be changed without affecting its policy content. In practice, the two most important and variable accounting details are (1) the timing (as distinct from the time value) of particular inclusions, deductions, or credits; and (2) the nominal incidence (as distinct from economic incidence) of any specific tax benefit or burden, such as those provided through inclusions, deductions, and credits.

a. Timing

The principle of present value equivalence holds that, from any point in time, an infinity of distinct cash flows can have the same present value. To the extent of well-functioning capital markets, a dollar today is worth the same amount as a dollar plus market interest at any point in the future. Thus, in a steady-state, flat-rate tax system, changing the taxable year of an inclusion, deduction, or credit should not affect the relative tax burdens borne by different individuals, assets, or transactions, so long as the amount that is includable or deductible is suitably modified to reflect the change in timing. Given present value equivalence, changing the sequence of specific cash flows that a given transaction will generate as between a taxpayer and the government does not result in a policy change except insofar as one changes the time value of the cash flows, rather than simply their timing.

Thus, consider the distinction between income and consumption taxation. Definitionally, an income tax conditions liability on the taxpayer's consumption plus change over time in net worth, whereas a consumption tax conditions liability only on consumption and thus generally makes the timing of consumption tax irrelevant. This is a real policy difference. Suppose we have two individuals with the same year 1 labor earnings, one of whom consumes the earnings immediately while the other invests them at the market interest rate for a year and then consumes the earnings plus the interest return in year 2 (Kaldor 1958, 79–87). A well-designed income tax will burden the saver more than the immediate consumer (assuming positive interest rates), while a well-designed consumption tax will burden them the same.[11] This difference matters to allocation and distribution.

Now suppose further that the income tax is implemented through rules such as economic depreciation and capitalizing inventory costs, whereas the consumption tax is implemented by expensing. Under economic depreciation, outlays to acquire assets are deducted over the assets' useful lives in accordance with the rate at which the assets lose economic value. Under inventory capitalization, outlays to acquire goods that are held for sale to customers are not deducted until the goods are sold. By contrast, under expensing, all business or investment outlays are deducted as soon as they are made. These rules implement the policy difference between income and consumption taxation, but also create a mere accounting difference. Deductions under the two systems now differ in timing, wholly apart from their difference in time value.

Thus, suppose that on December 31 of year 1, I spend $100 to purchase an asset that yields $110 on December 31 of year 2 (consistent with a generally prevailing interest rate of 10 percent). Once I receive the $110, I immediately spend it to buy dinner that same night. Under the above-described implementations, both taxes would require me to include $110 in year 2. However, under the income tax I would deduct nothing in year 1 and $100 in year 2, whereas under the consumption tax I would deduct $100 in year 1 and nothing in year 2.

There is thus a sizable timing difference between the two systems as implemented. For each of two successive years, the amount deductible under one differs by $100 from the amount deductible under the other. Thus, if the tax rate under both systems is a refundable 40 percent, I will fare $40 better under the consumption tax than the income tax in year 1, and $40 better under the income tax than the consumption tax in year 2. The real time value difference between the systems is considerably smaller. It is confined to the present value difference of $4 (at a 10 percent interest rate) between recovering $40 from the tax collector at the end of year 1 versus the end of year 2.

The timing difference, considered without regard to the time value difference, is mere accounting. After all, one would still have an income tax if one allowed cost recovery in year 1 that had the same present value as the $100 deduction at the end of year 2. At the 10 percent interest rate, this would involve a deduction of $90.91 on December 31 of year 1. Likewise, one would still have a consumption tax if the deduction was deferred until year 2 but had the same present value as expensing. Given the interest rate, this would involve a year 2 deduction of $110.

In practice, therefore, a shift from an income tax that uses economic depreciation to a consumption tax that uses expensing is both a policy change and an accounting change. As we will see in chapter 9, both of these changes may have retroactive consequences. It would be possible, however, to make only one of the two changes. To make only the policy change, one would retain all prior income tax rules concerning the timing of cost recovery but increase the amounts deductible to include interest on any deferral relative to expensing. To make only the accounting change, one would require immediate cost recovery for all outlays, as under expensing, but with deductions that had the same present value as those that would be provided over time under a conventional income tax.

It is important to recognize how my use of the term *accounting*—here, to describe timing changes insofar as they are not time value changes—differs from some common usages. For example, consider what are called *accounting rules* within the present income tax—say, the choice between the cash and accrual methods of accounting for receipts and expenses. Suppose that in December 2003 a calendar-year taxpayer renders $500 worth of services to a client and submits a bill, but the bill is not paid until January 2004. Depending on additional facts not pertinent here, this amount might be includable in the service provider's 2003 taxable income if he uses the accrual method (which comes closer to following the economics of the transaction), and in 2004 if he uses the cash method. Here there is both a policy and an accounting difference between the two systems, since the $500 inclusions differ in both time value and timing. Yet the fact that someone might call this a choice between two "accounting methods" has no bearing on the application of my terminology.

Or suppose the income tax was implemented by annually measuring each taxpayer's Haig-Simons income, defined as the market value of his consumption and change in net worth during the taxable year (Simons 1938, 50). Under this direct measure of income, it would no longer be necessary to consider such things as the cost-recovery period for given outlays. The Haig-Simons system would abstract from determining the proper accounting treatment of particular transactions, and instead simply measure people's change in net worth for the year given all pertinent facts. Thus, in a common sense of the term, the tax system would no longer have "accounting rules." Within my usage, however, it would still be using a specific accounting rule—one of including economic income in the specific year when it arises—to accomplish the policy aims of income taxation. After all, the policy would remain the same if we permitted taxpayers to defer or accelerate their Haig-Simons income to different taxable years at a market interest rate—just as it would remain the same if we allowed people to borrow or prepay, at market interest, the tax liabilities computed under Haig-Simons.

Suppose that in 2003 there was a tax on current-year Haig-Simons income, but that in 2004 this was changed to a tax on previous-year Haig-Simons income plus interest. This would not be a policy change, since the tax liability for each year's Haig-Simons income would still be collected, only a year late with interest. However, it would impose an accounting change retroactive tax if Haig-Simons income that accrued in 2003 was taxed twice by reason of it.

b. Nominal Incidence

A standard economic principle holds that the economic incidence of a tax, or who really bears it, may differ from its nominal incidence, or who sends the Treasury the requisite check. Thus, consider the payroll tax that is notionally used to fund the Social Security system. As a matter of law, half is paid by employers and half by workers. Economists generally agree, however, that this rule allocating nominal incidence between the two is economically irrelevant to how the tax burden is actually shared between them. The real economic incidence of the payroll tax depends instead on relative elasticities of supply and demand in the labor market. If workers' labor supply is close to inelastic while the demand for their labor is highly elastic, they will essentially bear the whole tax burden, at least in the short run, whether the law allocates none, half, or all of the nominal tax liability to them (Rosen 1995, 285).

The mechanism for differences between nominal and economic incidence is price changes. Thus, suppose that an employer pays $60 for my services and I receive $50, with the difference resulting from a $10 payroll tax, and that I will bear the full tax burden without regard to its nominal incidence. If the tax is nominally on the employer, he will pay $50 to me and $10 to the government. If it is nominally on me, he will pay $60 to me and I will pay $10 to the government. If we each nominally pay half, then the employer will pay me $55 and we will each pay $5 to the government. Thus, the bottom line is the same in each case, because the size of the check the employer writes to me adjusts to reflect the size of the checks that we each must write to the government. The after-tax amounts on each side, since they reflect broader market forces (assuming competitive markets), are resilient enough to withstand formal changes in how Congress purports to allocate between us the net tax consequences of our transaction.

This suggests that the policy content of a tax rule—meaning, again, its effect on resource allocation and wealth distribution—is a function of the net burden that it imposes on particular transactions. For a given transaction, holding this burden constant and assuming that full price adjustments occur, the nominal allocation of tax consequences between the parties is a mere accounting detail, necessary to resolve somehow in the course of administering the tax but having no effect on its steady-state consequences.

Suppose instead that prices cannot fully adjust. This could happen, for example, if the employment transaction was subject to a minimum-wage law that ignored the payroll tax unless paid by the worker (and thus included in the nominal wage). If the employer's cost and the worker's receipt really had to go up as a result of shifting the nominal incidence of the payroll tax to the employer, then the shift would at least partly result in a real policy change. However, it would still involve an accounting change to the extent that the nominal wage could and did decline by reason of the shift in nominal payroll tax incidence.

Two further examples of mixed policy and accounting changes from changing the nominal incidence of a tax may help to clarify the concept. First, suppose that a wine tax of $5 per bottle sold, payable by the seller, is replaced by a $6 tax payable by the buyer. Here we have both a policy change of $1 in the wine tax and an accounting change in the tax's nominal incidence.

Second, suppose Congress changes the rules that determine when a transfer between divorced ex-spouses meets the tax definition of alimony, thus making a transfer deductible by the payor and includable by the recipient rather than nondeductible and nonincludable. For a given prospective transfer that the rule might affect, the parties' net taxable income from the transaction is zero either way. Thus, if their marginal tax rates are the same, and the net tax liability from any transfer is therefore zero either way, we have a pure accounting change, which makes no difference so long as the parties adjust nominal payments to reflect the allocation of tax consequences between the parties.

However, if the parties have different marginal tax rates, then we have part policy change and part accounting change. The new rule both alters the net tax consequences of payments between ex-spouses (the policy change), and makes a merely nominal shift in tax liability to the extent unchanged. Thus, suppose that the ex-husband has a 40 percent marginal tax rate and the ex-wife has a 30 percent marginal tax rate. For a $100 payment from the man to the woman that now newly counts as alimony, the new rule decreases the former's tax by $40 while increasing the latter's tax by $30, thus merely shifting $30 (the accounting change) but reducing the net tax by $10 (the policy change).

Mere accounting changes in nominal incidence can result in accounting change retroactive taxes despite their steady-state irrelevance. Thus, in the alimony case, suppose that an expansion of what constitutes alimony applies retroactively to prior divorce agreements. For a given divorce agreement that did not provide for adjusting the nominal payment in the event of such a change, this may give the payor a transition gain and the recipient a transition loss—a pure accounting change retroactive tax if their marginal rates are the same. Or suppose we alter the wine store example so that a $5 tax on the seller, payable at the time of sale, is replaced by a tax on the buyer of $5 plus interest since the time of sale, payable when he opens the bottle. We now have two accounting changes, one going to timing (but not time value) and one to nominal incidence, but no policy change. These accounting changes could result in the imposition of an accounting change retroactive tax on bottles of wine that were sold under the old law and opened under the new law.

2. Determining the Scope of a "Rule Change" in Order to Determine Its Policy Change and Accounting Change Elements

The fact that any given tax rule combines policy with accounting content suggests that, for any rule change, one can specify both the policy change and the accounting change. There is one conceptual difficulty, however—even leaving aside computational problems such as determining the economic incidence of a tax burden or the proper interest rate for measuring present value equivalence. Determining how policy and accounting have changed requires two fixed points to compare—the "before" and "after" states—and thus is sensitive to how one defines the scope of a distinct rule change. Movement that starts at Rule A and ends at Rule B can be decomposed differently, depending on how many stops, constituting completed rule changes, one assumes have been made along the way.

Thus, suppose that we start with current law for municipal bonds and end with a rule whereby bondholders expense the cost of the bonds upon purchase and then include the interest income. Assuming constant tax rates and interest rates, this has the same present value as expensing, thus indicating that there has only been an accounting change. However, if we treat repeal of the interest exemption as one rule change and the introduction of expensing as a separate rule change, then we have a pure policy change followed by a change in both accounting and policy.[12]

Or suppose that we instead repeal the municipal bond preference in two stages, first converting it into the present value equivalent version characterized by expensing and interest inclusion, and then repealing expensing. Whereas one-step repeal would have been a pure policy change, here we have a pure accounting change followed by a change in both accounting and policy.

This problem relates only to the definition of rule changes, rather than to decomposing them into their policy and accounting change elements. In practice, it should ordinarily pose little difficulty. If the proponents of a given rule seek their preferred end-state all at once (perhaps so that they need only once overcome the burden of legislative inertia), or at least fully describe the end-state that they seek, then one has the needed information to perform the decomposition. Obviously, the difficulty would increase if decomposition had legal consequences rather than simply being a useful analytical exercise.

3. Identifying Policy Change and Accounting Change Retroactive Taxes

In this book, the difference between policy and accounting changes matters because of the distinctive retroactive taxes that they impose. It is therefore worth discussing further how to identify these retroactive taxes—keeping in mind that, in a given case, both may be found, and their effects be hard to untangle. Policy and accounting change retroactive taxes are distinct conceptually, however intermingled in practice.

a. Policy Change Retroactive Taxes

The test for a policy change retroactive tax is that its retroactive and steady-state allocative and distributional effects are of the same character. Again, the prospect of ungrandfathered repeal of the municipal bond preference simply extends the reach of the steady-state policy, by making the bonds less attractive than otherwise. Similarly, the prospect of enacting a consumption tax encourages saving even preenactment insofar as it would increase the after-tax return to saving.

One way to test for a policy change retroactive tax is that support for the policy change implies support for it (ignoring transition risk) subject to these qualifications:

1. Good policy may be different from period to period. Again, it is conceivable that one would want investors in 2003 to assume that their municipal bond preferences are safe, even if one might want to repeal the preference as to investment decisions in 2004.

2. If a subsidy or penalty was initially too large or small and then was overcorrected in the opposite direction, it is possible for the new enactment to be better than prior law, and yet for retroactivity to be undesirable because it would further extend the overreach.

3. Even if one likes a given policy change retroactive tax in principle, the politics of enacting the underlying policy change may dictate placating opponents by not imposing it.

4. If one believes that policy change retroactive taxes are generally undesirable and that current outcomes affect future practice, one has a "constitutional" reason for opposing their imposition even in cases where one supports the underlying policy change.

b. Accounting Change Retroactive Taxes

The most general test for an accounting change retroactive tax is that one could eliminate it (even if other transition consequences remain) by making a mere accounting change to the new rule, while keeping the new policy constant. Thus, in the case of income to consumption tax transition, the potential wipeout of outstanding basis due to the shift from economic depreciation to expensing is conditioned on this mere accounting difference between the two systems as implemented. It would disappear if the consumption tax used the same timing for cost recovery as the income tax, modified only to allow interest on deferral relative to expensing.

When the accounting change at issue involves timing, one can apply an additional test for accounting change retroactive taxes. Here, the test is that the retroactive tax would not arise if the rule change were given full nominally retroactive application. Thus, in the case of income to consumption tax transition, shifting from economic depreciation to expensing would not result in any permanent loss of cost recovery deductions for preenactment outlays if all *past* years' tax liability were recomputed to apply expensing.

When the accounting change involves nominal incidence, an additional test is that the retroactive tax could have been eliminated by price adjustments between affected parties. Thus, suppose that nominal liability under the payroll tax is fully shifted either to employers or to workers, thus creating transition gain and loss on existing employment contracts that did not specify an adjustment to nominal wages in the event that this occurred. This is an accounting change retroactive tax, apart from its interaction with other rules such as the minimum-wage law and wage computation under the income tax, in that its effect could be eliminated by adjusting nominal wages.

Since policy and accounting are distinct, the desirability of a given rule change's policy content generally has no bearing on the desirability of any accounting change retroactive taxes that it happens to impose. This may be important to advocates and opponents of a given policy change, who should recognize that their views on the policy change may have no bearing on their view of these particular transition effects. Nonetheless, my definition of an accounting change retroactive tax is intent free. If Congress replaced the present income tax with a consumption tax solely as a device to wipe out income tax basis and despite otherwise preferring income taxation, the wipeout would still constitute an accounting change retroactive tax. For the basis wipeout to reflect a policy change, the new policy would have to be one of prospectively denying cost recovery generally, and thus (at least in this respect) taxing gross income or gross receipts.[13]

D. Accounting Change Retroactive Taxes outside the Tax Law Setting

Accounting changes and consequent retroactive taxes are not unique to the tax laws. I earlier defined the "accounting content" of a tax rule as "details in its implementation that could in principle be changed without affecting its policy content." Obviously, however, any government rule will have implementation details that could change. Thus, suppose a form X that one must file when registering to vote is replaced by form Y, thus potentially disenrolling all voters who do not reregister. This would be a mere accounting change to the extent that the substantive requirements for registration remained the same. Or suppose the Supreme Court changed, in some trivial way, the exact words of the Miranda warning that police investigators are required to give the suspects in their custody whom they interrogate, thus potentially triggering retroactive findings of constitutional violation if (under constant doctrine) the Court demanded precise adherence to whatever wording it prescribed. I earlier gave the examples of a currency change and a new permit requirement under the Clean Air Act that involves no general steady-state change in environmental policy.

Because disentangling policy from accounting change can be complex, a real-world nontax example may be worth describing briefly. In 1990, when Congress amended the Clean Air Act to create sulfur dioxide emission permits, it did not merely create a new form of documentation, it also changed policy in at least two key respects. First, although permits were generally distributed to existing polluters as a conscious exercise in grandfathering, there was not a precise match between prior rights to pollute and the receipt of a permit. Some new limits were placed on lawful emission, and the allocation of permits reflected complex political negotiations between competing interests (Joskow and Schmalensee 1998). Second, permits (unlike prior rights to pollute) were made tradeable, and the resulting move towards "market-based" environmental regulation was indeed the reason for introducing them. Thus, the introduction of permits involved policy change as well as accounting change.

By issuing the permits for free rather than selling them at a market price, Congress forebore levying what—for any recipient that valued the ongoing right to pollute more than the new ability to sell this right—would have been, in the main, an accounting change retroactive tax. As it happens, the incentive effect of this tax would have been the same as that from a policy change retroactive tax in the form of newly taxing all sulfur dioxide emissions. By contrast, when Congress first enacted the Clean Air Act, it rejected compensation and imposed a policy change retroactive tax with similar incentive effects to this foregone tax, insofar as it newly banned certain emissions that had previously been permissible.

FOUR

Problems of Political Choice and Their Bearing on Transition Issues

A. Public Political Choice Compared to Private Consumer Choice

At least for policy change retroactive taxes, one might think that the optimal transition policy is easy to discern. Why not simply assume that the new policy is a good one—as its proponents surely will—and thus approve of it? If one makes this assumption, and transition risk concerns do not appear unusually significant (as they might in a case of systematic risk), one presumably should conclude without further ado that policy change retroactive taxes should generally be allowed.

This, of course, is the "new view," exemplified by Michael Graetz's comparison of public political choice to private consumer choice, when he asked why it should matter that "a change in tastes or societal conditions is reflected through the political process, rather than in the market" (1977, 65). Again, the reason for letting the owners of an ice cream parlor absorb the loss from a decline in the public's taste for ice cream is that it may induce them to try harder to determine what the public wants. If this increased effort is socially valuable, it is because satisfying consumer taste, as evidenced by the set of market transactions that we observe, is deemed valuable for its own sake. In a world of scarce resources, we are glad to have less ice cream produced if people show that they want it less, even if nothing about ice cream (or our knowledge about it) has changed in any objective sense.

Does the same analysis apply to a change in the political taste for the projects that are financed by municipal bonds, as evidenced by the fact that Congress decides to expand or contract the municipal bond preference? Suppose that the marginal project that the bonds would finance (if the prospect of ungrandfathered repeal does not bid up the interest rate) is an airport. Is an apparent change in national voters' taste for subsidizing projects of this kind self-validating in the same sense as a change in consumers' taste for ice cream, thus leading us to want it to influence financing costs and investment decisions *ex ante*?

It should be clear that these two ostensible manifestations of taste differ in important ways. Take first the ice cream parlor, under the strongest possible assumptions supporting the self-validating character of the change in taste. Here, we have nothing but voluntary transactions between the various parties—consumers, workers, dairy producers, and so forth—in which resources presumably flow to the highest valued uses. These transactions take place on a fully disaggregated basis. For example, given prices, each consumer separately decides how much ice cream to buy. There are no important externalities, such as uncompensated harm to people living down the block from the ice cream parlor or the dairy farm. Income disparities in the society do not distort these transactions as reflections of the intensity of public taste for different commodities—or, if they do, overall wealth redistribution is the best response. Consumers are better situated than anyone else to make the best choices for themselves. Thus, if ice cream is bad for their health, they have rationally decided that they enjoy it enough to bear this cost.

These are admittedly strong assumptions. To the extent that they do not hold, however, the case for the self-validating character of a change in taste may become debatable. For example, we might not want ice cream production to increase (leading to more ice cream parlors *ex ante* if anticipated) if consumers are acting on the basis of uncorrectable ignorance about the health risks, or cannot make rational tradeoffs between pleasure and health, or if the price of ice cream ignores important externalities, such as harm to the global environment when pasture for dairy cows replaces carbon dioxide–absorbing forest. The fact that the assumptions do not always hold may justify frustrating consumer preferences in some cases, such as by requiring the use of seat belts, the purchase of car insurance, or a doctor's prescription to receive various medicines.

Now consider the political decision concerning municipal bonds that underlies the airport example. Here, insofar as some people who do not want the airport will nonetheless pay higher taxes by reason of the bond exemption, we have involuntariness and externalities. The majority coalition votes everyone's tax dollars, not just their own, through a single collective decision, rather than a host of disaggregrated private decisions. We also may wonder whether information about the costs and benefits of the choice are as good as in the case where I am deciding whether or not I should eat ice cream. To what extent do voters understand or observe the long-term cost to themselves that is implied by the government's intertemporal budget constraint? How well can they evaluate contestable claims about the airport's stimulative effect, as compared to the subjective benefit of eating ice cream? Do they generally even know what is being decided on their collective behalf?

For an account of the significance of these problems, consider what Graetz (1997) himself has recently written about tax politics:

> The public has great difficulty resisting . . . [claims that] a tax cut for every-one . . . would so stimulate economic growth as to reduce or eliminate budget deficits. The temptation to believe that hard choices can be avoided remains too great (181).
>
> The tax law also changes in response to . . . political fads, vivid stories, and recently from misguided numerical constraints (184).
>
> Today, public polls serve as the guide to policymaking; special interest money is the 800-pound gorilla of the tax legislative process; and politicians with political courage are an endangered species (277).
>
> [Since it] simply is not practical in our system of government to remove congressional discretion over the tax law . . . we should change our political culture to eliminate the tax law as a playground for special interests. . . . A political system is sick when changing the tax law, or threatening to change it, is the most effective way to fill the campaign coffers of members of Congress. But that is the way it is (288).

This hardly sounds like the sort of process that (as the new view posits) yields decisions that ought to be anticipated on the ground that they are generally good, whether on consumer sovereignty and revealed preferences grounds or otherwise. Plainly, then, concern about the defects in collective political choice goes beyond mere right-wing "theology" (Graetz 1985, 1825). Such concern is, indeed, central to the last 50 years of political science and public choice literature, not to mention a tradition of constitutional thought, going back to James Madison, that emphasizes the need, in some settings, to constrain rather than empower the government.

The core defects of public political choice that discourage adopting optimistic new view assumptions about government decisions are threefold—involving what I call problems of aggregation, organization, and information. These are worth briefly considering in turn, not just to drive home (perhaps redundantly) the point that political outcomes are not presumptively good but also to provide an underpinning for my "constitutional" analysis of transition policy.

1. Problems of Aggregation

In the absence of dictatorship, collective choice requires aggregating people's preferences rather than giving each one the result he wants. Hence, the point that 49 percent of the people can buy their own ice cream but not pass their own law. Amongst other implications, aggregation is likely to reduce the level of voter investment in attempting to make good decisions. While I will ineluctably decide how much ice cream I eat, my vote will almost certainly not alter the outcome of an election, or even affect the winner's margin of victory more than infinitesimally.

The value of a single vote is so low that, under conventionally narrow rational behavior models, it seems paradoxical that people vote at all. The only plausible way to resolve the "voting paradox" is to invoke consumption motives involving symbolic or expressive behavior. That is, people vote because it feels good to perform a perceived duty, or to experience a sense of participation, or to express their feelings about particular candidates or issues. Yet motives of this sort may induce voters to act frivolously, such as by choosing amongst politicians with more regard to the immediate appeal of slogans and television personalities than to what the winner would actually do (Shaviro 1990a, 79).

Further aggregation problems arise from the fact that voting, unlike the use of money to buy consumer goods, is ordinal rather than cardinal. Each voter provides the same bare information about the order of his preferences, without directly indicating how much he cares. One possible consequence is majoritarian tyranny. A law that slightly helps 51 percent of the electorate while grievously harming the other 49 percent may nonetheless pass if everyone simply votes his own narrow self-interest. More generally, however, the ordinal character of voting creates a pervasive disconnect between societal preferences and political outcomes, as has been explored in an extensive political science literature. Most famously, Arrow's Theorem shows that voting often cannot succeed in combining individual preferences into a coherent collective choice (Farber and Frickey 1991, 39; Easterbrook 1987, 547). For example, suppose that there are three mutually inconsistent alternatives (A, B, and C) and three legislators who rank them in the following orders of preference:

Legislator 1: A, B, C

Legislator 2: B, C, A

Legislator 3: C, A, B

Under these circumstances, absent strategic voting, the results of pairwise votes will be that A defeats B, B defeats C, and C defeats A (Arrow 1963, 3).

Add in strategic voting and the instability remains, since the legislator who is worst off under any temporarily prevailing outcome can always make an offer to a member of the majority coalition that improves the outcome for both of them. For example, if legislators 1 and 3 ally in support of outcome A (with 3 aiming to fend off outcome B), legislator 2 can respond by offering 3 a better deal, involving a switch to outcome C. Now, however, 1 can buy off 2 by suggesting a switch to outcome B, whereupon 3 proposes to 1 that they ally in support of outcome A, and the process begins again.

This is no isolated or arbitrary example. It may generally occur in legislatures with dozens or hundreds of members and innumerable issues, and even more so in the electorate. It suggests that the final "results achieved under 'democratic' voting rules are arbitrary" (Eskridge 1988, 284), and that endless cycling between outcomes may occur unless procedural rules, perhaps under the control of a dictatorial agenda setter, permit one outcome to endure. Yet such an outcome lacks presumptive superiority as an embodiment of underlying societal preferences.

What is more, Arrow's Theorem provides but one of many grounds for expecting a frequent disconnect between legislative outcomes and the changing sum of underlying societal preferences. Anthony Downs, for example, has analyzed how, in a two-party political system, fortuities of how the parties situate themselves within a bipolar ideological spectrum can lead to outcomes, and changes in outcomes, quite divergent from the weighted average of people's preferences (Downs 1957, 114–25). To use a recent example, once the Republicans in 1995 had shifted to the right, President Clinton could benefit politically from likewise shifting to the right, almost without regard to whether voters had shifted. More generally, changes in party positioning that reflect mere leadership tactics and the fortuities of Downsian processes in the parties can shift political equilibria, even assuming static societal preferences.

The various paradoxes of collective decision making seriously challenge the presumption that legislative changes generally represent welfare improvements, even in the *de gustibus* sense of reflecting changes in public taste. Enactments that instead reflect mere cycling, or changes in the agenda setter or in political tactics, may better be viewed as random and purposeless from a general social welfare perspective. Accordingly, policy change retroactive taxes are not presumptively desirable. One needs either case-by-case inquiry into the merits of particular enactments or a "constitutional" analysis of the likely long-term effects of alternative transition regimes.

Because of their random quality, aggregation problems often lack systematic implications for the establishment of constitutional rules and norms, whether in transition policy, the tax laws, or elsewhere. They counsel normative skepticism but do not indicate a predominant direction of likely error that one can try to offset. One possible exception, lying beyond the scope of this book, goes to the possibility that one would want to discourage cycling or rule change generally, on the view that it imposes transition risk to no generally desirable end.

2. Problems of Organization

Legislation often involves gain to some groups and loss to others. Rivals can compete to express their preferences in the political process. Thus, their relative capacities to organize and act in a politically effective fashion, and to form or join majority coalitions, have important consequences.

At one time, political scientists of the "pluralist" persuasion largely ignored problems of relative organization, arguing that democratic outcomes tend to reflect in a generally balanced fashion the interests of all individuals and thus society (Truman 1951, 51–52; Lindblom 1965, 229, 276–85). More recently, however, it has been recognized that relative organization is extremely uneven. Even apart from the fact that some individuals, such as the wealthy, may have disproportionate influence across the board (Schattschneider 1960, 35), on particular issues, the opposing sides' interests may be unequally represented due to differences in organizational capacity.

The type of organizational disparity that has attracted the greatest attention in the literature is that between large groups whose members have low individual stakes in an issue, and small groups whose members have large individual stakes. Consider interest group theory, which holds that democratic politics tends to produce transfers from the many to the few. The underlying mechanism is collective action problems. The incentive to shirk advancing the interests of one's group, or even to find out where these interests lie, is not proportionate across society. All else equal, it tends to be more severe in large groups than small, given the former's greater internal monitoring and coordinating challenges. This suggests that transfers from the many to the few will be readily adopted (Olson 1965; Peltzman 1976, 213). Or perhaps the strength of members' identification and internal affiliation, rather than group size, is critical—helping to explain the frequent success in political battle of such relatively large groups as the elderly, farming interests, and oil and gas interests.

While pure wealth transfers are efficiency neutral—disregarding the "rent-seeking" costs of people's seeking and opposing them—the need to conceal them often necessitates the adoption of what Gordon Tullock calls "inefficient technologies" that may almost assure net societal loss. Farmers, for example, may be unable to procure the adoption of legislation that entails nothing more than the government's writing substantial checks to current members of their interest group. Rather, they may need to make the transfer less "raw" by cloaking it in the guise of a plausible farm policy—leading to such adverse allocative consequences as overinvestment in farming or the use by farmers of inferior technologies (Tullock 1989, 14, 19). Similarly, localities may find that to get extra money from a central government, they need to propose pork barrel spending, the value of which to them is less than its cost to the society. Once localities generally are doing this, each locality may have no better choice than to add its own wasteful project to the list, rather than oppose all the other wasteful projects (Tullock 1959).

While interest group theory predicts systematic exploitation of the many by the few, the opposite result is possible as well. Consider Fred McChesney's (1987) theory of rent extraction, based on the observation that politicians can extort tribute from well-organized groups in exchange for not harming them, rather than just accept bribes in exchange for helping them. McChesney's model turns interest group theory on its head, making organization a potential detriment rather than benefit for the same reason that rich people are more likely than poor ones to have their loved ones kidnapped and held for ransom.

Rent extraction is only one example where narrow groups with concentrated interests systematically suffer rather than benefit. Consider the Supreme Court's famous reference to "discrete and insular minorities," such as the members of distinctive racial, national, or religious groups, that need special judicial protection from the legislative process because they are prone to be singled out for hostile treatment (*United States v. Carolene Products Co.,* 304 U.S. 144 (1938), 152–53 n. 4). This reversal of interest group theory—since racial discrimination, for example, surely imposed far higher costs on the average African American than its benefits, if any, to the average Caucasian—needs only the right set of circumstances, such as animus towards a highly visible group that lacks good opportunities to join a majority coalition, to prevail.

Thus, small groups with concentrated interests can disproportionately either win or lose in the political process, depending on details of group organization and broader coalition formation. In cases where the members of a group face organizational barriers (such as anonymity or dispersal), lack natural allies, or are targets of general animus, they may be excluded from prevailing majority coalitions and have their interests systematically trampled on. Yet in other cases they may be extraordinarily effective in procuring negative-sum transfers from the rest of society. The one constant is that prevailing policy, or any changes thereto, may reflect such organizational disparities rather than general social welfare. Hence, it follows once again that policy change retroactive taxes, like the underlying policy changes, need not be desirable, and that a case-by-case or constitutional analysis is necessary.

To a greater extent than aggregation problems, organization problems have systematic implications for transition policy. If one can identify a situation where small groups' concentrated interests seem likely to be either favored or disfavored, one can try to respond by creating constitutional impediments to the expected direction of abuse. Thus, the rules in the United States Constitution barring the enactment of *ex post facto* crimes or the taking of private property without compensation mainly respond to concern about the hostile singling out of isolated groups or individuals to suffer narrowly targeted harm (Tribe 1988, 605; Ackerman 1977, 79–80). While those cases reflect concern that narrow groups will be too weak, James Madison's *Federalist Paper No. 10* famously argues that, in many respects, our political system is designed to prevent "factions" from being too strong.

Organization problems may importantly affect both tax law politics, as in Graetz's (1997, 277) description of "special interest money [as] the 800-pound gorilla of the tax legislative process," and retroactive taxes. An important and recurrent retroactive tax issue concerns the imposition of *ex post* capital levies or subsidies. The question of whether or not to impose, say, an ostensibly one-time wipeout of the income tax basis for existing assets or, alternatively, a substantial enhancement of such basis's value, typically places the concentrated interests of a narrow group (the directly affected property owners) against the diffuse interests of a large group (other present and future taxpayers). Thus, one's constitutional approach to capital levies and subsidies may be importantly affected by whether one thinks the minority's power is likely to be too great or too small, although one must consider as well the general efficiency and distributional characteristics of capital levies and subsidies.

3. Problems of Information

As a general matter, people are likely to make worse choices than otherwise when they are ill-informed. While information problems can always be invoked to challenge consumer sovereignty, they may be especially significant in the realm of public political choice, due to aggregation problems that affect individual investment in gathering accurate information, along with the sheer complexity, as well as the remoteness from one's own experience, of the empirical issues on which good public policy often turns. Again, it might be the case that comparing the costs and benefits of the extra state and local government spending generated by the municipal bond preference is harder than comparing the costs and benefits of eating ice cream.

Information problems come in two genres: those where information is simply bad, albeit with no particular expected direction of error; and those where it is systematically biased, or likely to err in a particular direction. Thus, take the question of how much we should spend on national defense. The problem of neutrally bad information arises if we are likely to spend the wrong amount, leading with equal likelihood to waste if we spend too much and adverse international consequences if we spend too little. The problem of systematic bias arises if we are generally likely to spend either too little or too much, thus making one of the two harms more likely than the other.

In some respects, neutrally bad information (if not cost-effectively correctable) may leave one at a loss as to how to respond. Thus, if information about our defense needs is neutrally bad, it is hard to say whether we should seek—through constitutional rules, institutional design, or the like—to encourage either increased or reduced defense spending.[1] Problems of neutrally bad information may nonetheless have general implications for transition policy. They provide an additional reason for expecting that policy decisions will not be very good, and thus for skepticism about the general desirability of policy change retroactive taxes. Moreover, suppose information problems vary in severity with the subject area or the form taken by the government decision—as in the cases where defense needs are either easier or harder to assess than education needs, or regulatory mandates are either more or less transparent than tax and spending rules with similar substantive effects. One's preferred transition policy might conceivably be affected by one's view of information quality in a particular area.

Additional implications may arise when bad information has a systematic direction, and thus one knows in which direction (such as the level of defense spending) policy decisions are likely to err. Claims of systematic error conflict with a rational expectations view, but they may be supportable in cases where the heuristic biases discovered through behavioral research, such as the endowment effect (underestimating opportunity costs relative to out-of-pocket costs), are implicated. A well-known example from the public finance literature is fiscal illusion, or voters' tendency to underestimate tax burdens that take particular forms (Buchanan 1967, 137–43). Consider, for example, corporate income taxation, if one believes that the difficulty of determining its incidence, or the fact that it is nominally paid by a legal entity, leads voters collectively to underestimate (not just be unsure about) its burden on them as individuals (Shaviro 1990a, 60–61).

Fiscal illusion and other systematic errors can lead to bad policy by distorting the comparison of cost to benefit. The greater the magnitude of such errors, and the more that they involve asymmetry between estimation of the cost and benefit sides, the greater the likely adverse effect on the quality of policy decisions. One implication for transition and other policies is that it might make sense to try to counteract expected errors. Suppose, for example, that people were likely to undervalue defense spending. This might make fiscal illusion in paying for such spending desirable, so that the errors would tend to cancel out and voters would come closer to making the right decisions (Lerner 1964, 95, as discussed in Shaviro 1997, 41–42).

The ultimate degree of policy failure in any case depends not just on information problems but also on how these problems interact with the other political choice problems. It may matter a great deal, for example, whether organization and information problems are complementary (both tending to distort political outcomes in the same direction) or offsetting. Also of great importance is the institutional setting. As we will see, a legislature, executive agency, and court may tend to act very differently in the same decision area, with significant implications for transition policy.

B. General Implications of Political Choice Problems for Transition Policy

Once one accepts that the mere fact of a policy change's adoption does not provide strong evidence of whether it—and therefore its policy change retroactive taxes, if any—is good or bad, political choice problems have no direct implications for a case-by-case analysis. Taking as given the decision to make the policy change, and disregarding how a given transition choice might affect future political decisions, all that one needs to know about that choice is how the alternatives would affect efficiency and distribution. Political science predictions about the likely character of political decisions under alternative transition regimes can be left to one side.

As soon as we take a more long-term view, however, the political science issues become important. This book is particularly concerned with the "constitutional" question of how alternative transition norms may influence policy. Yet one's interests need not be quite so global for the long-term perspective to matter. Avinash Dixit (1996, 25) has noted that, because "individual policy acts . . . often create facts, institutions, and expectations that have their own momentum and acquire at least some of the same durability as a change in the constitution itself," the distinction between case-by-case and constitutional analysis is blurry. All political decisions "combine some features of [long-term] rulemaking and some of [case-specific] individual acts, in varying degrees" (29).

Thus, at least to some extent, the constitutional perspective is always implicated by transition decisions. For example, each time investors argue to Congress that their reliance on prior law entitles them to transition relief against an adverse policy change, the political decision to accept or reject this argument may cast a shadow over future similar choices. A relatively stable transition regime may emerge in which arguments of this kind predictably have greater or lesser weight, even if short-term political considerations assure that transition outcomes will not be entirely consistent and predictable. The principle that transition relief ought or ought not (as the case may be) to be granted acquires force as an independent political norm, available for invocation each time by the parties whose interests or preferences it serves, to the extent that it is honored in practice.

The "constitutional" aims that transition policy therefore has can be divided into two categories. The first aim is to encourage better decisions regarding steady-state policy by affecting political incentives and information in light of the transition consequences that a new enactment would likely have. The second aim is to encourage the adoption of transition decisions that are themselves good policy rather than bad, taking into account both transition risk and retroactive taxes.

These aims, one could argue, are limited by what I call "scaling." Suppose that Congress is considering enacting a municipal bond preference because it wants to convey a particular quantum of benefit to bondholders. The underlying motive could reflect either public policy, such as shifting societal investment allocations by a specified amount, or interest group politics, such as giving campaign contributors a handout of a specified value. In principle, Congress can fine-tune the preference upon enactment to take account of the anticipated transition rule in the event that the preference is later repealed (assuming that this is more likely than expansion). Thus, in the case where the prospect of ungrandfathered repeal would otherwise reduce the preference's value in half from the desired level, Congress can respond by making it nominally twice as large (or accelerated) as in the case where grandfathering is expected, thus keeping the preference's value from being affected by the transition regime.

To the extent that such scaling occurs, policy change retroactive taxes, as merely the fortuitous means of implementing policies that Congress would have implemented in any event, lose their independent significance. Only questions of transition risk are pertinent. Some commentators—apparently considering only policy change retroactive taxes—have argued that full scaling should generally be expected (Ramseyer and Nakazato 1989, 1167–69). If enactments are simply a contract between legislators and investors regarding investment allocations, or perhaps between legislators and interest groups regarding the exchange of campaign contributions for payouts from the Treasury, then all that matters is the "expected net present value" that an enactment offers, which thus will be held constant through scaling without regard to the expected transition rule (1167).

However, this view—in a sense, like Michael Graetz's suggested analogy between changes in enacted public policy and private consumer taste—overlooks the distinctive features of public political choice, in particular those reflecting problems of information. Legislative decisions, even if reflecting particular policy aims or interest group input, are made in the shadow of a broader public audience that not only may object to interest group giveaways that are "just too raw" (Tullock 1989, 19) but that also more generally responds to legislation's symbolic properties and superficial appearance.

Take the case of municipal bonds. While one would think that the degree to which municipal bonds are tax favored should depend on exactly how much investment response (or interest group gratitude) Congress wants, the practice over time has been more rigid than this. Qualifying municipal bond interest has generally been 100 percent exempt from tax—not, say, 89 percent exempt, or 114 percent exempt. This rigidity reflects the fact that 100 percent exemption not only is administratively simpler but also "looks" more natural. Providing results better than exemption would expose supporters of the tax preference to extra criticism. This is simply another example of Tullock's point about the "inefficient technology" that those seeking government transfers—or even to have a principled influence on government policy—must adopt given limited information and perceptual biases amongst the general public.[2] Thus, there may be limits to the extent to which scaling can occur in response to the expected transition policy.

A related point is that politicians may not sufficiently care about the real effects of their enactments to adjust the nominal value conveyed to take account of the expected transition rule. Even if interest groups cannot be fooled into overvaluing the real benefits conveyed to them, there is the less attentive general public to consider. Legislation may be proposed simply as a form of position taking, to make the proponent look like a good person—say, a supporter of "education" or "competitiveness." Or it may be an end in itself, serving mainly to enhance one's prestige as an important political "player" (Shaviro 1990, 9, 86–87). When this is the case, the actual effects of an enactment (and particularly those conditioned on someone else's subsequent political initiative) may not be important enough to the enactor for scaling to be an important consideration.

A final point goes to the role that revenue estimating has recently played in the legislative process. Under the "PAYGO" rules that are mandated by laws governing the budget process, proposed tax and spending changes can be ruled out of order, and thus fail to be considered, unless they are accompanied by offsetting tax increases or spending cuts that make them appear revenue neutral on balance. The underlying revenue estimates do not adjust for the prospect of repeal (except insofar as a proposal is explicitly "sunsetted" during the estimating period, which has political costs of its own). Thus, adjusting a proposed enactment to compensate for the prospect of ungrandfathered repeal may increase the procedural burdens or other political costs incurred by the proponents.

If not for these factors, non–policy change retroactive taxes presumably would never arise, except where Congress would have imposed them even without the accompanying policy change. As we will see, however, seemingly anomalous non–policy change retroactive taxes are pervasive— arising even, say, when Congress merely changes tax rates without intending thereby to shift income-generating activity from one taxable year into another, or to help or harm tax-exempt municipal bonds. This reflects the complexity of determining transition consequences, along with the lack of strong incentives for any given actor to undertake the necessary inquiry or corrective measures. I conclude that, while one surely would expect scaling to occur to some extent, it is sufficiently incomplete for retroactive taxes to exert a significant influence on overall policy.

Unfortunately, just as in assessing the private incentive effects of retroactive taxes, it is fruitless to generalize about which transition policy is best across the board. Instead, one must examine how the organizational and informational elements play out in particular areas. Tradeoffs can be indeterminate, and even when a direction of predominant distortion is discernible, it may vary with the setting. I next briefly illustrate this before turning to the tax law setting, where perhaps more definite conclusions can be drawn.

1. Narrow Groups Unduly Advantaged versus Disadvantaged in Seeking Transition Gain or the Avoidance of Transition Loss

Often, the transition gain or loss that would most directly result from a policy change is focused on a narrow group. Hence, the offsetting loss or gain, while equal in the aggregate to the extent of gain-loss symmetry, is spread more diffusely. In these circumstances, does the narrow group tend to be unduly advantaged or disadvantaged, thus possibly calling for correction through the promulgation of an offsetting "constitutional" transition norm? The answer is that it depends.

Undue advantage to the narrow group's concentrated interest is, of course, the standard prediction of interest group theory. Thus, Saul Levmore argues that capital levies that would be efficient if underanticipated are unduly disfavored in the political process. Ostensibly, "powerful interest groups protecting their turf" not only have directly opposed efficient capital levies to great effect but also have even "unfortunate[ly] . . . succeeded in coloring our views about the efficiency and fairness of retroactivity" through their "repeated assertions" of the old view in support of transition relief (Levmore 1993, 291).

Even if Levmore is correct about the overall political bias against capital levies (leaving aside the question of whether and when they are efficient to begin with), it is easy to think of counterexamples. Consider the singling out problem of animus against isolated groups. Again, as a historical matter (but perhaps reflecting sound judgment), concern about this problem underlies such constitutional limits on transition policy as the bars on *ex post facto* crimes and bills of attainder, and the requirement that full-fledged government takings be compensated.

Questions of transition risk aside, there plainly would be a strong argument for allowing *ex post facto* criminal legislation, but for concern about singling out. When criminal legislation responds to a perceived *malum in se* rather than simply establishing specific requirements for lawful behavior that are in some sense arbitrary (such as specifying the date on which tax returns must be filed), retroactive application tends to involve policy change retroactive taxes, and thus to improve incentives if the enactment is good. Consider a bad act that was technically lawful when committed due to prior mistake or oversight in drafting the criminal laws. The prospect of its being made punishable after the fact might both improve *ex ante* deterrence of doing bad things and serve the interests of retributive punishment *ex post* (Krent 1996, 2154–55). Nonetheless, many agree that the retroactive taxes that would be permissible in the absence of an *ex post facto* ban would, with undue frequency, be bad ones, motivated by the impetus to threaten or inflict harm on individuals whom the legislator disliked. And this concern may be particular to the legislative process, having less (if any) application when judicial decisions criminalize behavior *ex post* via the common law or statutory interpretation (Krent 1996, 2173 n. 162).

Takings compensation has been prominently defended on political incentive grounds even without regard to the singling out or animus problem. Consider the case where a highway agency is deciding what private land to seize in the course of new construction, and the question is whether it should be required to pay compensation. The choice lies between imposing a concentrated cost on the few landowners whose property would be taken, or a diffuse cost on taxpayers generally to finance compensating those landowners. Interest group theory notwithstanding, it has been persuasively argued that the former alternative would be politically easier, and indeed too easy (Blume, Rubinfeld, and Shapiro 1984; Fischel and Shapiro 1988). The argument is twofold. First, despite the concentrated nature of their interest, uncompensated landowners have key organizational disadvantages. So long as the prospect of an uncompensated taking is low *ex ante,* of unpredictable incidence, and unlikely to recur as to any given victim, the costs of political organization may deter effective opposition. Hence, concentrated incidence fails to create the organizational advantages enjoyed, say, by the American Medical Association or steel industry when its members' interests predictably conflict with those of the general public. One cannot, for example, imagine the otherwise unconnected individuals whose property is subject to being taken by a highway authority engaging in "agency capture" in the manner of a regulated industry that comes to dominate the regulator.

Second, political attention to the landowners' plight may be reduced by fiscal illusion. In many cases, off-budget costs without explicit dollar amounts attached to them may receive less sympathy and attention in general political debate than those appearing on the budget and with explicit costs. But here the problem is accentuated by regulatory structure. Both explicit takings, as by local government highway authorities, and partial regulatory takings (whether or not compensable) typically involve an administrative agency that is empowered to act in a particular sphere, subject to a budget constraint that is set by the legislature. Such agencies generally attach less weight to off-budget costs than to those they must pay for out of their limited resources (Fischel 1995, 207). Moreover, given fiscal illusion, they generally cannot expect increased budget authorizations to fully offset increases in their explicit costs by reason of a compensation requirement.[3] Note that this argument critically relies on the role of an administrative agency in deciding whether to take property. A legislature, when not motivated by animus, may be especially reluctant to anger even a few constituents a great deal by denying them compensation when their property is taken (Farber 1992, 292)—except, perhaps, in cases where it can shrug its shoulders and blame the whole thing on an agency that it does not directly control.

The recent controversy concerning legislation (the Omnibus Property Rights Act of 1995) that, if enacted, would have required compensation for certain regulatory takings under the Endangered Species Act (ESA) provides a sort of market test supporting this argument. In general, advocates of more extensive species protection opposed the legislation, while those preferring less protection supported it, apparently based on their agreement that it would significantly reduce the level of regulatory activity by the Fish and Wildlife Service. Thus, both sides agreed that the payment of compensation to directly affected landowners would tend to reduce the level of regulatory activity, notwithstanding the standard predictions of interest group theory.

2. Effects of Transition Policy on Interest Group Politics: Enactment versus Repeal

A similarly complicated, but perhaps even more indeterminate, set of issues emerges when one turns to legislative politics and asks whether, in the ebb and flow of interest group legislation that is subject to repeal as well as expansion, it is better over the long run to provide transition relief upon repeal or deny it. Perhaps the best-known discussion of the problem comes from Gordon Tullock (1975). Tullock describes the "transitional gains trap," arising when the value of an inefficient special subsidy or monopoly is capitalized into asset values and then relied upon by "innocent" purchasers. Thus, suppose that farm subsidies bid up the price of farmland and increase the size of the agricultural sector until, despite the subsidy, it offers only normal economic returns. Now, repeal of the subsidy without transition relief will both impose a transition loss on farmers that some might argue is unfair, and lead them vigorously to oppose repeal even though the subsidy no longer offers them above-normal returns (1993, 67).

Under my analysis in chapter 3, there is no reason outside politics to consider this a "trap" at all. Ungrandfathered repeal would yield a policy change retroactive tax, reaching farmers in a way that is desirable precisely because repeal of the subsidy is good policy. Anticipation of this tax would tend to reduce the allocative response to the subsidy from the moment of enactment forward. The only drawback to imposing the retroactive loss on farmers upon repeal goes to transition risk, and thus is not significant to the extent that they either want to "bet" against repeal or can readily diversify or hedge against it.

However, Tullock is mainly making a political claim, to the effect that repeal of the subsidy will be difficult for transitional reasons even though it no longer offers farmers extra-normal returns. He notes that a policy of compensating current farmers for the elimination of the subsidy would address the political problem, but he dismisses the prospect that this will happen as "very small" (1975, 678). One could imagine, however, Tullock's account of the transitional gains trap being invoked to support a practice of granting transition relief upon the repeal of inefficient subsidies on the ground that it is a needed political lubricant.

A similar argument has prominently been made in the tax transitions literature, but it takes a somewhat different form. Mark Ramseyer and Minoru Nakazato (1989) rely on McChesneyean rent extraction to argue that society would benefit from guaranteeing interest groups transitional protection against the repeal of their subsidies. Ostensibly, this will reduce the socially wasteful post-enactment lobbying costs that the groups would otherwise incur in responding to politicians' extortionary retroactive repeal threats, without affecting enactment-period lobbying costs. Ramseyer and Nakazato reach this conclusion despite recognizing that the prospect of post-enactment lobbying may "dissipate large portions of [the apparent] gains" from the subsidies (1172). They offer the assumption that, no matter what the specific terms of the deal underlying enactment, the interest group will receive a fixed expected net present value per dollar of bribes paid to legislators. Thus, just as a short-lived subsidy can be made as valuable as a long-lived one by adjusting the value per year, so Congress can adjust for expected post-enactment lobbying costs by increasing the nominal subsidy.

This is plainly mistaken, however, if Congress faces any sort of overall budget constraint on subsidy payouts from the Treasury. Assuming some such budget constraint, the prospect that post-enactment lobbying costs will dissipate much of the value of Treasury payouts makes enactment-period lobbying less attractive than otherwise. Congress simply cannot provide as much "bang" for the available "bucks." An effective guarantee of transition relief would therefore yield an ambiguous tradeoff, rather than the clear societal gain that Ramseyer and Nakazato posit: more (rather than constant) enactment period lobbying in exchange for less post-enactment lobbying.

The same tradeoff applies to the argument one could deduce from

Tullock, to the effect that transition relief upon the repeal of inefficient subsidies is desirable as a political lubricant to repeal. While such relief may indeed facilitate desirable repeal in particular cases, its long-term effect is to increase political demand for initial enactment of the subsidies, assuming incomplete scaling. Hence, one is left at a loss regarding which transition regime, compensation or no compensation, yields better decisions over the long run, or even in any particular case where the short-term advantages seem clear.[4]

We are left, therefore, with an indeterminate political incentives problem, at least in the abstract. This once again shows the difficulty of generalizing about how questions of politics should affect transition analysis. One needs to confine one's political and related constitutional conclusions to particular contexts. I next briefly examine two non–tax law areas in order to illustrate how the political analysis can interact with the economics, before turning to the setting of tax legislation.

C. Effect of Politics on the Transition Analysis in Some Non–Tax Law Settings

1. Outright and Regulatory Takings

As we have already seen, the question of whether outright or regulatory takings by an administrative agency should be compensated is complex and controversial. Such compensation is constitutionally mandated for outright takings, with unclear but fairly narrow extension to regulation that goes "too far" in limiting the use of property (*Pennsylvania Coal Co. v. Mahon,* 260 U.S. 393 (1922)), thus at the limit rendering it "valueless" (*Lucas v. South Carolina Coastal Council,* 505 U.S. 1003 (1992)). However, legislation can create a right to compensation where the Constitution does not. The proposed Omnibus Property Rights Act of 1995 would have done so where certain regulatory mandates, including under the Endangered Species Act (ESA), reduced property values by more than a threshold percentage, and several states have passed similar compensation rules with respect to their own agencies.

In principle, an issue of compensation (or benefit taxation) arises whenever government regulation affects the value of property. While the issue is itself bookworthy given the level of relevant institutional detail across the regulatory landscape, the basic analytical considerations (apart from administrative cost) have already been set forth here. Economically, as suggested in chapter 3, the prospect of compensation raises two main issues. First, recall the example where an owner, in making investment decisions with regard to property, could disregard the prospect that the highway might come if, in the event that it came, she would be compensated for any resulting loss of value. The broader point is that owners' incentive to minimize adjustment costs depends on keeping their compensation (if any) independent of their decisions' effects on sunk cost investment. Thus, if zero compensation and fair market value compensation (and not, say, site value or some measure of value to the government) are the only available options, the former is clearly preferable from the standpoint of inducing minimization of adjustment costs.

Second, recall the ESA example where compensation would reduce owners' incentive to head off any restriction on land use by clearing their land of any possible rare species before the regulators could arrive and enjoin them from doing so. The broader point is that incentives may be distorted if actions that the owner takes may affect the subsequent imposition of an uncompensated loss (or receipt of a gain). Thus, for outright takings, if even fair market value compensation is below the owner's true reservation price, the same type of problem as under the ESA would arise if, say, highway authorities promised not to take any land containing buildings at least 10 stories tall. Or consider the Omnibus Property Rights Act of 1995, which, by limiting compensation to cases where more than a threshold percentage of property value was lost, would have encouraged owners to engage in development that increased the chances of suffering a sufficient percentage of loss to trigger compensation for the whole (Litan 1996, 68).

Accordingly, from the standpoint of private incentives, the aim of a rule concerning compensation should be to minimize these two sources of inefficiency. Unfortunately, they can have inconsistent implications, as in a case where a promise of full compensation is needed to prevent one's taking steps to forestall the exercise of regulatory authority, and yet induces overinvestment (given the possibility of such exercise) in other respects. How best to resolve any such dilemmas depends on case-specific information that is beyond my present scope. For example, where regulatory takings by local zoning boards are at issue, it might matter exactly what unilateral freedom of action owners actually have.

The analysis of private incentives seems unusually incomplete, however, in the takings as opposed to other transition settings. What makes it so is that this is an area for "constitutional" rules *par excellence*—by which I mean not that particular legal documents called "constitutions" may happen to address takings but that the area involves repeated low-level exercises of agency authority that may aptly be required to meet criteria that are set in advance. (In this sense, the Omnibus Property Rights Act of 1995 would have changed the "constitutional" regime for certain exercises of regulatory authority.) Due to this constitutional aspect, the economic analysis of takings compensation must be supplemented by the political, as in the discussion from earlier in this chapter of administrative agencies and concentrated interests.

The earlier discussion suggested that agencies—as distinct from legislatures—are often inclined to undervalue the costs that their decisions impose if compensation is not required and they are not facing organized interests. (Scattered property takings of unpredictable incidence are therefore different from imposing costs on regulated industries that may have considerable influence over their regulators.) The conclusion sometimes drawn from this analysis is that a requirement of full compensation, even if undesirable with respect to private incentives, will tend to improve agency decisions through the mechanism of greater cost internalization via inclusion in the agency's explicit budget (Blume, Rubinfeld, and Shapiro 1984; Shapiro and Fischel 1988).

The conclusion that greater cost consciousness will improve government decisions does not always follow, however. Thus, suppose that the Fish and Wildlife Service, in determining what regulatory mandates to issue under the ESA, systematically underestimates the benefit as well as the off-budget cost of protecting endangered species. Improving just its estimate of the cost might paradoxically lead to worse decisions. Thus, in a sense, both supporters and the foes of the 1995 compensation statute may have been right, by their respective lights, in preferring the financing rule that, given their other assumptions, seemed likely to yield "better" political results.

For outright and regulatory takings more generally, it is hard to be certain when compensation improves political incentives overall even if one agrees that, for reasons of fiscal illusion and agency structure, it will increase the perceived cost of regulatory activity. To some extent, the creation of a specialized agency inherently offsets the tendency to underappreciate diffuse benefits, and thus to provide too little regulation. Consider William Niskanen's (1971) influential work on administrative behavior and incentives, which suggests that agencies generally try to maximize their control over resources for reasons of empire building or expanding their power or prestige. Thus, even if the constituency for clean air and water is generally inactive because it is dispersed, at least the Environmental Protection Agency is on hand looking for new regulatory initiatives. Or even if too few people organize to demand useful highways, the local highway commission can be expected to have an interest in stirring up activity.

Yet whether this counterbalance to the diffuse benefit problem is too strong or too weak may vary with the setting. One might, for example, consistently believe that highway authorities tend to do too much, that whether local zoning boards do too much or too little depends on their internal politics (Fischel 1995), and that endangered species are so important and underappreciated by voters that the Fish and Wildlife Service does too little. Someone who thought this might conclude that the aim of improving agency decisions over the long run would be advanced by favoring compensation always in the first, under specified circumstances in the second, and never in the third of these categories, despite the analytical similarity of the structural political issues. Or one might seek a more general constitutional norm that was aimed at improving political incentives most of the time without resting on controversial views of specific policy areas.

2. Pollution Permits

While United States environmental policy rests mainly on a "command and control" approach specifying when pollutants can and cannot be emitted, many economists have called for a more market-based approach, such as one using classic Pigovian taxes or else tradeable emissions permits (Joskow and Schmalensee 1997, 37–38.) The 1990 Clean Air Act amendment creating tradeable sulfur dioxide emissions permits remains the only important example of such an approach, but there has been talk of extending it to other areas—for example, carbon permits to address global warming (Cramton and Kerr 1998).

The creation of a permit system poses the transition issue of whether permits should be issued for free to those currently permitted to emit pollutants, or auctioned to the highest bidder. The former is grandfathering, while the latter imposes a retroactive tax on polluters' sunk cost investment.[5] Economists have tended to favor the retroactive tax, but in the 1990 Clean Air Act case, the political system selected grandfathering.

Economically, the case for auction is quite powerful. An initial consideration is that transaction costs may be reduced by enabling the highest-valuing users to get the permits right away (Stavins 1995). More fundamentally, however, a retroactive tax on polluters, like a prospective tax, has desirable incentive effects to the extent anticipated. Thus, a retroactive tax on emitting sulfur dioxide, even if on that occasion a complete surprise, might be a precedent suggesting that, say, companies emitting carbon gases that contribute to global warming would face a similar retroactive tax if carbon permits are introduced.

By contrast, the likely lesson of the 1990 decision to allocate sulfur dioxide permits via grandfathering was that, in other areas where permits might be introduced, one may benefit from positioning oneself to be a permit recipient. The specifics of this behavior would depend on the precise contours of the preexisting regulatory regime in a given area, but could include increasing or at least accelerating one's currently lawful emission of pollutants and sunk cost investment therein.

Politically, the question most directly raised by imposing retroactive taxes upon the introduction of a permit program is whether it would tend to move actual pollution taxation closer to or farther from the optimal Pigovian level. In theory, a problem analogous to overtaking by the highway authorities could arise if the prospect of revenue enhancement through permit auctions were sufficiently enticing to Congress to induce it to set overall pollution taxes too high. Permit auction prices can be excessive from the Pigovian standpoint because they reflect the value of being able to pollute, rather than the external harm caused by pollution. Similarly, it would be inefficient to auction, say, permits to have windows in buildings, since this presumably causes no harm at all.

In practice, however, the argument that permit auctions would lead to excessive pollution taxes appears quite unrealistic. Not only are such taxes little imposed today, but the transition losers from a permit auction, such as companies that have in effect bet against retroactive pollution taxation through their investment decisions, are likely to be members of well-organized industry groups that have considerable legislative influence. In addition, the fact that the natural beneficiaries of grandfathering are less well defined here than, say, when the issue is one of preserving income tax basis suggests that significant resources may be dissipated in rent-seeking battles concerning the allocation of free permits. This appears to have happened when sulfur dioxide permits were handed out in 1990 (Joskow and Schmalensee 1997, 38).

Thus, an established practice of imposing retroactive pollution taxes through permit auctions would likely improve political outcomes. Perhaps the main counterargument is that the somewhat pretextual nature of using the introduction of tradability as the occasion for imposing transition loss— reflecting what is in part a mere accounting change in how authorization to pollute is evidenced (as discussed in chapter 3)—might tend to encourage undesirable accounting change retroactive taxes in other areas. In addition, it is obviously possible in a given case that grandfathering would be necessary to grease the wheels politically for a desirable reform—although this, in turn, might tend to encourage undesirable grandfathering in other future cases.

D. IMPLICATIONS OF POLITICAL CHOICE PROBLEMS IN THE TAX LAW SETTING

We now turn to the implications for transition policy of political choice problems in the tax law setting, where I aim to give the analysis greater institutional detail. This section makes two political choice claims in the tax law setting that end up mattering to my constitutional analysis. The first is that tax legislative politics is quite bad, even by the standards of legislative policy making generally, with adverse consequences for the quality of the decisions that are made. The second claim is that, in the legislative setting in which tax (among other) laws are made, decisions to provide grandfathering or other transitional adjustment are biased in favor of compensating transition losers, rather than eliminating the gains of transition winners. Thus, with losses more likely to be compensated than gains taxed away, a norm in support of transitional relief (even if defined symmetrically as between gain and loss) is likely to increase the scope of this asymmetry. The constitutional implications of both claims are further discussed in chapter 5.

1. The Special Problems with Tax Politics

For decades, there has been a widespread consensus among those who closely follow tax policy that the legislative process in this area is seriously flawed, even by the standards of collective political choice generally. More specifically, it is among the especially flawed areas, although it is not necessarily uniquely flawed. While this view is perhaps partly sour grapes from those whose policy preferences, such as support for a more comprehensive tax base, Congress does not share (Surrey 1957; Shaviro 1990a; Graetz 1997), the underlying critique is shared by political scientists who come to the area without a strongly held tax policy orientation (Lowi 1964; Manley 1970; Hayes 1981; Witte 1985). Tax politics suffers from severe problems both of organization and of information.

It has long been widely recognized that tax politics tends to be dominated by interest groups that seek favors for themselves and that, through a norm of logrolling, almost never oppose favors for each other (Surrey 1957, 1166; Manley 1970, 335–36; Davies 1985, 285–86; Shaviro 1990a, 55). These interests need not be small in membership—consider homeowners, who benefit from deducting home mortgage interest while excluding the related imputed income from their homes—but they nonetheless skew political outcomes given underrepresentation of the general revenue interest that is always the other side of the coin. This diffuse general interest remains unorganized and little heard.

In Theodore Lowi's influential terminology, tax politics (when progressivity debates are not at center stage) is mainly *distributive* (1964, 692–695; Hayes 1981, 48–49).[6] Other examples of distributive politics, with similar pathologies resulting from the dominance of the forces seeking particularized benefits, include tariff legislation when subject to Congress's direct control (as in Schattschneider 1935) and pork barrel spending. In both of these areas, the inherent shortcomings of the legislative process have come to be recognized, and to some extent have been addressed institutionally. Consider the use of commissions to recommend domestic military base closings, and the shifting of substantial tariff authority to the executive branch, which is less prone to favor protectionist interests at the expense of consumer interests (Witte 1985, 383). Thus, one is not being parochial about tax politics—to the contrary, one is aptly fitting it into a broader perspective—when one complains that it is an area of particularly destructive interest group influence.

However, problems of organization are not all that make tax politics seriously flawed, even by the standards of collective political choice generally. A crucial added element lies in the informational realm. An initial problem is simply the arcaneness of determining what would be, say, neutral treatment of competing investments. Yet arcaneness, like interest group politics, is hardly unique to tax politics. The root of the problem goes beyond complexity to affirmative fiscal illusion. People are seemingly unable to accept the arithmetic equivalence between a $1 "tax expenditure" and a $1 direct expenditure that are made for the same reason (Surrey 1973, 1). Indeed, the publication for many years of an official "tax expenditure budget" seems to have made little difference in this regard.

The core reason for this undue distinction in people's thinking is the endowment effect, which induces people to draw an exaggerated distinction between money that is never paid in to the Treasury and money that is first paid in and then taken back out. Due to this heuristic bias, demands for targeted tax benefits tend to have greater political appeal than would the same proposals if they were repackaged with no significant change in overall substance and appeared in the guise of proposed direct outlays by the government. And this is notwithstanding the fact that special income exclusions or deductions change in value as the taxpayer's marginal rate bracket changes—an element of program design that would often be generally regarded as perverse if replicated with respect to direct outlays (Surrey 1973, 134–38).

In some cases, the endowment effect furthers interest group power by reducing the perceived cost of targeted giveaways. In other cases, its ill effects have little to do with interest group politics. Politicians who are inclined to peddle frivolous proposals, whether as symbolic gestures to impress a largely inattentive general public or simply to establish themselves as important "players" within the Washington policy community, often find it most convenient to use the tax system as the proposed situs for their initiatives. One does not, after all, look as much like a practitioner of the rhetorically infamous "big government" if one purports to cut taxes rather than to increase spending—even though this distinction is purely formal if a substantively identical program can be packaged either way. Thus, pervasive information problems add to the unfortunate organizational effects on tax policy of tax politics' generally distributive structure, to make tax politics an area in which legislative decision making is notoriously poor in quality.

2. Gain-Loss Asymmetry in Relieving the Transition Consequences of Tax Law Changes

An important empirical question with regard to tax law changes is whether, on balance, Congress tends to be biased between compensating transition losers and burdening transition winners. Assuming incomplete scaling, a bias in either direction would suggest that transition norms that affected the general political appeal of transition relief, without affecting the relative political appeal of compensating losers versus burdening winners, would have systematic long-term effects on the overall tax system.

For example, suppose that problems of organization and information make Congress inherently more prone to compensate transition losses than to eliminate transition gains. All else being equal, this asymmetry will tend to result in an overall *ex post* capital subsidy from rule changes. The "old view" that retroactive taxes are unfair might tend to increase the capital subsidy, while the "new view" that *ex post* changes are generally unobjectionable might tend to reduce it. Reversing the direction of bias between transition gains and losses would tend to reverse the relative impact on wealth holders of the old and new views.

At a broad theoretical level, it is indeterminate whether the political system will lean towards taking away transition winners' gains or towards compensating transition losers. While interest group politics may suggest the latter, recall the prior discussion of outright and regulatory takings in which I suggested that agencies are particularly prone to impose transition losses, due both to the organizational barriers faced by uncompensated losers and to fiscal illusion if the agency is mainly scrutinized by the legislature as to its explicit cash budget. Or consider the suggestion in the time-inconsistency (such as Kydland and Prescott 1977) and rent extraction literatures that governments may be opportunistic, in the sense of imposing burdens rather than benefits on anyone who precommits in reliance on a previously announced policy and thus becomes a convenient target of *ex post* taxation.

Nonetheless, in the area of legislative tax law changes, it should be clear that the political impetus to compensate transition losses exceeds that to deny transition gains—even though there is some degree of offset between interest group organization and fiscal illusion, in the sense that transition losses can be used to pay for lower explicit tax rates while transition gains might require such rates to be increased.[7] Two key differences from the takings example are that here a legislature, rather than an agency, is the decision maker; and that the groups facing transition loss, such as from the repeal of a tax preference or the elimination of income tax basis, can organize more readily than can the dispersed individuals who are unpredictably subjected to takings. However, the main evidence for the asymmetry is empirical rather than theoretical.

An initial suggestive point is that the tax transition literature, ranging from the more academic to the more practice oriented, overwhelmingly focuses on relieving transition loss rather than eliminating transition gain *and* loss (Kaplow 1986, 553–54). Even the term that is conventionally used to describe transition devices such as grandfathering—transition relief—refers to the loss situation. Just as aspirin relieves a headache but a hangover would not ordinarily be said to relieve one of not having a headache, so it is verbally awkward to speak of "relieving" one's transition gain.

When one specifically looks at congressional practice, the asymmetry between the treatment of transition gain and loss grows no less striking. It is true that new tax rules whose formal application is directed to specific assets—say, depreciation for buildings, as distinct from the corporate tax—typically apply only to those placed in service after a general effective date. It is true as well that significant retroactive losses are sometimes imposed through the nominally prospective application of new rules to prior investments. Consider the passive loss rules from the Tax Reform Act of 1986, which imposed sizable transition losses on preenactment purchasers of various tax shelter investments.

Nonetheless, congressional practice reveals a strong asymmetry between the treatment of transition losses and gains, through the mechanism of specifically denominated "transition rules" that typically operate as exceptions to the general effective dates of new provisions. These transition rules pervasively favor the particular taxpayers to whom they apply (Jones 1988; Zelenak 1989). They come in two main forms. The first is generic rules of broad application, which typically hold that property placed in service after a new provision's effective date will nonetheless be taxed under the provision that it replaced, so long as the taxpayer had a binding contract to construct or acquire the property by a specified date. These "binding contract" exceptions to the effective date are almost always used to benefit qualifying taxpayers when the applicable tax rules change to their detriment—not to burden such taxpayers when the rules change to their benefit. Thus, Congress enacted a generic "binding contract" exception when tax depreciation rules were made less favorable in 1986 but not when they were made more favorable in 1981 (Joint Committee on Taxation 1981, 107; Joint Committee on Taxation 1987, 110).

The second genre of transition rules are those called "rifleshots," because they are deliberately drafted to apply to only one or a few taxpayers. One such provision from the Tax Reform Act of 1986 applied to "a [and presumably any] 562-foot passenger cruise ship . . . the approximate cost of refurbishment of which is approximately $47 million." Another specified a corporation "the parent of which was incorporated in California on April 15, 1925," and that, "on May 22, 1986, merged into a Delaware corporation incorporated on March 12, 1986" (Bittker 1989, 703). Rifleshot transition rules, like generic binding contract rules, are nearly always used to extend favorable treatment to the taxpayers they describe, and are widely recognized as products of distributive interest group politics at its most blatant (Birnbaum and Murray 1987, 146, 240).

While these asymmetric effective date rules represent a discrete practice of limited general significance, they arguably bespeak an important broader attitude. Consider the frequently discussed possibilities of shifting from an income to a consumption tax and of adopting corporate integration. Depending on how they were implemented, in the absence of deliberate transitional adjustment, the former might involve a retroactive loss for holders of old capital generally, and the latter a retroactive gain for holders of old corporate equity. As we will see, proposals have been made to implement each change both with and without transitional adjustment. Nonetheless, many observers of tax policy and politics agree that the retroactive gain from corporate integration would have a much higher probability of being allowed, in the event that the underlying rule change was adopted, than the retroactive loss from income to consumption tax transition. The latter, it is widely assumed, would arouse both more concentrated opposition (Bradford 1996, 136; Hall and Rabushka 1995, 79) and greater general perceptions of unfairness. As we will further see in chapter 5, this political distinction between the willingness to impose transition loss and allow transition gain has important consequences for predicting the likely marginal effects of promulgating alternative transition policy norms.

FIVE

Constitutional Norms for Tax Law and Tax Transitions

With the prior three chapters' economic and political background, we can now consider constitutional norms for tax law transition. Again, by "constitutional," I refer to a stable long-term rule or aspiration that constrains or at least influences political behavior. The tradition of constitutional economics in this sense goes back at least to the nineteenth century economist Knut Wicksell, although it was most extensively developed by Nobel Laureate James Buchanan, Gordon Tullock, and others in public choice theory's "Virginia school."

Constitutional economics often involves the idea of binding precommitment. For example, voters who recognize that during the course of ordinary politics they might be inclined to abridge each others' free speech rights, potentially making everyone worse off *ex ante* if it is unpredictable who will succeed in oppressing whom, may agree in advance to an enforceable constitutional bar on such abridgment (Shaviro 1997, 89). However, a similar analysis may extend to promulgating norms that lack any formal legal status but may influence behavior insofar as they are considered appealing. Indeed, the distinction between binding constraints and suggestive norms is not as sharp as it may initially appear, given the literal impossibility of precommitment. Even an ostensibly binding legal rule can be repealed, or it can be simply ignored if people cease to respect it. Likewise, a mere norm can serve as a powerful restraint under some circumstances. Buchanan has argued that a norm favoring balanced budgets except in wartime and severe recession was regularly observed by the United States government from enactment of the Constitution through the 1930s, when Keynesianism, amongst other factors, caused the norm to lose intellectual prestige (Buchanan and Wagner 1977). In the income tax realm, a norm defining "tax reform" as eliminating special tax preferences commands enough esteem to influence policy from time to time, however lacking in binding force or even general public assent. The Tax Reform Act of 1986, for example, moved the tax system significantly in this direction, in part because the media defined "reform" (presumptively a good thing) as eliminating special tax preferences (Conlan, Wrightson, and Beam 1990, 250–51).

Ideas importantly affect the play of interests and even shape how people define their interests. Thus, in the transition setting, consider the power of the norm holding that nominally retroactive tax law changes are inappropriate. It is unclear whether Congress could constitutionally provide, say, in 2002 that certain deductions for the year 2000 were not allowable after all (Levmore 1993, 270 n. 12)—although, if it could not, this would owe less to binding precommitment than to the anti–nominal retroactivity idea's influence on judges. As things stand, however, nominal retroactivity of this sort is generally beyond the pale of what is even discussed.

While ideas thus matter, ongoing practice matters as well. For example, the enactment of one nominally retroactive policy change would probably make the next such change more likely, creating the possibility that the norm would be gradually eroded. More generally, any time that Congress provides or declines to provide transition relief, its decision casts a shadow over subsequent similar cases, perhaps most likely in the form of a precedent that invites imitation, with the definition of "similar cases" depending on the categories that people actually draw. This is why one might support applying a constitutional norm in cases where it seemed to yield the wrong answer. The error cost of applying it that time might be less than the long-term benefit of reinforcing its use in other cases.

This chapter first discusses what I call the "comprehensive tax base" norm for tax policy generally. While not specifically linked to tax law transitions, it helps to orient good tax policy in that setting. I then propose and discuss three particular norms for tax law transitions, pertaining to policy change retroactive taxes, accounting change retroactive taxes, and nominal retroactivity.

A. Steady-State Tax Policy: A Comprehensive Tax Base of the Income or Consumption Tax Genre

1. Widespread Expert Support for the Comprehensive Tax Base

For many decades, a widespread consensus among tax policy thinkers has held that society would benefit from the use of a more comprehensive tax base (CTB) of either the income tax or the consumption tax genre. The comprehensive income tax ideal was long dominant,[1] but the consumption tax's reemergence as a prominent rival left intact the principle of internal comprehensiveness (as in Andrews 1974; Bradford 1986, 312–34).

Under the alternative CTBs, items constituting economic income or consumption, as these terms have been developed in the literature, would generally be taxed uniformly, rather than being tax favored or tax penalized in particular cases. Achievement of the CTB would be limited by administrative considerations (such as the difficulty, under the income tax, of measuring unrealized asset appreciation) and might be subject to deliberate exception in specific cases. However, the aim of applying CTB treatment where feasible would be given much higher priority than under present law.

Accordingly, under a CTB norm, the actual tax base would move considerably closer to one or the other CTB. Thus, we would not see as much bias as under present law between effective tax rates on different industries, different forms of consumption (such as home versus non-home), or corporate versus noncorporate investment. Similarly, given the CTB norm's real, if limited, influence (as reflected in the Tax Reform Act of 1986), the income tax base might grow narrower still if the norm lost intellectual prestige.

In this book, I will accept this consensus view and assume that the CTB norm has good effects, and thus that movement towards a CTB of either the income or consumption tax genre is generally desirable.[2] However, rather than defend the CTB norm in detail—a project for another day—I will note only that its plausibility importantly depends on claims about tax politics, not just about the efficiency and distributional concerns that are typically invoked in its favor. The theory of the second best (Lipsey and Lancaster 1956) suggests that once a system has any distortions—such as an income tax's bias against work and saving, and a consumption tax's bias against work—adding further distortions need not make things worse. In addition, externalities can justify what might otherwise seem nonneutral treatment. A Pigovian pollution tax, for example, might increase efficiency even if it were folded into the current income tax.

CTB advocates may recognize this point, insofar as they do not generally oppose all government interventions in the economy. They therefore must at least implicitly be relying on the problems with tax politics. Given the pervasive organizational and informational problems that I discussed in chapter 4, it is plausible that Congress's decisions would be improved if, when writing tax laws, it generally sought to define and tax consumption or economic income, rather than making particularized case-by-case decisions about appropriate tax treatment.

To be sure, the CTB norm requires arguing more than just that most of the non-CTB rules in the tax law that it would deter are bad. If these proposals simply changed form to operate through direct spending or regulatory policy, or else were replaced by other, equally bad policies that could more conveniently take those forms, little would have been gained by eliminating income tax preferences. Bad policy would simply have been exported from the tax laws to other areas of government policy making.

While this possibility is hard to disprove, the view that the CTB norm would yield overall policy improvement is more plausible. If a particular bad policy would have been implemented through the tax laws but for the CTB norm, then presumably this was the most politically convenient way, at the margin, to implement a bad policy.[3] Taking away a convenient tool for bad policy should raise the cost of implementing them generally, even if other tools remain; hence the argument that a pro-CTB constitutional norm would have desirable marginal effects.

So far, however, I have ignored the seemingly crucial problem of choosing between the income and consumption tax versions of the CTB—and thus, for example, determining whether an asset's tax treatment should shift in present value terms towards economic depreciation or towards expensing. This choice has riven tax policy debate for decades, and seemingly would prevent broader consensus that more than one of the two leading alternative CTBs is worth seeking. As I discuss next, however, this divide is considerably less important than it may appear.

2. Choosing between the Income Tax and Consumption Tax CTBs

Under both income and consumption taxation, market work and consumption are disfavored relative to nonmarket work and leisure, causing inefficiency and distributional error. The reason for adding, in the income tax, a further distortion and distributional error based on people's intertemporal consumption preferences and choices is unclear. Yet the theory of the second best suggests that this added error does not necessarily make things worse, given the first error. Once we overburden workers relative to nonworkers, how strong is the prediction that making the burden worse still for worker-savers, but not quite as bad for worker-nonsavers, will increase either efficiency loss or horizontal distributional error?[4] What is more, even if the consumption tax fares slightly better in efficiency and horizontal distributional terms, there might be a counterargument, grounded in political economy and subject to administrative questions such as about the efficacy of tax planning, that in practice income taxation will tend to be the more progressive system, even though in principle one could equalize progressivity between the two through the choice of rates. Thus, neither system is unmistakably superior in the abstract.

It is important to realize, however, that the abstract difference between the two taxes is significantly smaller than most commentators have long assumed. Rather than extending to whether or not all of what we may colloquially call investment returns are taxed, the two systems differ purely with regard to whether they tax the real (that is, inflation-adjusted) riskless return to waiting (Bankman and Griffith 1993; Bradford 1996; Gentry and Hubbard 1996; Warren 1996; Cunningham 1996; Bankman and Fried 1998). This is best appreciated by notionally dividing the return from an investment—say, Bill Gates's initial stake in Microsoft—into the following categories: (1) the risk-free return to waiting (which he could have earned by investing in short-term Treasury bonds rather than Microsoft); (2) the risk premium, generally available for risky investments because the marginal investor is risk averse; (3) the inframarginal return to having a good investment idea; and (4) the wage for working on Microsoft's behalf to implement the idea, to the extent paid through stock appreciation rather than cash salary.

In principle, only the first of these items, the risk-free return to waiting, is taxable under an income tax and exempt under a consumption tax. The risk premium is exempt under both if taxpayers can make offsetting adjustments to their pretax bets. Thus, suppose that while investing some of my assets risk free (for arithmetic convenience, at a zero return), I also want to invest $100 for an instantaneous but highly risky expected return of $110. This investment will yield, with equal probability, either $220 or 0. I observe, however, that the tax rate (under either system) is 50 percent. Assuming that losses are fully refundable at the 50 percent rate,[5] the taxes have in effect given me unwanted insurance. After paying tax on the profit or deducting my loss, I will be up only $60 or down only $50, leading to an expected return of only $5.

Given the bet that I preferred, however, it is plausible under both taxes that I will respond through an adjustment to my overall investment portfolio that involves doubling my risky bet (Bankman and Griffith 1993, 393–95). I thus shift $100 from the risk-free to the risky investment, which now totals $200 and will yield either $440 or 0 before tax. After application of the 50 percent tax rate to my $240 gain or $200 loss, I once again am up $120 or down $100, for an expected gain of $10. I have therefore succeeded in fully disinsuring and eliminating either tax system's effect on both the risky return I expected *ex ante,* and the actual return I received *ex post.*

Admittedly, some of the above assumptions seem heroic. Can and will I borrow risk free once I have shifted my entire portfolio into risky investments? Will I recognize and adjust for the effects of the tax, rather than being lulled by the nominal pretax return? Yet these objections apply under both taxes, and thus do not affect the conclusion that income and consumption taxation reach risk premia to the same extent, if at all.

The inframarginal and implicit wage elements of investment returns in the colloquial sense, such as Bill Gates's profits from Microsoft, are reached by both the income tax and the consumption tax. Here the key distinction from risk premia is that one cannot scale up the investment in response to the tax. Risk aside, one presumably would already have sought the maximum pure profit, or worked as much as one wanted given the tax burden. To help show that the consumption tax, no less than the income tax, reaches the added value from Microsoft's extraordinary success, consider that its profitability comes from selling consumer goods, or inputs to produce such goods, that any general consumption tax would reach.

Another way of making the point that income and consumption taxation differ only in their treatment of the pure return to waiting is more abstract still. The main difference between these taxes is one of timing (as in the distinction between expensing and economic depreciation for one's capital outlays). Risk and inframarginal returns are not functions of timing; they could, in principle, be instantaneous. Only the return to waiting is inherently a function of time.

The implications of recognizing that income and consumption taxation differ only in their treatment of the pure return to waiting can be surprising. Historically, the real riskless rate, if one deduces it from the returns offered by short-term Treasury notes since 1926, has averaged less than 1 percent per year (Bankman and Griffith 1993, 387; Bradford 1996, 129). Even if this figure is unduly low—perhaps reflecting an anomalous period when inflation frequently outstripped expectations, or the federal government's exploitation of its own valuable "brand name" as a permanent and reputable bond issuer—it suggests that the abstract difference between the two systems is far smaller than has generally been thought. And given that income and consumption taxation differ purely in their treatment of a given item—the return to waiting—even thinking of them as separate systems may be more confusing than illuminating. Instead, one should simply ask whether or not this particular item should be included in the tax base, thus giving the debate much the same scope and spirit as, say, the debate over the proper tax treatment of medical expenditure.

This understanding of the closeness of income and consumption taxation underlies the growing scholarly consensus that the abstract choice between them is far less important than has been commonly thought. Achieving one's preferred tax treatment of the return to waiting is less important than eliminating inter-asset distortions that—even given second-best problems and externalities—are likely to be undesirable under either system (Gentry and Hubbard 1998, 43–44; Shaviro 1992, 27–28).

Under the current income tax environment, this implies that advocating movement towards a CTB in which (to the extent feasible) all current returns to saving are fully taxed may be the most promising policy aim to adopt, absent any other strongly indicated route for equalizing the taxation of different alternatives. Under such a view, special tax preferences and dispreferences are alike presumed undesirable from the neutrality standpoint. Thus, even though the exclusion of municipal bond interest and the benefit of the realization requirement for appreciated assets reduce the tax burden on investment, whereas the double taxation of corporate income and the taxation of nominal or inflationary gain increase it, all should be disfavored by income and consumption tax advocates alike.[6]

3. Consequences of the CTB Norm for Tax Law Transitions

The CTB norm primarily relates to the definition of good steady-state tax policy. Its main relevance to tax law transitions is twofold. First, by generally defining good tax policy, it may shed light on whether particular retroactive taxes, whether resulting from policy changes or accounting changes, should themselves be presumed good or bad. Second and less obviously, the CTB norm suggests that good policy in designing the tax base should be deemed not to change over time. Thus, if the municipal bond preference is always presumptively bad policy, then consideration of ungrandfathered repeal need not be complicated by the possibility that it was once good policy and has only now become bad.

B. NORMS FOR TAX LAW TRANSITIONS

1. Norm 1: Allow the Imposition of Policy Change Retroactive Taxes

Within the present income tax, the CTB norm suggests that tax preferences and dispreferences that discriminate between alternative forms of same-period consumption or investment are generally undesirable. Hence—to give a few examples—the municipal bond preference, deduction for home mortgage interest (given the exclusion of imputed rental income from home ownership), deferral of unrealized asset appreciation, and double tax on corporate investment are all presumptively bad policy. While each might be defensible, they belong to a broader grouping of tax rules that are mostly bad policy.

This in turn provides a rough metric for evaluating whether particular tax law changes are good or bad. When they move towards a comprehensive tax base, as by curtailing or repealing the above income tax preferences and dispreferences, they are presumptively good policy. When they move in the other direction, they are presumptively bad policy. This seems to suggest the following rule for policy change retroactive taxes: Transitional protection should be denied when preferences and dispreferences are curtailed, and granted when they are expanded.

In illustration, consider municipal bonds. The prospect of repealing the preference without grandfathering has good incentive effects since it reduces the investment response, while the prospect of ungrandfathered expansion has bad incentive effects. Transition risk is unlikely to be significant either way, since people can easily hold diversified investment portfolios. Thus, one might like to have in place a constitutional norm holding that outstanding bonds should be grandfathered against preference expansion but not repeal.

Unfortunately, such a constitutional norm seems unlikely to achieve significant influence. Its underlying basis, hostility to income tax preferences and dispreferences, is expressly rejected whenever anti-CTB legislation is enacted. One can hardly hope for much success in arguing to enacting legislators that, since the legislation is probably bad policy, it should be denied retroactive effect that would have been granted to an opposite enactment. Moreover, given the norm's transparently "heads we win, tails you lose" character, the main consequence of trying to communicate it might be to discredit the speaker rather than popularize the norm.

We need, therefore, to consider constitutional norms for policy change retroactive taxes that might be more practical. In developing possible alternatives, two underlying assumptions seem reasonable. The first is that any widely acceptable norm must extend the same treatment to preference curtailment and expansion. The second is that, on average, the relationship between the actual income tax base and the CTB is in approximate equipoise. Given the lengthy period over which income tax politics has been unfolding, there is no general reason why we should expect things to be getting either systematically better or worse.[7] Applying this assumption in light of the CTB norm and related skepticism about tax politics, tax base changes are close to random from the standpoint of good policy; they are not much more likely to improve the tax law than to worsen it.

Under this assumption, the policy change retroactive taxes that result from tax base changes, considered as a group, have a mean desirability of close to zero. This suggests a stance not far from indifference, on average, to their imposition from the retroactive tax standpoint, potentially leaving transition risk as the most relevant variable. Accordingly, if such risk is socially costly, the best transition policy may be to avoid imposing it. Hence, the conclusion that initially seems to emerge is that the constitutional norm for policy change transition effects should perhaps be one of providing symmetrical "relief." Taxpayers should seemingly be "protected" against the risks both of transition gain if the tax treatment of their investments becomes more favorable, and of transition loss if it becomes less favorable. And one could in good faith publicly argue for such a norm in conventional, "old view" terms of stress reliance, so long as the norm is understood to apply symmetrically to transition gains from preference expansion and losses from preference curtailment.

If adherence to this norm for policy change retroactive taxes could be made mandatory, the above analysis might indeed be persuasive. Recall, however, that Congress is inherently more disposed to eliminate transition loss than transition gain when it changes the tax laws. Accordingly, in practice, the norm's main effect might be to increase the extent to which taxpayers are induced to anticipate movement *away* from the CTB through a "heads you win, tails we lose" practice whereby grandfathering dispro-portionately applies to preference curtailment as compared to expansion.

Admittedly, this claim is quite uncertain. Congress's predilection to eliminate transition loss rather than transition gain is an aspect of its average behavior. The question of how an old-view-type norm, stressing reliance and certainty, would affect the real tax base over time goes instead to marginal effects on its behavior. Thus, suppose that, under any politically plausible set of norms, Congress would eliminate transition loss more frequently than transition gain, and that, prior to the promulgation of a strengthened pro-transition relief norm, it was relieving loss rather than gain in two-thirds of the cases where it provided transition "relief." There is a theoretical possibility that, within the set of extra cases in which the new norm now induced it to provide such relief, gain would be more common than loss. If this were so, then despite Congress's continuing greater predilection to eliminate transition loss rather than transition gain, an old-view-type norm would actually reduce the overall asymmetry between preference curtailment and expansion and move the real tax system that people observed over time closer to the CTB.

Despite this theoretical possibility, I think it considerably more likely that the marginal effect of an old-view-type, pro-transition relief norm would match the average effect, thus increasing the asymmetry between the elimination of transition losses and transition gains. The forces demanding relief against transition loss do not always win, but at least they are heard. When, as Kaplow (1986, 555) says, "losers cry for compensation while winners never cry for taxation," and when even the academic literature mainly ignores transition gain, it is plausible that, in almost any representative set of cases where transition relief is being seriously considered, the loss cases will tend to outweigh the gain cases.

If this is so, then the best politically feasible constitutional norm for policy change retroactive taxes is one that rejects reliance and holds instead in new-view-type terms that taxpayers ought to bear the consequences of policy changes, thus encouraging anticipation. To be sure, the real reason for advocating this norm—that in practice it may reduce Congress's predilection, through its transition policy, to favor tax preference expansion over curtailment—might lack broad appeal when stated forthrightly. Yet one can argue for the norm in Graetzean "new view" terms that are likely to sound more pleasantly in Congressional ears. After all, the same norm holds (albeit on different grounds) insofar as Congress's tax base decisions are generally good.

Hence, I conclude that the constitutional norm for policy change retroactive taxes should support allowing their imposition and denying transitional adjustment to mitigate either gain or loss.

2. Norm 2: Prevent the Imposition of Accounting Change Retroactive Taxes

Whenever a change in tax rules affects the tax system's use of such accounting conventions as those concerning timing and nominal incidence, accounting change retroactive taxation may result. Perhaps the best-known example in current debate is the capital levy that would result from replacing the present income tax with a consumption tax, if this resulted in the overnight disappearance of unrecovered income tax basis. As we will see in the remainder of this book, however, accounting change retroactive taxes are pervasive when income tax rules change, due mainly to the intricacy of the annual accounting rules on which the tax system relies.

Investors who are subjected to a transition gain or loss have no financial reason to care whether it results directly from a policy change or instead is a byproduct of an accompanying accounting change. The distinction is nonetheless important. To policy makers, the byproduct element means that one's view of it need not follow from one's view of the underlying policy change. Thus, an income tax advocate might like, and a consumption tax advocate dislike, the capital levy that could result from income to consumption tax transition. By contrast, for a policy change retroactive tax, such as exposing old municipal bonds to preference repeal, one's view of the enactment ought generally to dictate one's view of inducing anticipation.

The distinction between policy and accounting change retroactive taxes is of general normative import as well. Accounting change retroactive taxes are inherently a kind of byproduct, occurring only at the crossover point between succeeding policies, because they generally are not plausible as an ongoing matter. For example, neither an income tax nor a consumption tax advocate is likely to favor a regular rule either denying basis recovery for business outlays, and thus imposing the tax on gross receipts, or allowing all outlays to be deducted twice while inflows are counted only once. Yet these are essentially the results that switching back and forth between the two systems might have at the crossover point, absent transitional adjustment.

Similarly, consider Kaplow's (1986, 613) example of a shift from calendar-year accounting to the use of a fiscal year that ended on June 30, potentially causing six months of income to be taxed either twice or not at all in the year of the change. Or recall my earlier example of a currency change, wiping out the value of existing currency in the absence of transition relief, and resembling the income to consumption tax case because it is the fact that money (like unrecovered income tax basis) has been acquired but not yet used that triggers the loss. These are retroactive taxes that seem undesirable whether they take the form of positive taxes that are capital levies, or negative taxes that are capital subsidies. In the fiscal-year example, why either specially reward or penalize economic activity during the six-month period that is at issue? In the currency change example, why impose special tax consequences on the act of holding money at a particular moment?

In short, accounting change retroactive taxes tend to be undesirable without regard to their direction. By contrast, for policy change retroactive taxes, in the context of an income tax where the notion of economic income plays an orienting role, one would expect some to be good (such as when the municipal bond preference is curtailed) and others bad (such as when it is expanded), perhaps with a mean desirability of about zero. Hence, the analysis there appropriately focused on likely asymmetries in imposing transitional taxes under alternative constitutional norms. By contrast, it seems desirable to avoid the application of accounting change retroactive taxes in all directions—against gain and loss alike, and when resulting from good and bad enactments alike.

The reason for providing such relief is not just one of eliminating anomalous transition risk, such as the double-or-nothing bet in Kaplow's fiscal-year example. While that example just involves risk if one can equally imagine the transition decision going either way, in many cases it is clear whether the potentially approaching accounting change retroactive tax would be positive or negative. No one thinks, for example, that unrecovered income tax basis will be double recovered, rather than eliminated without compensation, as an accounting byproduct of income to consumption tax transition. When a particular accounting change retroactive tax that people anticipate or observe has a systematic direction, an undesirable positive or negative tax is actually being anticipated, wholly apart from the problem of uncertainty or variance.

I therefore conclude that, for accounting change retroactive taxes, a constitutional norm should support opposing their imposition. This, of course, is the opposite of the conclusion I reached for policy change retroactive taxes, and it echoes the old view rather than the new view. One further consideration should be mentioned, however. The analysis thus far has disregarded Congress's predilection to eliminate transition loss more readily than transition gain. Given that predilection, it is plausible that this norm would at the margin reduce *ex post* capital levies more than capital subsidies.

The main reason for disliking such an effect—once one rejects the Auerbach-Kotlikoff "free lunch" view of capital levies—is that it might undesirably reduce the overall progressivity of tax-transfer policy. Here the claim would be that, for reasons of political economy, accounting change retroactive taxation's effect on progressivity was not likely to be fully offset by other adjustments, such as to preannounced marginal tax rates. If one further concluded that the likely inefficiency of most accounting change retroactive taxes was a price worth paying for increasing overall progressivity, one might want to advocate a new-view-type position supporting their imposition. My own belief, however, is that the arguable progressivity effect, while indicating the presence of a genuine tradeoff, is too slight and speculative to alter the previously stated bottom-line conclusion.

Hence, I conclude that the constitutional norm for accounting change retroactive taxes should support preventing their imposition and providing transitional adjustment to mitigate both gain and loss.

3. Norm 3: Prevent the Imposition of Nominally Retroactive Taxes, as Loosely Defined by Current Practice

A norm opposing nominally retroactive changes (henceforth, the "ANR" norm, for "anti–nominal retroactivity") is strongly rooted in popular sentiment, legislative practice, and perhaps even the Constitution as the courts are likely to interpret it. Thus, while Congress in May 2002 might change tax rates for part or all of that year, we would not expect it at that time to change the tax rates for 2001. Similarly, while it might in 2002 repeal the municipal bond preference without grandfathering existing bonds, we would not expect it to hold that municipal bond interest paid in 2001 or earlier was taxable after all, thus requiring some such adjustment as the filing of amended returns for past years.

An initial set of cases where the ANR norm should be relatively uncontroversial pertains to the selection of black-letter "rules of the road," serving administrative convenience despite arbitrariness in their details, and requiring notice in order to function effectively. Requiring that drivers stay either on the right or on the left of opposing traffic, as the case may be, is a standard example. For another, suppose that the traffic laws concerning safe driving speed evolve in three stages. First there are no rules (even under the general provisions of tort law). Then a rule is enacted requiring reasonable speed under the circumstances. Finally, to reduce accidents by coordinating the speeds of different drivers who are on the road at the same time, the legislature specifies a precise numerical speed limit that applies, in addition to the reasonableness requirement, without regard to road conditions.

One would certainly want drivers to anticipate the "reasonableness" enactment, so that they would exercise due care even before any legal obligation was created. Yet there might be no reason either to want or to expect them to pick the numerical speed limits that were arbitrarily chosen to coordinate people's driving speeds. In particular, this would be clear if no speed was inherently better than any other, and coordination at *some* (any) arbitrary number was the legislature's sole aim. To be sure, in practice, almost any rule of the road is likely to have some incentive qualities. For example, inducing anticipation of a lower rather than higher speed limit might have some desirable effects. Yet the distinct analytical element of arbitrary particular detail remains one that may be both hard to anticipate (implying high transition risk) and not particularly worth anticipating.

Applying the "rules of the road" concept in the tax realm, it might make little sense to give nominally retroactive application to a newly prescribed annual filing date for income tax returns. Likewise, even if nominally retroactive changes in the income tax rate or includability of municipal bond interest were deemed permissible, it might make little sense to levy underreporting penalties (beyond market interest) for people who now owed more for past taxable years as a result of the nominally retroactive change.

However, the ANR norm goes well beyond preventing nominal retroactivity merely in cases where an arbitrary rule of the road is involved. Nonetheless, as popularly understood, it does not condemn *all* applications of a newly enacted rule to preenactment periods. One exception is that income or loss accruing economically before enactment, but not yet taken into account for income tax purposes, is not subject to the norm. While the norm forbids reversing the municipal bond exclusion for interest paid last year or taking back last year's depreciation deduction, it apparently permits applying this year's capital gains rate to the appreciation of an asset that occurred economically last year, so long as the asset is sold this year.

The ANR norm also permits preenactment application through the selection of an earlier effective date. Usually, the effective date is specified early in the legislative process and corresponds with when some official act was taken by proponents, such as announcing a legislative proposal or formally introducing it in the House of Representatives. The resulting preenactment application of the new statute (if it passes) is commonly defended both as consistent with "old view" reliance, on the ground that the announcement provided notice, and as necessary to deter taxpayers from either rushing to engage in "under-the-wire" activity before tax rules become less favorable or sitting on their hands until it becomes more favorable.

A rarer and more controversial practice is choosing a January 1 effective date for the year of enactment, even without official preannouncement. Thus, income tax rate increases enacted on August 10, 1993, were made applicable as of January 1, at which time President Clinton, who proposed it, and the 103rd Congress, which adopted it, had not yet taken office. This attracted vehement protest, although it was neither unprecedented (Logue 1996, 1168–69) nor much of a surprise given the publicity that Clinton's tax increase plan had received during the 1992 presidential campaign.

Even the harshest critics of this effective date, however, presumably would have been angrier still had the rate increase applied to 1992, or before Clinton was even elected. Moreover, many critics apparently accept same-year retroactivity so long as the tax rate is going down rather than up. In 1995, the House of Representatives passed a procedural rule allowing members to raise points of order blocking consideration of retroactive tax increases of the 1993 genre (*Adopting the Rules of the House of Representatives for the 104ᵗʰ Congress,* 104ᵗʰ Cong., 1ˢᵗ sess., H. R. 6, 1995). However, the Republican leadership that stood behind this rule also proposed, as part of that year's "Contract with America," that the capital gains rate be reduced retroactively to January 1 of that year (Manning 1995).

These borderline ambiguities aside, the ANR norm may seem both to have a clear effect and to make a clear demand. The apparent effect is that each period's events be taxed under the rules in force at the time. The apparent demand is that no past period's events be revisited by applying to them the rules from a later period. As it happens, however, neither of these statements about the norm is fully correct.

The problems with the above statement about the ANR norm's effect are twofold. First (expanding on the case where a new capital gains rate applies to prior appreciation), the tax system often waits many years to take full account of prior economic occurrences. Accordingly, midstream rule changes may qualify as nominally prospective even if they change the tax consequences of a completed past event. Suppose I acquire a business machine with a five-year depreciable life for income tax purposes and that, one year later, all depreciation deductions for the machine are repealed. The last four years' depreciation deductions could be disallowed without nominal retroactivity (if not without complaint). By contrast, had cost recovery been allowed in full in the year of acquisition, through an up-front deduction with the same present value as the five years of depreciation, then a subsequent rule change that denied any portion of this deduction *ex post* would have constituted nominal retroactivity. Hence, what may be mere arbitrary accounting details of how deductions of a fixed present value (ignoring the prospect of a rule change) are provided can affect the manner and extent of their protection by the ANR norm.

Second, even if the tax treatment of an economic occurrence is fixed in stone by immediate full allowance, it may be ineluctably linked to events in other tax years—hence the familiar point that retroactivity, in the sense of changing the consequences of past decisions, need not depend on nominal retroactivity (Graetz 1977). Consider the purchase of a tax-exempt bond, predictably triggering a series of cash flows in subsequent taxable years. Or consider the cash inflows in later years that may result from the current-year use or sale of a business asset. Tripling the tax on this later income, or indeed expropriating the asset, generally would not fall within the definition of nominal retroactivity.

Thus, mere accounting considerations govern the definition of nominal retroactivity. The ANR norm's seeming arbitrariness grows greater still, however, when one considers the variety of ways in which a past-year tax result can, in effect, be reversed. Suppose Congress nominally permits last year's tax returns to stand but requires an explicit related adjustment to next year's returns—for example, a "look back" recapture of items previously deducted or excluded (Levmore 1993, 270). Starting from this clear case, the fit between this year's inclusion and last year's deduction could gradually be loosened, as by imposing a special tax on assets of a given vintage and character (and thus statistically correlated with claiming the past deductions), with the result more or less approximating direct reversal of the earlier tax treatment. No bright line distinction can be made between the changes that constitute indirect nominal retroactivity and those that do not, since this depends on the degree of fit between past benefits and current detriments (or vice versa).

For another ambiguity problem, suppose that in year 1 Congress announces a 50 percent tax rate for year 2, but subject to providing that only 30 percent will be collected right away, and that Congress will decide definitively in year 3 whether to collect the extra 20 percent for year 2 (Levmore 1993, 270). If this is not nominally retroactive, perhaps Congress can eliminate the ANR norm altogether by simply announcing that, henceforth, all tax rules are provisional and subject to *ex post* (but given the notice, no longer "nominally retroactive") alteration. Or perhaps, if notice can be inferred from behavior, then as soon as Congress makes a single nominally retroactive change, the ANR norm is gone and need not be lamented. After all, taxpayers can no longer assert a lack of actual notice.

Despite their theoretical difficulty, however, these problems have done little to impede the ANR norm's application in practice. Its scope has generated little controversy beyond the limited dispute about 1993-style effective dates. Yet the arbitrariness of its boundaries invite one to question whether, and if so why, it should be thought appealing.

This challenge can be deepened by explicitly generalizing what the above problems show. Nominal retroactivity is inherently a formal, rather than a substantive, economic category. The principle of present value equivalence suggests that, ignoring the prospect of rule change, a deduction of $X in year 1 has the same incentive and distributional effects as a deduction of $X plus the applicable interest rate in year 2. Hence, it cannot be the case that, as of the beginning of year 2, the economic consequences of (nominally retroactively) changing the deduction if allowed in year 1 will differ from those of (nominally prospectively) changing it if allowed with interest in year 2. The risk-plus-tax analysis will be the same either way. For example, the deduction's nominal timing should have no effect on whether anticipation of repeal is desirable.

An initial point in defense of the ANR norm is that it obviously serves important administrative purposes. Could one really imagine requiring taxpayers to keep on hand all of their past tax records, and then periodically undergoing the tedious task of recomputing past years' tax liabilities, at least on some occasions when the tax law changed? While this consideration is obviously crucial in practice, I will disregard it here because administrative concerns are not all that underlies the norm, and surely would not (and should not) trump the "right" answer in all cases if nothing else were involved. Sometimes, it surely would not be prohibitively difficult to apply tax changes nominally retroactively—for example, by having the IRS determine the tax consequences (based on reported taxable income) of altering the applicable rate tables after the fact.

It may further seem that one could defend the ANR norm as simply a facilitator for transactional flexibility and cheaper contracting. Given that it exists, it provides a convenient device for fine-tuning the extent to which current tax rules are guaranteed, thus aiding investors and the government (on behalf of taxpayers generally) in the achievement of preferred risk allocations. However, even insofar as we value transactional flexibility despite political choice problems, one could ask why it needs to take this particular form. Why not simply let legislation state the extent to which particular rules are (or will become) guaranteed, without requiring that this turn on when particular items actually accrue under applicable tax accounting rules? In some cases, as where taxpayers have imperfect access to capital markets, it might be inconvenient for the level of guarantee to depend on when an item is actually included or deducted.

The most general defense of the ANR norm can only lie in the realm of political choice. Here, two main considerations come to mind. The first goes to the level of legislative discretion to affect distribution. The power to impose retroactive gains or losses greatly increases the legislature's power to redistribute wealth between individuals. This may seem good insofar as we favor particular redistributions that we are sufficiently hopeful the legislature will actually enact. However, the enhanced power to redistribute is undesirable insofar as we expect the legislature to choose bad redistributions or use its enhanced power to engage in rent extraction. Given the difficulty of authorizing only "good" redistribution and limiting rent extraction directly, we might conclude that various crude quantitative limitations on the legislature's redistributive powers are desirable, both to mitigate transition risk that serves no systematically good purpose and to ameliorate political rent seeking. One such limitation is the takings clause, which requires levies on particular individuals to have sufficient generality and bars regulatory takings if their impact on a property's value is sufficiently severe. Barring nominally retroactive rule changes may be another such device.

To see how significant a limit on legislative power the ANR norm may be, suppose that it did not exist and that there also were no statutes of limitations constraining how far back a tax return would remain legally open for redetermination. At the limit, the tax treatment, say, of municipal bonds for 1975 would never be finally settled, at least so long as that year's bondholders (or their traceable descendants) lived. Indeed, in principle, no one's wealth would ever be secure, since whatever one had could be wiped out (or vastly augmented) by changing one's tax liabilities for past years. The ANR norm provides a type of continually updated closure on the portion of one's wealth that the legislature can conveniently reach, and thus limits the government's capacity to redistribute, in a way that is arguably valuable (despite the case for progressive redistribution) for the same reasons of maintaining private incentives and limiting government abuse that are widely thought to justify some measure of protected property rights.

The choice of this particular device to limit redistribution may still seem arbitrary. If the most defensible underlying aim as to permissible redistribution is purely quantitative, why choose this device rather than some other, and why assume that it achieves an appropriate quantum (neither too low or too high) of remaining permissible redistribution? Given, however, the brute fact that the ANR norm is in place and that it appears to have strong psychological support—presumably from the endowment effect, which makes us all the more attached to explicit tax results (at least the favorable ones) from past taxable years—the problem of arbitrariness compared to some hypothetical alternative may be unimportant.

A second political justification for the ANR norm relates to its use as a device for fine-tuning transactional flexibility. Suppose we want Congress to be able to make credible binding commitments (and not just by the cumbersome practice of executing contracts) but that, given our concern about its incentives, we want to ensure that it pays a political price for doing so. Compared to simply letting Congress state the extent to which a given tax benefit or detriment should be considered guaranteed, reliance on the ANR norm has two distinct advantages that may offset its burdening the timing choice. Once in place, it makes a guarantee more credible by limiting future Congresses' power to revoke it without paying a political price. At the same time, however, by requiring that tax benefits be provided relatively soon in order to be considered secure, it forces a Congress that operates in a world of short-term federal budgetary accounting to pay a more explicit budgetary price.

A good example of the latter is provided by the experience of the 1995 Republican congressional leadership in seeking to implement the "Contract with America" that it had promulgated in the previous year's elections. Apparently to avoid increasing the measured federal budget deficit within the time window subject to official estimation, the Contract had offered depreciation deductions with the same present value as expensing, but to be provided many years in the future. Despite the principle of present value equivalence, business leaders failed to support the depreciation plan. They apparently understood the significant prospect that the deferred deductions would be repealed before being allowed. In short, since the Republican leadership was unwilling to take greater political responsibility for expensing equivalence by allowing deductions within the time window for official measurement, it was unable to make the promise politically credible.

In sum, one can plausibly argue that the ANR norm, with its bar on nominally retroactive tax law changes under the circumstances that I have described, has desirable constitutional consequences that are not easily replicated by alternative means, even though its effect depends arbitrarily on the mere accounting details of tax rules. The ANR norm will be crucial to subsequent analysis even when unmentioned, due to its screening function. It limits the transition rules that can even be considered and, in some cases, prevents solutions that might be clearly desirable if they did not tend to pave the way politically for other, less appealing nominally retroactive policy changes.

C. APPLYING THE TAX TRANSITION NORMS

The previous section suggested three basic constitutional norms for tax law transitions, applying equally to transition gain and loss: (1) allow the imposition of policy change retroactive taxes; (2) prevent the imposition of accounting change retroactive taxes; and (3) prevent the imposition of nominally retroactive taxes. Before proceeding to the case studies that take up the rest of the book, some clarifying points are in order:

1. Retroactive taxes generally increase transition risk, since future policy decisions are inherently unpredictable. Hence, norm 1 can reduce social welfare in a particular case even if the particular retroactive tax involved

is a good one, if the risk is sufficiently socially costly. However, while a case-by-case analysis would involve balancing the risk against the tax in addition to assessing whether that particular retroactive tax is a good one, my proposed norm overlooks the risk problem on the ground (discussed in chapter 3) that taxpayers can often fairly readily achieve their preferred risk positions, which in any event need not reflect unlimited risk aversion. A constitutional norm inherently must be pitched at a sufficient level of generality to yield the wrong answer in particular cases.

2. Norms 1 and 2 are not directly in conflict, since any specific retroactive tax should be classifiable as resulting either from a policy change or from an accounting change, depending on whether it reflects steady-state differences between the old and new tax laws or is instead a one-time byproduct of accounting changes at the boundary. As we will see, however, a given change in the tax law can simultaneously yield both policy change and accounting change retroactive taxes. Moreover, even if the two can be disentangled analytically, doing so in the design of transition policy may prove at times extremely difficult. Hence, there may be instances where the norms suggest conflicting outcomes and there is no easy resolution.

3. Norm 3 (the ANR norm) directly conflicts with norm 1 in any case where levying a policy change retroactive tax would require nominal retroactivity. For example, upon repeal of the municipal bond preference, norm 1 would counsel, but the ANR norm oppose, revising all past years' tax returns to require that municipal bond interest be included in taxable income. In such cases of conflict, the ANR norm is meant to prevail. While my arguments for it are merely suggestive, general adherence to the norm is in any event a brute fact of political life.

4. The ANR norm often contributes to the imposition of accounting change retroactive taxes. If changes were always made nominally retroactive, norm 2 would be unnecessary in the timing cases that provide the bulk of the real-world tax law examples, since the retroactive taxes that it counsels eliminating would not occur to begin with. For example, the shift from income to consumption taxation would not result in the denial of any cost recovery for business outlays if all past years' tax liabilities were recomputed to reflect a consumption tax that applied expensing. Hence, the ANR norm will often impede or even prevent accomplishing what norm 2 counsels. Once again and for the same reasons, the ANR norm is meant to prevail in the event of conflict.

D. JUDICIAL AND REGULATORY CHANGES

Since this chapter's constitutional analysis is based on assumptions about legislative behavior, its conclusions need not apply to rule changes that result from the decision of a court or administrative agency. Those decision makers may face different political incentives than legislators, and they are allocated a different, generally more interpretive and interstitial, sort of authority by the American legal system. It thus might be the case, for example, that good policy dictates that judges conceive of themselves as doing something other than trying to make good policy. While the subject of judicial retroactivity in particular has spawned a large literature turning in part on issues of judicial role that lie beyond this book's scope, the implications of my general transition analysis are nonetheless worth considering briefly.

1. Retroactive Application of Judicial Decisions

It has long been a truism that "statutes operate only prospectively, while judicial decisions operate retrospectively" (*Rivers v. Roadway Express, Inc.,* 511 U.S. 298 (1994), 311–12). More precisely, while legislation generally follows the ANR norm even if it has retroactive effects, courts are permitted and indeed expected to issue holdings that explicitly apply to prior events. Thus, while the United States Constitution (Article I, Section 9) forbids the legislature to criminalize people's acts *ex post facto* or direct "bills of attainder" against them, it is part of the judicial function to determine whether particular individuals are guilty of particular crimes—arguably a sort of nominally retroactive finding.

To some extent, the nominally retroactive application of judicial decisions is logically inherent in what we call the judicial function. The traditional legal view, famously expounded by Sir William Blackstone, that "[t]he judge, rather than being the creator of the law was but its discoverer" (*Linkletter v. Walker,* 381 U.S. 618 (1965), 623) describes a function that someone must perform and that correlates to some extent with what courts, as distinct from other, more directly politically accountable Anglo-American government institutions, commonly do.

This correlation between the courts' limited political accountability and their being assigned the function of nominally retroactive law "discovery" is no coincidence. Rather, it reflects a theory about political choice. The notion, presumably, is that, at least given widespread cultural norms about judicial behavior, the judiciary's relative insulation from direct political control by the voters improves the reliability of its purported findings about what the law already is. Thus, even if one considers the Supreme Court highly politicized, one might nonetheless consider the Justices more likely than the Congress to attempt honest statutory interpretation. In addition, the courts' insulation, along with their limited power (since they can only decide cases brought before them, and must purport to engage in mere interpretation), ameliorates concern about the sort of undue singling out, whether hostile or favorable, that nominal retroactivity facilitates.

We have, therefore, a theory and, to some extent, a practice of judicial behavior in which nominal retroactivity is considered necessary and acceptable—in sharp contrast to the common view about legislation. Accordingly, even when case precedents are explicitly overruled, policy change retroactive taxes imposed by courts do not evoke the same criticism as those imposed by legislatures. Moreover, given nominal retroactivity, accounting change retroactive taxes may be relatively uncommon.

Nonetheless, adherence to this view of unlimited judicial nominal retroactivity has long been incomplete. Commentators recognized from early on that courts do not and indeed cannot merely find the law; at the least, they must engage in interstitial law making to fill in statutory gaps or indeterminacies. This function looked sufficiently like law making, rather than law finding, to prompt occasional judicial decisions that, at least when prior case authority was reversed, the new authority should apply only nominally prospectively (*Linkletter v. Walker,* 624) and perhaps subject to some sort of grandfathering.

In the United States Supreme Court, a doctrine proclaiming that discretionary limits could be placed on a decision's retroactive application was pronounced with new decisiveness in the Warren Court era and its immediate aftermath (*Linkletter v. Walker*; *Chevron Oil Co. v. Huron,* 404 U.S. 97 (1971)), only to be repudiated in the 1990s (*Harper v. Virginia Dep't of Taxation,* 509 U.S. 86 (1993)). This fluctuation owed much both to the Court's relative comfort in the two eras with viewing itself as a policy making body that could logically be viewed as subject to old-view-type notions of reliance, and to the difficulty it experienced in trying to develop workable rules limiting retroactivity (Fisch 1997, 1059–61).

To the extent that one considers courts discretionary policy makers (whether they want to be or not), the argument in this book suggests that old-view-type reliance is not a convincing ground for denying to their decisions a retroactive, and even nominally retroactive, effect. Rather, the analysis should turn on assessing the transition risk and retroactive tax effects of allowing retroactive application. Thus, if one believed that judicial decisions were generally policy improvements, one might want to encourage full retroactivity as a way of encouraging anticipation (subject to concern about transition risk).

Any such detailed analysis of constitutional norms for judicial retroactivity is beyond this book's scope. Two narrow points are worth making, however. First, one's view concerning the extent to which courts cannot help being, or indeed should positively embrace being, policy makers need not correlate with one's view of judicial retroactivity. Consider the Warren Court, which in some instances was reluctant to give full retroactive effect to newly announced protections in the law of criminal procedure that might have required freeing numerous incarcerated prisoners upon their bringing *habeas corpus* petitions. Perhaps, ignoring calculations about political acceptability, the Warren Court should have been willing to free prisoners who had been convicted under what it considered inadequate procedural safeguards in order to strengthen police and prosecutor incentives to anticipate the expansion of these safeguards. Likewise, perhaps the contemporary Court should conclude that, insofar as it dislikes but cannot wholly avoid policy making, it should limit its own effective powers by avoiding retroactive application when convenient. The value of unlimited retroactivity is logically distinct from questions concerning the proper level of judicial activism as a discretionary policy maker.

Second, some of the cases from the 1960s and 1970s that limit nominal retroactivity may suggest a more persuasive ground for doing so. I noted previously that nominal retroactivity makes little sense with regard to black-letter "rules of the road," prescribed for administrative convenience, that rely on advance notice and are not particularly anticipatable in their details. In some cases, something like this appears to provide the reason for limiting a decision's retroactive application. Thus, in *Chevron Oil Co. v. Huron,* the Court's reversal on a point of statutory interpretation concerning whether state or federal law applied to a particular tort claim was held not to apply retroactively to bar causes of action by reason of the state's shorter statute of limitations. Given prevailing legal authority at the time, the suing party had reasonably believed at the time that it had the longer federal period to sue, and the switch in applicable law presumably was unrelated to any policy view about which of the (in a sense arbitrary) statutes of limitation should apply.

Similarly, in *Linkletter v. Walker,* the Court declined to free prisoners by giving retroactive application to *Mapp v. Ohio* (367 U.S. 643 (1961)), which had applied the federal "exclusionary rule," barring the use of evidence obtained in unlawful searches and seizures, to state prosecutions. The Court in *Linkletter* noted that *Mapp* had extended the exclusionary rule on what one might call administrative grounds, founded on the view that other ways of protecting Fourth Amendment rights had proven ineffective. As such, *Mapp* was somewhat distinguishable from cases giving full retroactive application to newly announced bans on practices such as the use of coerced confessions that were "abhorrent at the time" (*Linkletter v. Walker,* 638)— although, to be sure, the *Mapp* protection was not purely (or perhaps even primarily) an arbitrary rule of the road, as distinct from a substantive expansion of defendant rights.[8]

It is certainly debatable whether *Chevron* and *Linkletter* in fact concerned mere arbitrary "rules of the road" that there was no particular reason to induce litigants to anticipate. One could also debate the workability of a judicial rule limiting nominal retroactivity solely for decisions that are deemed to establish arbitrary rules of the road. Yet this ground for limiting the nominally retroactive reach of judicial decisions has some appeal, for the same reason that, even in the absence of the general reasons for the ANR norm, one would not want to punish taxpayers for failing to anticipate that, say, the date for filing income tax returns might be moved up from April 15 to some earlier date.

2. Retroactive Application of Treasury Decisions

In general, the prevailing retroactivity regime for administrative decisions simply applies the conventional view that legislative decisions should be (at least nominally) prospective, while judicial decisions can and should be nominally retroactive. Some regulations are considered merely "interpretive"; that is, like judicial decisions, they specify the meaning of laws already on the books, and thus ostensibly "find" rather than "make" law, leading to the view that they should apply nominally retroactively (*Anderson, Clayton & Co. v. United States,* 562 F. 2d 972 (5th Cir. 1977), 985 n. 30). Other regulations are "legislative" and create new rules by exercising power delegated by Congress. These regulations accordingly are limited to nominal prospective application, like new statutes. This distinction, already well-grounded in American law although obviously murky in application, became a specific statutory requirement in 1946 with the enactment of the Administrative Procedure Act (APA). Section 553(d) of the APA provides that new regulations, unless merely interpretive, cannot take effect until at least 30 days have passed from the date on which (at least in initial proposed form) they are made public.

Tax regulations and other Treasury decisions, however, are subject to a specific retroactivity rule, section 7805(b) of the Internal Revenue Code (IRC), that probably precludes any application of section 553(d) on this point (*Redhouse v. Commissioner,* 728 F. 2d 1249 (1984), cert. denied, 469 U.S. 1034, 1253; *Stamos v. Commissioner,* 95 Tax Court 624 (1990), 637). Until 1996, section 7805(b) afforded the Treasury broad discretion to "prescribe the extent, if any, to which any ruling or regulation, relating to the internal revenue laws, shall be applied without retroactive effect."[9] In practice, the Treasury tended to observe the interpretive versus legislative distinction, and it was subject to judicial review for abuse of discretion when it applied new regulations retroactively (*Automobile Club of Michigan v. Commissioner,* 353 U.S. 180 (1957)). Nonetheless, commentators generally criticized the breadth of Treasury discretion to impose retroactive burdens, based on "old view" reliance, rejection of the Blackstonean claim that interpreters merely find the law, and distrust of how the Treasury might use its retroactive powers (Robinson 1987; Camp 1987; Nolan and Thuronyi 1983; Hoffman 1976).

In 1996, these criticisms bore perhaps unexpected fruit with the substantial modification of section 7805(b) by a provision of that year's "Taxpayer Bill of Rights" legislation. The new section 7805(b) generally limits regulations to nominally prospective application from the date of announcement. The main exceptions pertain to regulations issued within 18 months of the legislation to which they relate, or that are made retroactive to prevent "abuse." Thus, the Treasury may now have less rather than more retroactive power than other administrative agencies, since even interpretive regulations lose the Blackstonean assumption of preexisting truth if not issued with sufficient swiftness.

Under this book's analysis, neither "old view" reliance claims nor the naiveté of the claim that interpreters merely find preexisting law should have any bearing on the extent to which the Treasury is permitted to apply its regulations retroactively, or even nominally retroactively. (By contrast, distrust of the Treasury *is* pertinent.) As with legislative or judicially imposed retroactivity, the analysis should turn on the transition risk and tax effects of allowing retroactive application, given the relevant political inclinations and incentives of the particular institution.

Thus, if one thinks that Treasury regulations generally improve the law, as by eliminating tax planning opportunities that produce inefficiency yet fall short of "abuse," then the 1996 change is probably regrettable. It reduces tax planners' incentive to anticipate that the socially costly opportunities they detect will be rendered ineffective after they have acted. By contrast, suppose instead that one distrusts the Treasury as overly inclined to maximize revenues, and fears that the courts will simply rubber-stamp its claims that retroactive application is necessary to forestall "abuse."

One who held this view might conclude that the 1996 legislation did not go far enough in limiting regulatory retroactivity.

The 1996 legislation preserves the Treasury's authority to determine the extent to which its pronouncements other than formal regulations will apply retroactively (IRC section 7508(b)(8)). Thus, absent a judicial finding of abuse of discretion it can retroactively revoke private rulings directed to particular taxpayers, along with published revenue rulings that state its current interpretation of a point of law. Historically, however, it has tended both to honor its private rulings, and to apply revocations of its published rulings only nominally prospectively (Nolan and Thuronyi 1983, 779–80). This practice presumably reflects the value to the Treasury (as well as to taxpayers) of its being able to commit credibly, when it so chooses, to an agreement in a specific case.

SIX

CHANGES IN INCOME TAX RATES

If one principle, beyond the bar on nominally retroactive changes, has been axiomatic in discussions of tax law transitions, it is that no adjustment is needed to prevent transition gain or loss from income tax rate changes (Slawson 1960, 232; U.S. Treasury Department 1992, 90). On one recent occasion, however, such an adjustment was prominently proposed. The "Treasury II" tax reform plan that helped engender the Tax Reform Act of 1986 contained an income inclusion that was designed to tax away transition gains of taxpayers who had previously deducted accelerated depreciation at high pre-reform tax rates, and would henceforth be including the associated gross income at reduced post-reform tax rates (U.S. Treasury Department 1985, 192–96). This proposal was swiftly and decisively rejected, but perhaps (reflecting its novelty) without a good understanding of the transition issues that it raised.

Given its reception, the 1985 Treasury proposal may strengthen, rather than undermine, the premise that transitional adjustment for rate changes is politically out of the question. Nonetheless, the issues are worth discussing here. Transitional adjustment for rate changes might become politically plausible if this book's aim of advancing expert understanding of transition issues were realized. Moreover, the transition issues here are more complex and ambiguous than has commonly been supposed, and have interest both for their own sake and to illustrate the complicated interplay between policy change and other retroactive taxes in the setting of an annual income tax.

To simplify the analysis, I confine my discussion to rate changes that are fairly straightforward. They apply to taxable income generally, rather than to special categories such as capital gains, and to all taxpayers at a given taxable income level. Average rates (tax liability as a percentage of taxable income) are assumed to change in the same direction as marginal rates (those applying to one's last dollar of taxable income). Marginal rates are assumed to lie below the revenue maximization, or "Laffer curve," point where rate increases begin to lose revenue and rate reductions to increase it.

In addition, I ignore changes in one's marginal or average tax rate that result not from changes to the rate tables that the tax system employs in different years but from fluctuations in one's annual taxable income under a graduated system. The latter is an important phenomenon—for example, it can induce one to shift taxable income between different years, or cause people with fluctuating incomes to pay higher taxes than people with steady incomes under a graduated rate structure—but it is analytically distinct from transition, since it could arise even if the tax laws never changed.

A. Retroactive Rate Changes as Imposing a Policy Change Retroactive Tax

To capture the full range of transition effects of income tax rate changes, it is useful to start with an abstract hypothetical and gradually add realistic elements. Suppose initially that we have not an income tax but a lump-sum endowment tax. This tax applies graduated rates to a measure of innate income-earning ability as determined at birth, but it happens to be collected through annual payments during one's life span. Here, a change in tax rate, even if it resulted in adjusting all past years' tax payments, would not be "retroactive" in the sense of affecting the tax consequences of preenactment decisions, since, by definition, a lump-sum tax is invariant to taxpayer decisions.[1] The prospect of a rate change would, however, have distributional effects. For example, the adoption of a rate increase for high-endowment individuals, financing a rate cut for low-endowment individuals, would transfer wealth from the former group to the latter.

The prospect of this change would expose all potentially affected individuals to a transition risk that some might want to counter through insurance-like arrangements if feasible. This imposition of transition risk might represent a social cost, at least in the form of higher transaction costs to counter it. However, the distributional effect when tax rates changed would directly advance the underlying policy aim of transferring wealth from high-endowment to low-endowment individuals.

Now suppose that the difficulty of measuring endowment has induced the use of a comprehensive income tax, on the theory that income provides the best available signal of endowment, despite also reflecting work effort and saving. The income tax inefficiently burdens work and saving (and overtaxes workers and savers relative to those with equal endowments but different tastes), but this is deemed an acceptable price to pay for taxing endowment to some extent. Thus, the burden on work and saving—while unfortunate and preferably minimized, all else equal—is part of the deliberate policy of income taxation. To the extent inseparable from partially achieving endowment taxation, it is a component in an overall package that is deemed desirable on balance.

Under this income tax, suppose that a rate increase is adopted for high-income individuals in order to pay for uniform cash transfers to all citizens. The latter are lump-sum and thus have no incentive effects, but the two new policies in combination are progressive, because high-income taxpayers pay for everyone's transfers. The result of adopting the new policies, therefore, is to transfer wealth away from high-income individuals, while also dampening their incentive to work and save. We thus have a combination of tax effects that are lump-sum as in the prior example—although here depending on people's tastes for market work and material consumption, not just endowment—with those that depend on prior and subsequent decisions.

Starting with the rate change's effect on future decisions, the increase in progressive redistribution comes at an efficiency price, but one that supporters of the change are evidently willing to pay. Now suppose that we are considering its possible retroactive effects on preenactment decisions, such as choosing a high-wage career over a low-wage but otherwise more pleasant career. Under the simplifying assumption of full anticipation, an *ex post* rate increase inefficiently deters work and saving even before enactment but achieves some progressive redistribution away from high-income individuals. This is precisely the same tradeoff as that embraced by supporters of the rate increase when future decisions are being affected. It should presumably be resolved the same way unless there is some difference between the relative costs and benefits in the two cases—a difference that one might think could go in either direction.

Thus, despite the clearly undesirable incentive effects of a retroactive (like a prospective) tax rate increase, it presents a straightforward case of policy change retroactive taxation. The same conclusion applies to retroactive tax cuts, although here the tradeoff lies between desirable incentive effects and what may be undesirable distributional effects. All else equal, therefore, the retroactive application of either direction of rate change should be welcomed both by its supporters and under my norm 1. And the same holds for newly introducing an income—or, for that matter, consumption, wealth, or wealth transfer tax—in the absence of any related accounting change. After all, newly introducing a tax is merely a special case of the rate increase scenario, with the rate increasing from zero to some positive amount.

Before making the story more complicated, however, it is worth considering whether the rate changes Congress adopts might tend to be good policy on average—even under my highly skeptical view of tax politics—thus suggesting an added constitutional argument for retroactive application. The strongest argument supporting the average desirability of enacted rate changes concerns cases where, in contrast to the above example, they change overall revenue rather than distributional policy. Thus, consider Congress's decision in 1942 to raise income tax rates in order to pay for World War II. It seems clear that this was good policy given the change in government revenue needs, and indeed that, in retrospect, rates ought to have been raised earlier (ignoring countercyclical considerations pertaining to the Great Depression). The lower tax rates in preceding years turned out to reflect a faulty assessment of long-term revenue needs. Had rates gone up earlier, they would not have had to go up as much in 1942, probably reducing overall distortion.[2] In principle, nominally retroactive application of the 1942 rate increase—to preenactment years, not just the post-enactment consequences of preenactment decisions—would have achieved such correction, thus potentially making it good policy if one ignores the administrative and political economy reasons for the ANR norm.

Perhaps the World War II example is exceptional. Yet surely it is reasonable to surmise that the average quality of political decisions to change rates, when reflecting the aim of overall revenue adjustment, is relatively high. This is an area where—unlike, say, in debating the desirability of the municipal bond preference—information actually improves significantly over time. It is hard to doubt that we will know more about revenue needs from the perspective of 2004 *in* 2004 than we did in 1994. The new information may also be relatively salient and observable, and of a sort that the politicians who are running the government at some point find it in their interest to heed.

What about rate changes that reflect changes in distributional goals? Here, the argument that they generally improve policy faces two objections. First, it seems unlikely here that new information would play the same role in improving political outcomes. Even if, say, economists develop better estimates of labor supply responses to attempting redistribution, this information is unlikely to be as salient and influential as evidence of changing revenue needs. One can perhaps derive some comfort from the fact that, in Theodore Lowi's terminology, tax politics concerning progressivity is generally "redistributive," rather than "distributive" like most tax base politics. It thus involves sufficiently active political competition between opposing interests to mitigate (if not eliminate) the organizational defects that are often so severe in the realm of legislative tax policy. Yet this may not be enough to prevent the level of progressivity from reflecting mainly aggregative changes, such as shifts in the parties' Downsian equilibria, and changes in public sentiment—depending, say, on whether the middle class currently feels greater resentment of the rich or the poor—that are more or less random from the standpoint of good policy.

Second, suppose that legislation changing income tax rates is systematically good, but in the sense of tracking shifts over time in the optimal rate structure, rather than moving ever closer to a fixed optimal target. Here, even though the policy changes are by hypothesis desirable, it is not clear that they should apply retroactively, given the apparent alterations in the tradeoffs that determine good redistributive policy. In illustration, suppose that in year 1, high-income individuals' work decisions are more tax elastic than in year 2. All else equal, tax rates ought to be more progressive in year 2 than year 1. Hence, a rate change that desirably increased progressivity for year 2 might be undesirable on balance for year 1. Under a rational expectations view, this would tend to discredit nominally retroactive application of the more progressive year 2 rates (if adopted) to year 1—even absent the ANR norm (which I have thus far been ignoring). One complication, however, is that year 2 income will to some extent reflect year 1 rather than year 2 decisions, and it would be impossible to have applicable tax rates depend on when a given decision was made even assuming this to be desirable.

Accordingly, for rate changes that reflect shifts in distributional policy rather than in revenue needs, perhaps the best reason for welcoming retroactive application to the consequences of past decisions remains norm 1, which advocates general support for policy change retroactive taxes. Up to this point, however, I have continued to assume that the rate changes pertain to a comprehensive income tax, which generally does not alter incentives apart from those concerning how much to work and save. If, instead, the income tax, like our existing one, is shot through with preferences and dispreferences, does this alter the analysis?

Departures from comprehensive income taxation interact with rate changes to the extent that they are accomplished through items, such as inclusions, exclusions, and deductions, the value of which depends on the taxpayer's marginal rate. Thus, one effect of raising income tax rates is to increase the value of the municipal bond preference, barring some compensating adjustment to its computation. In a world without information problems or transaction costs, one might expect that tax rate changes would nearly always be accompanied by pervasive changes to various tax preferences and dispreferences. After all, it would seemingly be an extraordinary coincidence if a Congress that wanted to double income tax rates—thus implementing a particular tradeoff between incentive and distributional goals—also happened to want precisely to double the value of all the various preferences and dispreferences that were dependent on tax rates. In actual practice, however, rate changes rarely prompt any compensating adjustment to these items.

Under the CTB norm, the retroactive tax on income tax preferences and dispreferences that results from reducing tax rates and thus reducing their value is good policy, while the opposite result from increasing tax rates is bad policy. Obviously, however, it is implausible that Congress would follow an asymmetric policy of allowing the items to lose but not gain value from rate changes. For our purposes, therefore, the most salient point is that here, too, we have a policy change retroactive tax. It results from a steady-state change in the value of a special inclusion, exclusion, or deduction, and thus would be enhanced, rather than eliminated, if the rate change were hypothetically given full nominally retroactive application.

Now, however, we need to add a final real-world complication. Rate changes invariably are not given nominally retroactive application, at least beyond the calendar year of their enactment. This is all to the good given the reasons of political economy that underlie the ANR norm, but it would be a brute fact of political life even if the norm were incorrect. Accordingly, the inevitable consequence of enacting a rate change is that different tax rates end up applying to different taxable years. This, in turn, creates three distinct varieties of transition issue.

First are what I call "boundary" issues. The accounting rules that the tax system uses to assign items to particular tax years become of vital importance once it is agreed that rate changes will only apply nominally prospectively. Second are problems of intertemporal distortion. Taxpayers may take steps to shift the timing of taxable income recognition, based on anticipating the application of different rates to different years. Third are "matching" problems. Taxpayers with reciprocal outlays and inflows, such as from purchasing an asset in one year to generate gross income in other years, may deduct and include these items at different tax rates if they are taken into account in different tax years, potentially yielding transition gain or loss. Each requires separate and fuller consideration.

B. Transition Consequences of Not Applying an Income Tax Rate Change to Preenactment Taxable Years

1. Boundary Issues in Determining the Reach of the Rate Change

As soon as we accept the ANR norm's limit on the retroactive application of income tax rate changes, we run into the problem of deciding to which items of taxable income or deduction a new rate will apply. While this depends in part on taxpayer responses to the rate change, such as shifting net income to low-rate years, suppose initially that the timing of taxpayer behavior is fixed, as in the case where I can decide whether to work but not when any resulting income will become taxable.

A new tax rate almost inevitably has some retroactive impact on taxpayer decisions, given the frequency with which decisions in one year (such as career choice) affect economic outcomes in later years. The exact degree of retroactive effect depends in part on contemporaneous transition policy decisions, such as the choice of effective date and whether full implementation of the new rate is delayed after enactment. (Grandfathering generally is not used with respect to rate changes, given the practice of applying tax rates to one's overall income computation for a given period.) In general, the aim of maximizing a new rule's range of application implies picking the earliest effective date that the ANR norm permits. This typically is the earliest date of some official statement by a proponent or sponsor, or, more controversially, January 1 of the year of enactment.

The degree of retroactivity also depends on the particular accounting conventions that the income tax happens to use to determine when particular items, such as inclusions or deductions, are taken into account. Thus, the choice between two accounting methods that are present-value equivalents in the absence of any rate change may turn out to have important consequences if a change occurs.

In illustration, consider the tax treatment of original issue discount (OID) bonds. These are bonds, typically yielding taxable interest income, as to which some or all of the accruing interest is not paid until the bond's maturity. Thus, if 10 percent is the applicable interest rate, I might pay $100 for an OID bond that will pay $121 in two years. At one time, OID interest was not includable until the bonds were paid off or sold. In 1969, however, Congress enacted rules requiring that the interest be included roughly as it accrued, thus eliminating the tax benefit of deferral. This enactment combined a policy change (increasing the present value of the tax liability) with an accounting change (moving forward the taxable years in which OID income was reported).

In principle, Congress could have made the policy change without the accounting change, by continuing to impose tax only upon a bond's transfer but charging interest on the deferral of tax liability. This is the method that Alan Auerbach (1991) and David Bradford (1995) have sketched out for appreciated assets with less-predictable value paths, in order to eliminate the tax benefit of deferral under the realization requirement. Likewise, Congress could, in principle, have made the accounting change without the policy change, such as by requiring current inclusion of some accruing interest and exclusion for the rest, in a manner that was calculated to hold constant the present value of expected tax liability.

Presumably, only administrative convenience dictated the particular accounting choice that Congress made as part of the 1969 reform. Yet one distinctive side effect of this choice was to narrow the subsequent application of rate changes to outstanding OID bonds. Thus, suppose that on January 1, 2001, I pay $100 for an OID bond that pays me $121 on January 1, 2003. If a rate change takes effect on the latter date, then, by reason of the 1969 accounting change, almost none of the interest on this bond, rather than all of it, ends up being taxed at the new rate.

Thus, accounting rules, by assigning inclusion and deduction items to particular taxable years, help determine the extent to which a given taxpayer decision ends up being affected retroactively by subsequent rate changes. Yet, while the extent of retroactivity depends on accounting, any retroactivity that results imposes a policy change retroactive tax. For example, in the OID case, the anticipatory consequences that I would bear solely under the pre-1969 accounting rule are those of the rate change generally (i.e., increased deterrence of saving and the possibility of added progressive redistribution if earning OID income is a signal of high endowment).

2. Problems of Intertemporal Distortion from Taxpayer Responses to a Rate Change

The analysis so far has ignored taxpayers' deliberate timing responses to rate changes. However, such responses are well known. Examples include shifting charitable gifts to high-rate years (Clotfelter 1992, 228–29), or market work and profitable asset sales to low-rate years. One consequence of such shifts is that a rate change's breadth of application ends up depending on the general timing elasticity of taxpayer behavior, as well as on the effective date and accounting rules. However, when the shifting behavior has real nontax consequences, it raises incentive and distributional issues wholly apart from the new rate's breadth of application.

In illustration, when Congress in 1993 increased the highest explicit marginal tax rate from 36 percent to 39.6 percent, presumably to alter the steady-state tradeoff between distribution and incentive effects, it also encouraged acceleration of wage-earning activity to the end of 1992 and gave a tax advantage to people who thus accelerated relative to those who were otherwise similar but did not. This was clearly unfortunate, leaving aside effects on the new rate's breadth of application. Not only did the incentive to shift income lack any allocative rationale, but inability to shift income is not a plausible signal of high endowment.

One possible response, at least to the efficiency problem, would be to defeat income shifting, thus making it not worth trying. Yet this is quite difficult to accomplish. If the behavioral shifts induced by tax rate changes were easy to observe, the obvious solution would be to disregard them. This could involve providing that the shifted inclusions and deductions would be reported in the taxable year when they would have arisen but for the shifting behavior, or that they would be taken into account at the tax rate that would have applied that year. Or, to increase the new rate's range of application at the expense of fully addressing income shifting, it could be disregarded solely when it moved tax items to the period before the rate change. Obviously, however, behavior that shifts tax items between taxable years in response to a rate change is hard to observe.

How best to respond to the observation problem is unclear. For tax law changes generally, a common response is to attempt to forestall income shifting by picking as early an effective date as the ANR norm permits.[3] Unfortunately, however, while the use of an early effective date has the advantage (from the proponents' standpoint) of increasing the new rule's range of application, along with the possible disadvantage of increasing interim transition risk, its capacity to reduce income shifting is unclear.

To the extent a rule change is anticipated (as in 1993, when it had been discussed in the previous year's presidential campaign), the use of an early effective date rather than, say, the date of enactment merely changes the boundary line that taxpayers must cross. It thus may reduce some taxpayers' income shifting while increasing that engaged in by others, leaving the overall effect ambiguous. To the extent a rule change comes as a surprise, an early effective date can indeed reduce income shifting in that instance by preventing taxpayers from making use of the new information (such as the announcement of a new proposal) that typically triggers it. Moreover, in such a case, so long as the use of early effective dates is symmetrical (such as between rate increases and reductions), it has no systematic implications regarding the difference between preannounced and true *ex post* tax levels. Instead, the lesson to taxpayers is that accurate advance information about approaching rule changes has value, thus potentially inducing increased investment in attempting to acquire it, with possible implications for the extent to which income-shifting behavior can actually be reduced over the long run.

Another possible response to the difficulty of observing income-shifting behavior is to attempt to infer its presence indirectly. Suppose, for example, that Congress in 1993 had wanted to eliminate the benefit sought by taxpayers who postponed charitable contributions from the prior year. One possibility would have been to provide that half of any excess of 1993 over 1992 charitable deductions presumptively indicated deliberate shifting, and thus could not reduce one's tax liability at more than the 1992 rate. This, however, might have induced further shifting, such as postponing charitable contributions from 1993 to 1994 or beyond.

3. Matching Problems When Related Deductions and Inclusions Are in Different Taxable Years

A final problem resulting when a rate change, applied no earlier than the year of enactment, causes different tax rates to apply to adjoining taxable years is that of "matching." Often, taxpayers have related outlays and inflows that arise at different times. For example, I may borrow, invest, and ultimately repay loan principal, triggering both interest deductions and taxable investment returns. Or I may purchase inventory that I subsequently sell to customers, or buy a depreciable asset and use it to generate gross income. A break-even transaction (or portion of a larger transaction) that should have no net tax consequences—say, paying and receiving $10—may end up having net consequences if the resulting inclusions and deductions are at different tax rates by reason of being assigned to distinct taxable years between which there has been a rate change.

Under a pure Haig-Simons income tax (Simons 1938, 50), in which taxable income was determined by measuring the taxpayer's consumption and change in net worth (including the present value of all expected future cash flows) during the taxable year, this problem would not arise. Such a tax would not require timing rules for specific outlays and inflows, as opposed to determining net worth at the beginning and end of the year given their occurrence. Thus, suppose that a $10 expenditure at the end of year 1 triggered an $11 receipt at the end of year 2—a receipt that was expected all along and that had a $10 present value at the end of year 1 because the relevant interest rate was 10 percent. This transaction would have no effect on Haig-Simons income in year 1 and would result in tax liability solely with respect to the $1 of interest-like income in year 2—leading only to a policy change retroactive tax if the tax rate changed between the two years, since the year 2 tax change would have arisen even had the rate change been applied nominally retroactively to year 1.

Now suppose that the difficulty of measuring the taxpayer's general net worth required the use of timing rules for specific transactions, but that these rules were designed with the aim of replicating Haig-Simons income as closely as possible. The most obvious way to account for the above transaction would be to require capitalization rather than deduction of the outlays in year 1, thus assigning to year 2 both the $11 inclusion and the $10 deduction. This, like direct application of the Haig-Simons measure, would result in levying a policy change retroactive tax on the $1 of net income in year 2.

Finally, however, suppose that the deduction was taken in year 1, while the inclusion remained in year 2. In practice, the most likely reason for such a disjuncture between the taxable years of the deduction and the inclusion might be the enactment of a deliberate income tax preference for the taxpayer's investment, thus inducing Congress to allow the outlay to be expensed. Yet allowing a year 1 deduction of any particular present value merely represents the choice of a particular accounting convention for cost recovery. Just as an income tax preference for this item (like an across-the-board consumption tax) could use a year 2 deduction of $11 to achieve expensing equivalence at a 10 percent interest rate, so a Haig-Simons-equivalent income tax could in theory allow a discounted deduction of $9.09 in year 1, thus providing the same benefit as a $10 deduction in year 2. Under constant tax rates, and assuming no controversy as to interest rate (or difficulty in borrowing and lending at this rate), there would be little reason to care about moving the deduction from year 2 to year 1 while keeping its present value the same. Once a year 1 deduction was being used, however, the enactment of a rate change for year 2 would result in a non–policy change retroactive tax for taxpayers whose inclusions and deductions straddled the two years.

In illustration, suppose that, for computational convenience, we simplify the example to make the interest rate zero, both in general and for this transaction, leading to the deduction of $10 in year 1 and the inclusion of $10 in year 2 whether the transaction is treated preferentially (from an income tax perspective) or not. If the tax rate is 30 percent in both years, the transaction bears the zero net tax rate that it clearly should under either an income tax or a consumption tax norm. That is, the deduction generates a $3 tax refund in year 1, while the inclusion yields a $3 liability in year 2, eliminating any net result even in present-value terms (given the zero interest rate). However, if the 30 percent tax rate for year 1 should change either to 20 percent or to 40 percent for year 2, then the transaction, despite being break-even before tax, will generate an overall tax liability of either positive or negative $1, depending on the direction of the rate change.

The resulting retroactive tax appears clearly undesirable. Not only does it give distributional consequences to a break-even transaction, but it is likely to distort behavior in year 1 insofar as the rate change is anticipated. The problem may merely be one of undesired transition risk if the prospect of a rate change is at that time considered symmetric. However, if investors in year 1 assign greater weight to the prospect of a rate change in one direction (either up or down), there is a further adverse implication for efficiency: tax-motivated delay or the discouragement of good investment if they anticipate a rate increase, and rushing to invest or the encouragement of bad investment if they anticipate a rate cut.

This is precisely the sort of problem to which the 1985 Treasury II depreciation recapture proposal would have responded. The combination of highly accelerated depreciation in the early 1980s with substantial rate reduction in 1986 conferred a sizable retroactive gain on taxpayers who, having gotten to deduct the depreciation at relatively high marginal tax rates, now got to include the offsetting gross income at significantly lower rates. Moreover, this was a function purely of the deductions' acceleration compared to the related income, rather than of their analytically distinct preferentiality. Accordingly, one need not have been hostile to pre-1986 depreciation policy to conclude that conferring transition gain under such circumstances had undesirable incentive effects.

In principle, therefore, the Treasury proposal had considerable merit. To be sure, a fuller assessment would require close examination of its administrative and compliance feasibility, and of how well its incidence correlated with that of the transition gain. Moreover, suppose that Congress, once embarked on the course of responding to the transition effects of rate changes on "unmatched" inclusions and deductions, adopted an asymmetric policy of addressing losses from rate increases more readily than gains from rate reductions. This would tend to increase the real scope of income tax preferences, since acceleration of deductions usually correlates in practice with preferentiality. Accordingly, there conceivably might be a constitutional argument against proposals like that of the 1985 Treasury.

A more definite conclusion is that, without regard to the degree of income tax preferentiality granted to particular types of investment, there is a benefit, from the standpoint of transition policy, to accounting rules that, like Haig-Simons-equivalent accounting, apply "matching"—generally allowing deductions in the same tax year as the related gross income that they produce. Thus, for example, it would be desirable, all else equal, to move towards a depreciation system that replicated economic depreciation in its nominal timing. Any desired degree of income tax preferentiality, such as equivalence to expensing, could be preserved by allowing unrecovered basis to grow at a suitable interest rate (Bradford 1997).

In practice, determining the course of economic depreciation, and thus replicating its timing without regard to preferentiality, may be difficult even without regard to its political feasibility. Yet depreciation is one of the easier cases for applying the matching principle. Thus, suppose that I am considering borrowing in order to make a particular investment. If I anticipate a possible rate change, the timing of my interest deductions should in principle be matched to that of the income inclusions that this investment would likely produce. However, observation problems make this difficult to accomplish. The fungibility between money borrowed in a specific loan transaction and all other funds available to the taxpayer makes it hard to determine which investment I was actually considering at the margin when I decided to take out a particular loan.

Nonetheless, moving towards matching has clear advantages from the standpoint of limiting anomalous retroactive taxes from rate changes. To be sure, it may also have disadvantages. Allowing outlays to be deducted sooner rather than later (at whatever present value) tends to move them out of Congress's reach, thus limiting the prospect that it will, say, double or eliminate the present value of an asset's remaining depreciation deductions. It thus may reduce transition risk if legislative adjustment to any outstanding deductions is sufficiently politically likely relative to the enactment of rate changes. Or earlier allowance may be desirable as a way of increasing the actual reach of the ANR norm's protection against retroactive policy change. Finally, deferring deductions makes their real value when claimed inflation sensitive, unless the tax system includes inflation adjustments that may be administratively complex or politically unfeasible.

Failing the use of matching, Treasury II–style adjustments for transition gains and losses from rate changes are worth considering as well, and ought to receive a more respectful hearing than occurred in 1985. As we will see in chapter 9, concerns of this sort would become particularly acute if the present income tax were replaced by a cash-flow consumption tax, since the accounting change away from taxable-year matching of inflows with outlays would make the transition problem from rate changes significantly worse.

SEVEN

INCOME TAX BASE CHANGES

Changes to income tax inclusions, deductions, credits, and special rates for particular types of income—henceforth, "tax base changes"—provide the bulk of tax law transition issues that arise as an ongoing matter. Obviously, such changes can exhibit infinite variety. Some unambiguously increase and others reduce conformity between the statutory tax base and the CTB. The effect of other changes in this regard is unclear, due either to the CTB's ambiguousness or their own indirection, such as denying a deduction that the CTB would allow, with the effect, in some instances, of offsetting an associated exclusion that it would not allow. For movement both towards and away from the CTB, some changes are policy improvements while others make things worse, reflecting that the CTB norm does not provide the correct answer all the time.

The tax base changes that Congress adopts also involve a varying mix of policy and accounting changes. However, some regularities can be detected despite accounting choices' arbitrariness (administrative convenience aside), due to conventions in tax rule design. Absent deliberate transitional adjustment, these conventions would do much to determine what policy and accounting change retroactive taxes are actually imposed when Congress enacts tax base changes. In practice, however, the imposition of retroactive taxes depends as well on deliberate transition policy. This, in turn, reflects not only the fortuities of ongoing politics but also a fairly consistent transition practice, in some respects at odds with my proposed constitutional norms for retroactive taxes. This chapter therefore begins by examining the conventions that underlie tax rule design and the provision of deliberate transition relief, before turning to normative discussion.

A. Commonplace Accounting Changes When Congress Modifies the Income Tax Base

As chapter 3 discussed, the policy content of a tax rule is analytically distinct from its accounting content. One could change either a rule's steady-state allocative and distributional effects or its conventions concerning such accounting details as timing and nominal incidence while holding the other constant. Thus, in principle, the two types of content could change independently and with equal frequency. In practice, however, accounting changes are considerably more constrained than one might surmise from their steady-state policy irrelevance. Both administrative and informational considerations—the latter going to how accounting details may affect political perceptions of a tax rule—impose sufficient regularity on tax base design to confine the settings in which accounting change is common, even in the face of policy change.

1. Nominal Incidence

Under the present income tax, nominal incidence in particular tends to observe firm conventions. For example, a person to whom economic income has unambiguously accrued generally is the one who must report it as taxable income. When I earn a wage, I rather than the employer must pay the tax (albeit that the employer may have to withhold), and when I recognize capital gain, I rather than the buyer must pay the tax. If I own an asset, then only I can claim the depreciation deductions (ignoring for the moment that they may mismeasure economic depreciation). This convention helps serve the policy aim of applying graduated marginal tax rates to different people's incomes, but it has a pure accounting element insofar as prices would adjust if one changed nominal incidence without changing the amount of tax due in a given case.[1]

The convention of holding nominal incidence constant often extends as well to the provision of various income tax preferences, to which one might think rate structure considerations were irrelevant. Thus, Congress has never seriously considered replacing the municipal bond preference with a subsidy directly to the issuer. Or consider the fact that preferential as well as economic depreciation can only be deducted by the tax owner (Shaviro 1989b, 435–37). While tax ownership is a term of art with limited economic content, a provision enacted in 1981 that made it almost purely elective, by permitting paper transactions called "safe harbor leases" to succeed in transferring it, proved so controversial as a device for overt deduction sale that it had to be repealed the next year.

Much of the time, therefore, income tax rule changes hold accounting constant so far as nominal incidence is concerned, thereby limiting the accounting change retroactive taxes that might conceivably be imposed in the absence of transition relief. Of course, this practice could conceivably change at any time. Even under current practice, however, there are settings in which nominal incidence is subject to change. In particular:

1. In transactions that generate net taxable income of zero because the amount includable by one party is deductible by another, changes in how that amount is measured may reciprocally shift tax liability between the parties (to no net effect if their marginal tax rates are the same). Thus, in the taxation of compensation that is paid in the form of stock options, the timing and extent of employee inclusion and employer deduction are often linked. Or suppose that a newly enacted inflation adjustment made only real, rather than nominal, interest includable and deductible. Both inclusions and deductions of interest would be affected, to no net tax effect in some cases. The enactment of the original issue discount (OID) rules in 1969 (and a significant revision to them in 1982) had reciprocal implications of this sort, and on each occasion Congress minimized retroactivity by applying the new rules only to instruments issued after the effective date (Bittker and Lokken 1989, 56-3–56-5).

2. Similar reciprocity arises when the basic characterization of a transaction determines whether it will result in both inclusion and deduction, or neither. Marriage-related transfers (along with others where there is arguably a gift) provide a good example. When Congress in 1984 changed the tax definition of deductible and includable alimony, it made the new rules applicable only to transfers under post-effective-date agreements, rather than to all post-effective-date transfers (Joint Committee on Taxation 1985, 716), thus preventing accounting change retroactive taxation.

3. For partnerships, allocating taxable income amongst the partners involves inherent difficulty. Even when taxable income equals economic income, the true economic split may be hard to ascertain. Taxable income that differs from economic income has not economically accrued to anyone, and thus has no real incidence. Partnership tax law nonetheless must provide a framework for determining how the partners split the taxable income, and a change in this framework could result in accounting change retroactive taxation from shifts in the incidence of tax liability within a given partnership.

2. Timing

When Congress changes the income tax laws, timing is perhaps more subject to change than nominal incidence. Nonetheless, for a broad class of cases, timing tends to remain constant even if there is a change in policy. Hence, for these cases, deliberate transition relief is not needed to avoid accounting change retroactive taxation.

The income tax laws employ a pervasive distinction between "yield-to-maturity" and "wait-and-see" taxation. Under the former, which mainly is used for fixed returns (although I define it to include explicit mark-to-market taxation of observed appreciation), income is taxed annually whether or not the taxpayer receives cash in hand. Under the latter, which mainly is used for contingent returns, no inclusion occurs prior to the occurrence of a realization event, such as sale (Warren 1993, 463). This is an accounting difference, although it correlates with a policy difference insofar as wait-and-see taxation generally omits any interest charge for the deferral and thus reduces the present value of tax liability rather than merely deferring its collection.

While the two-part accounting regime is not entirely fixed—for example, the OID rules changed the boundary between the systems—it does tend to be followed consistently even as Congress enacts deliberate policy changes pertaining to preferentiality. For example, one might predict that the tax treatment of municipal bonds and owner-occupied homes will exhibit constant timing, remaining on yield-to-maturity apart from gain or loss on sale, even if Congress moves towards CTB treatment for both by repealing the bonds' interest exclusion and taxing homeowners' imputed rent (thus rendering the mortgage interest deduction nonpreferential). Likewise, when Congress changes the capital gains rate, it makes a policy change with no associated accounting change. Tax liability continues to arise upon realization, rather than at some other time.

This is merely an observation about common practice; nothing requires it to be so. In principle, Congress could just as readily change timing while keeping policy constant as the reverse. Thus, suppose that the costs of purchasing municipal bonds and homes were made deductible, and the interest income and imputed rent thereafter taxed. This would roughly replicate current policy while altering timing. In some cases, Congress does indeed show accounting flexibility of this sort. Thus, for tax-exempt saving through individual retirement accounts (IRAs), some provisions offer deductible contribution followed by taxable distribution, while others provide roughly the same benefit via nondeductible contribution followed by tax-free distribution. Yet such examples of varying timing while keeping policy constant remain exceptional.

In two important types of cases, changes in policy *do* tend to involve changes in timing. The first is that of "accounting" rules in ordinary tax parlance, as distinct from my use of the term. Thus, recall the choice between the cash and accrual methods of accounting for outlays and receipts, which may affect one's tax liability in present-value terms but also causes specific items to be includable or deductible in different tax years. Congress has in recent years narrowed the availability of cash accounting. Or consider the installment method of accounting for sales, under which certain gain is deferred (an accounting difference), generally without any interest adjustment (a policy difference).[2] Repeal of the installment method might be likely to include acceleration of the gain.

Second, timing tends to change along with policy in the area of cost recovery, or the deduction over time of outlays that yield economic value beyond the current year—for example, depreciation deductions. In principle, the present value of cost recovery deductions could be entirely independent of their timing. Recall the examples of an immediate deduction with the present value of economic depreciation, or economic depreciation deductions with interest to replicate the present value of expensing. In practice, however, a convention holding that the amount deducted should nominally equal the amount spent requires changes in policy to use the mechanism of changing timing. Thus, to make the depreciation regime for a particular asset more favorable, Congress typically shortens the recovery period or accelerates deductions during this period.[3] Changes in the opposite direction typically involve lengthening and other deceleration. A good illustration of how engrained this practice is arose in 1995, with regard to the deferred, present-value-equivalent depreciation plan in the "Contract with America." A major reason why (as noted in chapter 5) business leaders discounted the plan as politically unstable may have been that it invited controversy by departing from the practice of limiting nominal deductions to amounts spent.

Accordingly, there remains a consistent practice of making accounting changes when there is a policy change pertaining to cost-recovery rules such as depreciation. Accounting change retroactive taxation would therefore result if newly enacted depreciation rules were made applicable to assets placed in service before the new rules' effective dates. Thus, suppose that cars used in a leasing business were initially treated as five-year straight-line property, so that the purchase of a $15,000 car would generate deductions of $3,000 per year for five years. Then suppose that at some point the cars were made three-year straight-line property, such that a newly purchased $15,000 car would generate deductions of $5,000 per year for three years.

In this example, the effect of retroactively (but not nominally retroactively) applying the new depreciation regime to a car that had been placed in service under the old regime and was in the fourth or fifth year of its depreciation life would be to disallow all further cost-recovery deductions. After all, zero is the amount deductible in years four and five under the new regime. Thus, a policy change presumably aimed at encouraging car investment would end up discouraging such investment before enactment to the extent anticipated, by reason of the accompanying accounting change. This is precisely the approach that most commentators—without considering current transition practice—assume would be followed in the absence of deliberate transition relief if Congress replaced the present income tax with a consumption tax that used expensing.

B. Regularities in Congressional Decisions on Whether to Impose Retroactive Taxes

Congressional policy with regard to imposing retroactive taxes upon the enactment of tax base changes has two main features. Accounting change retroactive taxes are pervasively avoided through grandfathering for pre-effective-date assets or transactions. Policy change retroactive taxes tend to be avoided, but subject to exception and depending to some extent on mere accounting elements of the old and new tax rules that are at issue.

1. Accounting Change Retroactive Taxes

Political practice with regard to the above-described accounting changes regarding depreciation is well known. Congress invariably avoids imposing the potential accounting change retroactive taxes by providing that the new depreciation rules it enacts will apply only to newly placed-in-service assets. It thus forestalls the nominal over- or underrecovery of basis that would result if the depreciation rule for an asset was changed in midstream and allowed to apply prospectively notwithstanding its non-application in preenactment taxable years.

This reflects a broader Congressional practice with respect to accounting changes. Recall, for example, that new alimony rules applied solely to post-enactment transfers, and that Congress, by applying newly enacted OID rules solely to new instruments, avoided giving old instruments "basis credit" on either the borrower or lender side for the income that would have been recognized if, counterfactually, the new rules had applied to preenactment taxable years. This practice also has good predictive value for the future. Thus, if Congress indexed interest on loans to reflect inflation, reciprocally affecting inclusions and deductions and to some extent affecting only nominal incidence, one would expect it to provide transition relief for pre-effective-date loans—particularly if marginal rates were close enough to limit the associated policy change significance of the new rule.[4]

The regularity of this practice may initially seem surprising, given the lack of general understanding of the distinction between policy and accounting change retroactive taxes. Perhaps the reason is that the accounting change retroactive taxes potentially resulting from tax base changes often are easy to spot and lack any obvious policy rationale. Why, for example, would one want two years of rental car depreciation to disappear in certain cases, merely because one is prospectively shortening the useful life for rental cars in order to make subsequent cost recovery more favorable? Why subject previously divorced spouses to unanticipated changes in tax incidence—thus inducing future divorce agreements expressly to provide for such changes—simply because one has decided to alter the reporting prospectively on a consistent basis?

2. Policy Change Retroactive Taxes

For policy change retroactive taxes, even though retroactivity might serve anticipatory purposes from the enactors' standpoint, grandfathering or other transition relief is the norm. For example, the enactment or repeal of a tax preference typically is limited to post-effective-date new assets or transactions. This practice presumably reflects widespread acceptance of "old view" reliance arguments, along with interest groups' resistance to direct retroactive repeal of their benefits (Levmore 1993, 283), and the political weakness of arguments they might make for providing them with incentives *ex post* (notwithstanding that such arguments might gain plausibility from a rational expectations perspective).

The example of depreciation may help to illustrate this practice. To avoid accounting change retroactive taxation of preenactment assets when the depreciation rules change, all Congress needs to do is use actual unrecovered basis as of the effective date to compute remaining deductions, rather than allowing the back-end deductions that would have been allowable had the new system been in place all along. Yet this does not foreclose policy change retroactive taxation, in the form of changing the timing of remaining cost recovery for old assets to conform more closely with the new regime. Thus, if the useful life for rental cars shortened from five years to three years, Congress could speed up the recovery of the remaining basis for pre-effective-date assets. In practice, however, Congress typically leaves unchanged the depreciation regime for old assets.

However, as noted at the end of chapter 4, Congress more assiduously eliminates retroactive loss from preference curtailment than retroactive gain from preference expansion. In illustration, consider home mortgage interest deductions. In 1987, when Congress enacted dollar limits on the face amount of mortgage debt that could give rise to deductible interest, preexisting debt was grandfathered (Internal Revenue Code of 1986, section 163(h)(3)(D)). It seems highly unlikely that any similar effort would be made to avoid transition gain if these debt limits were repealed.

Wholly apart from any such asymmetry, however, the practice of avoiding policy change retroactive taxation is far from absolute. Even to the extent that this practice carries the prestige of good policy, departing from it generally does not evoke the same level of outrage as nominal retroactivity. Moreover, the fact that policy change retroactive taxes are not generally as senseless from the enactors' standpoint as accounting change retroactive taxes helps make them a natural policy option to consider.

In practice, policy change retroactive taxation is typically considered respectable policy as a response to "abuse," however that flexible term may happen to be defined. Thus, the recent legislation that generally eliminated the Treasury's power to give its new regulations nominal retroactive application expressly retained this power "to prevent abuse" (Internal Revenue Code, section 7805(b)(3)). And the prevailing view that the need to correct "abuse" can justify greater retroactivity helps explain business interests' nervousness about the deferred expensing-equivalent deductions proposed under the Contract with America. If deductions nominally in excess of outlays did not look "abusive," one could presumably have been confident that the repeal of Contract depreciation, in keeping with depreciation changes generally, would have left untouched outstanding deductions that pertained to old assets.

In addition, policy change retroactive taxation is considered permissible when certain formal accounting mechanisms are used to accomplish it. The mere accounting attributes that may cause it to be regarded as innocuous rather than offensive are twofold. First, it can be imposed indirectly, or through rules that affect, say, a deduction's ultimate allowability rather than its formal computation. Second, where the tax system uses wait-and-see accounting, changing *ex post* the tax treatment of past economic events is deemed unobjectionable.

a. Indirect Retroactivity

A consistent practice of avoiding policy change retroactive taxation would presumably focus on particular items' effect on tax liability. For example, if the tax rate is 30 percent, the real significance of a rule permitting one to deduct a dollar next year is that it will reduce one's tax liability by 30¢. A consistent and thoroughgoing reliance-based view would presumably regard this economic value as the thing that needed to be protected.

As it turns out, however, the practice of discouraging retroactive taxation is considerably narrower and more formalistic than this. We have already seen the general lack of any adjustment for the effects of tax rate changes on the value of nominally fixed deductions—even in cases where this results in anomalous retroactive taxation due to the mismatch between deduction and related inclusion. It further turns out that so long as the formal step of computing a particular item, such as a deduction, remains unchanged, transition practice does not require that the deduction actually be allowed. Disallowance is permissible—albeit subject to criticism on grounds of undue retroactivity—so long as it results from the application of rules conditioning the computation of taxable income on the interplay of different items on the taxpayer's post-effective-date tax return.

A good example is provided by the enactment of the passive-loss rules in the Tax Reform Act of 1986, generally disallowing deductions in excess of current taxable income from suspected tax shelters that are classified as "passive activities." In the immediate post-enactment period, these rules' main effect was to defer otherwise allowable depreciation deductions from preenactment investments that had been deliberately structured to permit current use of those deductions against labor income (Rock and Shaviro 1987, 4).[5] However, because the rules involved applying a deduction limit to all current-year items from passive activities, rather than directly recomputing depreciation deductions under the prior law tables, it was deemed acceptable under prevailing practice.

Or consider home mortgage interest deductions. In 1990, Congress enacted a complicated percentage disallowance rule for various itemized deductions, including home mortgage interest. Under this rule, one must reduce these deductions by 3 percent of the amount by which one's adjusted gross income exceeds an indexed amount (initially $100,000), until one has lost 80 percent of the deductions (Internal Revenue Code, section 68).

While the rule was mainly designed to function as a disguised marginal rate increase, it does so by reducing the tax benefit from home mortgage interest deductions. One thus might think that it would raise the same concerns about retroactivity as the 1987 enactment that directly defined certain mortgage interest as nondeductible. Nonetheless, upon its adoption there was no grandfathering. Just as in the passive-loss case, the use of a Rube Goldberg mechanism that relied on the interaction of various current-year income and deduction items made retroactive disallowance politically more palatable.

b. Retroactivity When the Tax System Uses Wait-and-See Accounting

For a separate kind of example where the permissibility of policy change retroactive taxation turns on mere accounting, consider capital gains rate changes. These invariably apply retroactively (albeit nominally prospectively) to appreciation that accrued under prior law. Thus, if my stock appreciates at a time when the capital gains rate is 28 percent and I sell it on the first day after the rate has changed to 20 percent, I pay tax on the entire gain at 20 percent.[6]

In principle, such instances of policy change retroactive taxation ought to evoke the same reliance-based concerns as changing the depreciation regime for an asset after one has placed it in service. After all, one is changing *ex post* the tax consequences of past events (both the investment decision and the appreciation that actually occurred). However, due to the use of wait-and-see accounting for capital gains, such concerns apparently do not arise. Indeed, debate about capital gains rate changes typically emphasizes the likely revenue effects without the slightest sensitivity to the fact that, in the short term, this is almost entirely a debate about a retroactive rate change for previously accrued gain.

In ignoring the retroactive elements that, in other settings, are considered so important, people may respond to the lack of a formal accounting entry for the past appreciation, and the fact that taxation at the new rate is triggered by the "new" act of sale, thus ostensibly making it voluntary. Yet the former point is mere accounting, and the latter point loses its significance once one recognizes that what matters distributionally is the burden imposed by the tax system, not the act of tax payment. A rate increase affects burden even without a taxable event that triggers liability.

Suppose that the existing tax regime for capital assets had different accounting content but roughly identical policy content (taking into account the realization requirement as well as the capital gains rate). Since the tax benefit of the realization requirement and capital gains rate presumably have an expected value for any given asset—reflecting such factors as asset volatility and trading costs (Strnad 1991)—one could, in principle, leave initial investment incentives unchanged for all assets through a regime in which appreciation was taxed as it accrued and asset holders were allowed a stream of annual deductions that had exactly the present value needed to keep expected tax burdens the same as under present law. Ignoring administrative issues, this regime would be a Pareto improvement over the existing one, since it would provide the same investment incentives up front but avoid inefficiently deterring sales of appreciated assets (the lock-in effect).

If this tax regime were currently in place, one could impose a policy change retroactive tax by reducing the allowable future-year deductions for assets acquired before the effective date. So far as initial investment incentives (as distinct from subsequent lock in) were concerned, this would essentially be the same as increasing the capital gains rate under the actual tax law. Yet it likely would prompt stronger protests about undue retroactivity and the undermining of reliance—evidencing the role that mere accounting considerations play in determining when transition relief is considered appropriate.

C. Assessing Congressional Practice with Respect to Policy Change and Accounting Change Retroactive Taxes

1. Application of My Proposed Constitutional Norms

The above discussion of congressional transition practice reached the following conclusions: (1) accounting changes are relatively infrequent; (2) even when they occur, Congress generally avoids imposing accounting change retroactive taxes; and (3) Congress also generally avoids imposing policy change retroactive taxes, but with a bias towards relieving transition loss from preference curtailment, and with exceptions to the general practice for "abuse," indirect deduction disallowance, and tax rules that use wait-and-see or realization accounting.

How do these practices fare under this book's constitutional analysis? A simple reading of my proposed constitutional norms would suggest that practice concerning accounting change retroactive taxes is generally correct, while that concerning policy change retroactive taxes is incorrect in the general case and correct in the exceptions. Hence, transition practice ought to change in the direction of more readily imposing policy change retroactive taxes, without necessarily requiring the use of indirect methodologies, such as the passive loss rules, that may have disadvantages of their own. Thus, if the municipal bond preference or home mortgage interest deduction were repealed, indirection would not be required in order to reach pre-effective-date assets, and depreciation changes might involve altering the rate of cost recovery on old assets' remaining basis.

One should keep in mind two caveats, however. The first is that norm 1, supporting the imposition of policy change retroactive taxes, is intended merely as a marginal corrective, seeking to make transition practice less favorable to income tax preferences than under an old-view-type reliance norm. In effect, I assume that its main effect would be to produce a few more cases like the passive loss rules, perhaps without requiring the same degree of indirection. To help show why this might be a good thing, consider that those rules, by imposing surprisingly great retroactive losses on taxpayers who had purchased tax shelters prior to the 1986 Act, may have taught a lasting lesson. They showed that investments designed to generate large tax losses are susceptible to being addressed by Congress after the fact despite its frequent diffidence about retroactivity. In the next tax shelter era, one could imagine this lesson being remembered, inducing greater investor caution, and this might be all to the good.

If this surmise about the marginal effect of advocating norm 1 is incorrect, the case for it might evaporate. The norm might be undesirable if it was not reducing the overall scope of income tax preferences over time, or was doing so only slightly relative to its increasing transition risk by inducing anticipation of policy changes with a mean desirability of zero. Moreover, even if its main effect is as I surmise, it would still be inferior to a norm imposing policy change retroactive taxes solely for *good* changes (or pro-CTB changes), if not for such a norm's manifest unfeasibility.

The second caveat about applying my proposed norms is that constitutional considerations need not invariably outweigh those of the particular case at hand. On any occasion, the short-term gain from achieving a good transition (or steady-state policy) outcome that time, by departing from the dictates of the applicable constitutional norm, may conceivably be greater than the long-term harm to good constitutional practice. Given this point, I next apply a case-by-case analysis to a few prominent or recurrent examples of possible tax base change.

2. Examples of Case-by-Case Analysis

a. The Home Mortgage Interest Deduction

Amongst tax scholars, few provisions in the Internal Revenue Code are as roundly (and I would say correctly) condemned as the home mortgage interest deduction. Its defects, considered in combination with the exclusion from taxable income of the imputed rental value of one's home, include the following:

1. It distorts consumption (and therefore also investment) choices, both between home and non-home consumption and between home ownership and rental. The latter distortion matters for two main reasons. Home ownership tends to increase transaction costs for people who move frequently, and it can impede achieving optimal portfolio diversification, as middle-class homeowners have sometimes learned to their detriment when housing prices in their neighborhoods declined.

2. It causes the value of owning a home to depend in part on one's marginal tax rate, thus distorting the allocation of homes among taxpayers.

3. Given capitalization of the expected tax benefits into housing prices, it makes homes costlier to purchase. This would be irrelevant under perfect capital markets, since the lender would advance more given the tax benefits' effect on value, but in practice, it may impede home purchases by first-time buyers with limited credit (such as people whose only significant asset is their expected future labor earnings). Thus, suppose that lenders require security, in the form of net assets on hand, to advance more than 90 percent of a home's purchase price. Raising the price of a home through tax capitalization increases the prospect that a would-be first-time buyer will be unable to finance the purchase.

Nonetheless, few tax rules appear as politically sacrosanct as the home mortgage interest deduction. Thus, even many sweeping tax reform proposals leave it partly or fully in place. Yet marginal curtailment of the deduction is politically possible, as the 1987 and 1990 changes helped show. Indeed, the deduction's revenue cost, which exceeds $50 billion per year, makes it a natural target for further curtailment in the event of deficit reduction when fiscal pressures reemerge in the first decade of the twenty-first century.

Obviously, both a constitutional analysis based on norm 1 and a case-by-case analysis based either on the CTB norm or the view of this deduction expressed above suggest denying transition relief if the deduction is further curtailed. Indeed, what might make such relief all the more objectionable is the likelihood that, if the tax preference were expanded (such as by repealing the statutory ceiling on loan principal), homeowners would be allowed to enjoy the transition gain without limitation. This is not to deny that, in order to curtail the preference even purely prospectively, concerns of political feasibility might require extending grandfathering to existing homes or loans as the price of enactment. Yet viewing this not as good transition policy for its own sake but as a politically motivated concession—and one whose disadvantages included its possible "constitutional" influence on future transition outcomes—would help to put such an outcome in proper perspective.

An important counterargument concerning the case-by-case analysis is worth mentioning. In chapter 3, I downplayed problems of transition risk by noting both that some individuals want to "bet" about future policy by making a particular investment, and that if they want the investment without the bet they often can offset the risk through a variety of hedging or diversification strategies. Hence, from the perspective of determining optimal constitutional rules, it seemed justified to assume that analysis of retroactive taxes, rather than transition risk, generally should drive the analysis. Yet the home mortgage interest deduction presents a case where transition risk may be unusually significant.

For homeowners who are not in the wealthiest segment of the society, homes typically provide a significant percentage of the value of their gross assets. Thus, the ownership of a home often conflicts with what one might consider optimal asset diversification. Moreover, the existence of such asset concentration within homeowners' portfolios does not wholly rebut the possibility that they would prefer, all else equal, to spread the resulting risk of fluctuation in the value of their homes. Rather, they may lack convenient means to achieve their preferred risk positions, given their other reasons for wanting to own their homes and the transaction cost impediments to purchasing private insurance against the risk that their homes will lose value.[7] Hence, one could argue that, in principle, people would be willing to pay some positive amount of insurance, at least against the transition risk of an adverse policy change, even though we do not observe such protection being offered in the market. This, in turn, might provide an argument for transition relief such as grandfathering in the event that the home mortgage interest deduction was curtailed—although subject to the retort that private markets' failure to offer insurance against the political transition risk tells us something about demand for it relative to its cost.

Another version of the risk-based argument for transition relief would emphasize the possibility of disrupting credit markets if the deduction were sharply and unexpectedly curtailed. Conceivably, given the common practice of borrowing a substantial percentage of the purchase price with little security other than the home itself, such curtailment could trigger a situation where numerous home mortgage loans, perhaps with concentrated incidence in the hands of financial institutions that specialize in providing them, would cease to be adequately secured, raising the specter of a disruptive wave of defaults.

Such a scenario should perhaps excite some skepticism. There is good reason to believe that the impact on home values would not be great enough to cause a wave of defaults (Bruce and Holtz-Eakin 1998)—for example, due to partly offsetting gains such as that from reduced expected future competition from new home construction (discussed at the end of this chapter). Still, one cannot, at least as a logical matter, entirely rule out the wave-of-defaults scenario. Yet even if transition relief were therefore justified on balance, it would still come at an efficiency cost. Undesirable transition risk cannot be alleviated without reducing desirable taxpayer anticipation of the possibility that the home mortgage interest deduction will be curtailed.

A final transition issue raised by the home mortgage interest deduction goes to the design of transition relief if offered. Confining the analysis to grandfathering (I consider generic alternatives such as phase-in or delayed implementation in chapter 11), the most obvious alternatives are to grandfather deductions that pertain to an existing home either (1) unconditionally for the life of the home, (2) only for the current owner, or (3) only for the current owner's preexisting mortgage loans. The third and narrowest of these alternatives is the one that Congress used when placing a statutory ceiling on tax-favored home mortgage loan principal.

From the standpoint of addressing transition risk, the main difference between these forms of relief is simply how much transition relief they provide. Thus, suppose alternative (1) was narrowed to grandfather only 75 percent of all mortgage interest deductions for the life of the home, and that this happened to equalize the present value of all expected future deductions between alternatives (1) and (3). Alternative (1) would provide less relief than (3) with respect to current mortgage loans, thus perhaps making default under them more likely. However, such defaults as occurred would be transactionally costlier under (3) than (1), given that under alternative (1), the continuation of transition relief would increase the homes' value to prospective purchasers. Accordingly, it is ambiguous which alternative better addresses transition risk, apart from differences purely in the overall level of transition relief.

In principle, however, limiting the quantum of transition relief by restricting grandfathering to existing owners or loans seems clearly inferior to limiting it by providing deductibility across the board but for less than 100 percent of deductions. The difference is that the ownership and debt limitations tend to distort taxpayer decisions across an additional dimension—for example, by encouraging pre-effective-date borrowing or post-effective-date deferral of repayment as a way of increasing the transition benefits. Thus, the main argument for such limitations would have to be that, as a political matter, they cannot be "traded in" for quantitatively equivalent across-the-board restrictions on grandfathering, and that the efficiency cost of the additional distortions they cause is outweighed by the benefit of reducing overall (undesirable) transition relief.

b. Realization and Recognition Rules

The capital gains preference is only one example of an income tax rule that uses realization-based wait-and-see accounting, leading in practice to policy change retroactive taxation when there is a change in rule that keeps accounting constant (or changes it only prospectively). Other examples of possible rule changes that would involve wait-and-see accounting include the following:

1. Changes in the definition of what constitutes a realization event for income tax purposes. Consider 1997 legislation that newly defined certain "short-against-the-box" transactions, such as where one sells a borrowed security that one also holds, as sales for tax purposes (IRC section 1259). While this rule altered the nominal timing of gain recognition, it avoided accounting change retroactive taxation by applying solely to post-effective-date transactions (rather than giving taxpayers basis increases to reflect the tax that would have been imposed had it applied nominally retroactively). It did, however, impose a policy change retroactive tax by impeding continued deferral of previously accrued but untaxed gain by taxpayers who might have wanted to engage in short-against-the-box transactions.

2. Changes in the rule concerning unrealized appreciation at death. At present, property transmitted at death permanently avoids tax on the previously accrued gain, by the mechanism of an untaxed increase in basis to its then fair market value (IRC section 1014). A replacement rule might either make death a realization event, with tax consequences

for the decedent's final income tax return, or else provide that property transmitted at death, like that transmitted by *inter vivos* gift, would keep its prior basis.

3. Changes to statutory nonrecognition rules, under which a given realization event is disregarded and gain or loss therefore remains untaxed until another such event occurs. Examples include rules providing nonrecognition for certain exchanges of like-kind property (IRC section 1031), and of property for corporate stock (IRC section 351) or a partnership interest (IRC section 721).

For all such changes, my first constitutional norm suggests that one should welcome the practice of allowing the new rule to apply to previously accrued gain or loss, thereby imposing a policy change retroactive tax. (The ANR norm prevents nominally retroactive application to pre-effective-date transactions.) A case-by-case analysis, however, is more complicated here than with respect to, say, the home mortgage interest deduction. The reason for this greater complexity is that good policy is particularly hard to identify, and the CTB norm is unusually unhelpful, in the realization area.

One might plausibly interpret the CTB norm as suggesting that the capital gains preference be eliminated and that as many events or transactions as possible be deemed to result in gain recognition. (The implications for loss recognition are less clear-cut, given taxpayers' ability to engage in strategic trading, whereby they hold winners and sell losers.) One should keep in mind, however, that the realization requirement has mixed efficiency implications. Permitting gain recognition to be deferred without an interest charge (and with strategic trading opportunities) provides an income tax preference for certain investments. Yet conditioning the end of deferral on the occurrence of a realization event results in an income tax dispreference. For example, if I have an asset with a basis of 0 and a value of $100, I am not made any wealthier by selling it for $100. The realization tax is essentially an excise tax on the act of sale, and it distorts economic behavior through what is known in the capital gains literature as the "lock-in effect" (Shaviro 1992, 1–2, 25–26).

The layering of this dispreference on top of the initial preference gives rise to a difficult second-best problem: It both offsets prior distortions and creates new ones. Which of the two effects is greater can be a difficult empirical question, turning on details of taxpayer response that the CTB norm fails to enlighten. For example, a revenue-losing capital gains rate increase would tend to make everyone worse off by increasing the burden of those subject to it while also requiring others to make up the revenue loss. Similarly, the short-against-the-box rules are probably undesirable if in practice they produce little net revenue while substantially increasing tax-planning costs.

These are problems of determining what is good steady-state policy, without particular reference to retroactivity. Yet, insofar as rule changes that relate to realization would impose policy change rather than accounting change retroactive taxes, one would expect the steady-state and transitional issues to come out the same way. In this area, therefore, not only is transition practice relatively symmetric between expanding and curtailing tax benefits, but there is no particular reason to favor asymmetry in one direction.

c. Nominal Incidence Changes under the Present Income Tax

We have already seen that Congress generally avoids accounting change retroactive taxes, whether from changes in timing or in nominal incidence. In the case of a pure accounting change, such as adopting inflation in-dexing for loans in a world where all borrowers and lenders deducted and included all interest at the same marginal rate, this result seems utterly unobjectionable. Retroactively changing the tax law's effect on preexisting loans, such that constant net tax liability simply shifted between borrowers and lenders (since now only real interest would be deducted and included), would serve little purpose. The prospect that this might happen would expose borrowers and lenders to pointless transition risk, to which they might respond by increasing their transaction costs. For example, they might write lengthier contracts that specified how their deals would adjust in the event of a retroactive accounting change. Or for loans that permitted the borrower to accelerate repayment without penalty, they might go to the trouble of replacing old loans with new ones that had suitably adjusted nominal interest rates.

In practice, however, pure accounting changes that lack any accompa-nying policy content may be the exception rather than the rule. Adminis-trative concerns aside, the main reason to change accounting is presumably that it will facilitate, or is otherwise associated with, a policy change. Thus, for indexing loans, the motivation might be that some of the effects on tax liability would not be fully reciprocal, due to differences between includability and deductibility or in the marginal tax rates of borrowers and lenders. Suppose, for example, that indexing served to prevent taxpayers from exploiting the divergence between nominal and real interest to shift taxable income from high-bracket to zero-bracket taxpayers. Indexing is a policy change to the extent of these rate bracket differences, and anticipation of its applying retroactively would tend to deter these transactions even before the policy change was adopted.

The question therefore arises of what to do when a policy change and an accounting change are effectively intermingled. In principle, one might like to disentangle the two in order to impose the policy change but not the accounting change retroactive tax. However, while simple in principle, this may be hard in practice. Suppose that, for a given loan, the effect of retroactively applying indexing was to increase the borrower's tax liability by $10 while reducing the lender's tax liability by $4. To impose solely the policy change retroactive tax, one would instead keep the prior law result *except* that one or the other taxpayer's liability (or a combination of the two) would increase by up to $6. If the details of the two parties' tax computations were otherwise simple enough, one might simply add to either's tax liability an amount equal to the product of (1) the inflation component of the nominal interest and (2) the difference between their marginal rates.

In practice, this is likely to be hard to accomplish, except perhaps in cases where the lender is tax exempt and thus can be assumed to bear no tax consequences from the change. Even knowledge of the two parties' marginal tax rates—which they may be reluctant to share with each other and may not even know themselves until tax-filing season—may be inadequate in cases where interest deductions or inclusions affect the current-year allowability of other items (such as under the passive loss rules), or where interest expense is capitalized and its tax consequences are therefore deferred. Thus, in most cases one may be unable to separate the policy change from the accounting change in determining the scope of transition relief.

Perhaps the best that one can do in such a case is make an *ad hoc* judgment about the relative significance of the two retroactive taxes. Thus, inflation indexing might present a weak case for retroactive application to pre-effective-date loans if the clientele effect, whereby taxpayers systematically exploit the prior mismeasurement through increased loans from low-bracket lenders to high-bracket borrowers, was considered a small part of the overall loan picture. By contrast, a new partnership tax rule that rendered ineffective what were deemed abusive "special allocations" of deductions to high-bracket partners might sensibly apply to pre-effective-date partnership agreements, notwithstanding an accounting change element, if most of the retroactive effect was on taxpayers who had engaged in the costly tax-avoidance behavior that it defeated.

D. Boundary Issues and Problems of Intertemporal Distortion Presented by Tax Base Changes

A further set of transition issues posed by tax base changes go to a new rule's "boundaries," or breadth of application, and to problems of intertemporal distortion. Boundary issues relate to the set of tax items that, because they have not yet been taken into account, remain subject to retroactive change notwithstanding the ANR norm. For example, in practice, only depreciation deductions that remain unclaimed as of the taxable year of a rule change are subject to retroactive alteration. Problems of intertemporal distortion arise when taxpayers change the timing of their behavior in response to rule changes that apply only to post-effective-date behavior. Examples include rushing to invest when the depreciation rules are about to become less favorable, or waiting to invest when they are about to become more favorable.

As a result of the convention requiring the amount deducted nominally to equal the amount spent without regard to time value, preferential cost recovery almost always is more accelerated than economic cost recovery. Thus, preferential deductions almost always cease to be subject to retroactive change more rapidly than do those that are consistent with CTB treatment—although whether this is good or bad for the taxpayer depends on whether retroactive change is generally favorable or unfavorable. On the inclusion side, however, things are reversed. Since preferentiality often involves deferral, it tends to increase the period of possible retroactive change, although again with unclear implications.

The problems of intertemporal distortion that result from having different tax base rules for different periods are perhaps more significant. In general, whether a tax base change is good or bad policy, any incentive either to accelerate or defer some act in order to place it in the more favorably taxed period induces inefficiency. Unfortunately, these incentives cannot be entirely avoided once the ANR norm ensures that different tax rules will apply to different taxable years. As with tax rate changes, the usual legislative response is to use an early effective date, thus reducing short-term taxpayer intertemporal shifts to the extent of preenactment underanticipation, although the degree to which this practice actually reduces intertemporal distortion is unclear given the effect on taxpayer incentives to find out about approaching rule changes (as discussed in chapter 6).

Legislators can also change the tax treatment of as yet unreported items from pre-effective-date transactions so as to reduce the importance of "beating" the effective date in either direction. Thus, if the depreciation regime for rental cars becomes less favorable than previously, one can slow down cost recovery for as yet unclaimed depreciation deductions from pre-effective-date cars. If it becomes more favorable, one can speed remaining cost recovery for rental cars. In each case, this reduces the present value of the difference between the tax treatment of pre- and post-effective-date items, thus potentially reducing taxpayer responses within the period right around the effective date—although, again, not necessarily reducing intertemporal distortion over a longer period.

Current transition practice in setting effective dates has an unfortunate asymmetry for which there is little justification. As I noted at the end of chapter 4, the application of policy changes that are adverse to the directly affected taxpayer typically is limited by transition rules, either generic or limited to particular taxpayers with a friendly congressional sponsor, that create "binding contract"–type exceptions to effective dates. For example, a shift towards less-favorable depreciation (such as that adopted in 1986) typically does not apply to property placed in service after the general effective date if, by that date, the taxpayer had a binding contract to construct or acquire the property. By contrast, a shift towards more-favorable depreciation (such as that adopted in 1981) typically applies to all property placed in service after the general effective date, without regard to contractual obligations at that time. The result of this asymmetry, to the extent not negated by scaling adjustments to steady-state rules, is to expand the application over time of preferential as compared to economic tax treatment, contrary to the CTB norm. Given the likely political unfeasibility of an opposite practice, in which only 1986-type changes would have binding contract exceptions, the most one can hope is that practice will change in the direction of discouraging "binding contract" exceptions to effective dates, and simply applying early effective dates across the board.

E. Resolution of Bets Concerning the Supply and Demand Effects of Future Tax Rules

1. The Supply and Demand Effects of Future Tax Rules on Asset Values

A final set of transition issues raised by tax base changes concerns people's bets about the supply and demand effects of future tax rules. In general, by making a given investment, one bets that new information will increase rather than reduce the investment's value. Since current prices reflect expectations prior to the receipt of that information, one in effect bets that other people, on average, are being too pessimistic about the investment and will learn, when the information arrives, that they ought to have made more investments of the same kind.[8]

For this reason, an investment, say, in rental housing involves an implicit bet that other people would invest more today in competing assets if they correctly foresaw future tax law changes. In part, the investor bets that, on the whole, other investors are being too pessimistic about the retroactive effects that future tax enactments will have on current rental housing. In addition, however, one bets that, on the whole, other investors are being too optimistic about the tax regime that will apply to such housing's future competition, in the form of subsequently developed new rental housing.

The reason is as follows. For a durable asset such as rental housing, the level of future competition from similar assets that do not yet exist is one of the things that current investors need to anticipate. This level, in turn, depends in part on the tax regime for such investment, which is not yet known. Thus, suppose rental buildings placed in service in 2004 and thereafter receive unfavorable tax treatment due to political developments in 2003. This will reduce investment in the buildings in 2004 and thereafter, relative to the case where the 2003 political decision yielded favorable tax treatment. Someone who knew, or at least believed, several years earlier that, on the whole, other investors were too optimistic about the post-2003 tax rules for rental buildings would be able to garner an extra-normal return by investing in the buildings before their price reflected the information about future competing investment that would become generally known in 2003.

Something like this point has been widely made in the legal and economics literature, yet it has been, in a crucial sense, misunderstood. Various commentators argue that when Congress makes the tax rules for new assets of a given type less favorable than previously, old assets of the same type inherently gain value. Likewise, making the tax treatment of new assets more favorable than previously is said to reduce the value of similar old assets (Graetz 1977, 60–63; Feldstein 1981; Auerbach and Kotlikoff 1983; Bradford and the U.S. Treasury Tax Policy Staff 1984, 162).[9] Under this view, the retroactive effect on old assets can be substantial. Laurence Kotlikoff estimates that the Tax Reform Act of 1986, by repealing or reducing such income tax preferences for new assets as the investment tax credit and accelerated depreciation, "handed owners of [old] U.S. capital a huge capital gain—$747 billion in today's dollars," or 13.1 percent of the assets' prior value. The Economic Recovery Tax Act of 1981, by expanding many of the same tax preferences, ostensibly caused a 6.5 percent reduction in the value of old assets (Kotlikoff 1992, 179).

It should be clear, however, that these estimates involve a crucial and unexplained failure to approach the issue from a rational expectations perspective. Even if enacting the 1986 Act had the claimed effects relative to retaining present law, this merely tells us something about a betting outcome *ex post*. From such a perspective, it would be equally accurate to say that the 1986 Act handed owners of old capital an enormous capital loss compared to a hypothetical tax act that would have entirely denied depreciation deductions for new capital. Whether investors gained or lost from the new information that was provided by the ultimate political outcomes in 1981 and 1986 depends on how these outcomes compared to prior investor expectations concerning what would happen on each occasion.

Thus, suppose that the 1981 and 1986 changes had been irrevocably preannounced in 1970. It seems hard to deny that all investors would thereafter have received only normal returns, at least insofar as the course of the tax law was concerned. After all, they would have been investing at all times in light of an accurate understanding of what was actually going to happen. The fact that the 1981 and 1986 changes were not preannounced merely indicates risk or variance in predicting the outcomes, along with a possibility that investors on average erred on either occasion by under- or overestimating the extent to which the law would actually change on each occasion. The lack of preannouncement in no way undermines the point that, to determine the transition gain or loss to owners of old assets, one needs to examine the change in expectations, not the change in written law.

When these writers do not completely ignore expectations, they treat the degree of enacted change as an upper bound on the change that investors could have anticipated. Thus, Auerbach and Kotlikoff consider only the expectational range from myopically assuming that present conditions will continue indefinitely, to exercising what proves *ex post* to have been perfect foresight (1987, 9–10). They ignore the case where investors expect even greater change than occurs. They thereby import systematic bias in the direction of expecting the continuation of prior law, without apparent justification.

If the question were one of predicting the exact, line-by-line details of newly enacted laws, Auerbach and Kotlikoff might be correct to examine the range from complete surprise to full anticipation. After all, one cannot achieve better than 100 percent accuracy in predicting the details of a new enactment. By analogy, consider attempting to predict whether a given coin toss will come out heads or tails. In a sense, the outcome is always a "surprise" even if one can accurately gauge the probabilities. A given toss of an honest coin will come out 100 percent heads or 100 percent tails, thus diverging from one's prior estimate that this outcome was only 50 percent likely. Similarly, if at a given moment in 1986 the content of that year's tax reform legislation had become fixed but its enactment remained subject to doubt, there presumably was an *ex post* gain to old capital of the sort that Auerbach and Kotlikoff posit as the uncertainty was resolved by enactment.

Yet this sort of example is merely a special case of forecasting future law generally, and is most plausible for the immediate run-up prior to enactment or rejection of a fixed proposal during a given congressional session. For the period before the 1986 Act was close to enactment, nothing would have prevented people from having a range of possible outcomes in mind, potentially extending from no change (or even change in the 1981 direction) to greater change than actually occurred. Old capital would presumably have lost overall had the newly adopted rules, despite slowing down cost recovery for new investment, been watered down relative to what people expected. Again, changing expectations is what matters, not changes in the tax rules themselves.

In general, there is no inherent reason why people's view of future law should err systematically in the direction of assuming that the tax treatment of particular assets will change less, rather than more, than ultimately proves to be the case. This rebuts Auerbach and Kotlikoff's conclusion that newly enacted investment incentives generally "reduce the market value of old capital and, therefore, the economic resources of the owners of the existing capital stock" (1983, 147–48). One simply cannot generalize this way about the expectational effects of tax law changes in a given direction.

One could compare the assumption here to that by 1960s Keynesians, when they assumed that expanding the money supply would inherently reduce unemployment as firms and workers continually erred in the direction of expecting a constant money supply. As discussed in chapter 2, the rational expectations revolution in macroeconomics arose from the insight that expanding the money supply relative to expectations should prove increasingly difficult over time even assuming initial myopia. Similarly here, if a government actually decided to follow the Auerbach-Kotlikoff formula for encouraging capital accumulation by "simultaneously increasing investment incentives and capital income tax rates" (1983, 148), it would have to keep on exceeding expectations that presumably would evolve to reflect observation of the policy. Even if attempted only once, how would one credibly assure investors that it would not happen again?

As it happens, the Auerbach-Kotlikoff surmise of systematic error in the direction of expecting the continuation of prior law probably does correctly describe the path of expectations under the particular circumstances of 1981 and 1986. To be sure, each of those two enactments was predictable to some extent from the political climate, which was strongly emphasizing investment incentives in the late 1970s and income tax base broadening in the mid-1980s. Yet each enactment ended up going considerably further in the predictable direction than what must have seemed a sensible median expectation—in 1981, due to the development of a "bidding war" between President Reagan and congressional Democrats, and in 1986 because the tax reform movement succeeded to an extent that most people had considered unlikely (Birnbaum and Murray 1987, 18, xi).

Nonetheless, studies of the 1981 and 1986 Acts by Andrew Lyon (1989a; 1989b) fail to detect transition effects of the sort that Auerbach and Kotlikoff predict, and that indeed one ought to expect in the special case of underanticipation. However, Lyon offers a possible explanation for the negative finding. His studies examine the values of business firms around the two times of enactment, rather than asset values, and he surmises that the predicted asset value shifts may have occurred, but been offset by firm-level adjustment costs. Thus, in 1981, even if old depreciable assets lost value due to the adoption of more favorable cost recovery for new assets, the firms that owned most of these assets may have experienced an offsetting gain from the prospect of enjoying extra-normal returns from new assets of the same type during the period of capital market adjustment (1989a, 229–32).

In effect, then, Lyon suggests that firms investing in particular depreciable assets make two bets about how future tax law will affect supply and demand. In addition to the bet about future competition between new and old assets, which they win if the tax law grows unexpectedly less favorable, they bet about the future value of their expertise with respect to such assets, which they win if the tax law grows unexpectedly more favorable.

There is accordingly an implicit hedge, or offset, between the two bets. It is likely to be imperfect, however. Any one decision by a firm may implicate one bet more than the other. Moreover, the relationship between the two offsetting bets may vary between industries, over time, and between the firms in an industry. Thus, despite the element of offset, each bet has independent significance.

2. Normative Significance of Bets on the Supply and Demand Effects of Future Tax Rules

Since economists have mostly overlooked the repeated-play element in tax transitions, it should be no surprise that they have misunderstood the normative issues raised by the above bets about the supply and demand effects of future tax rules. In general, the view that is taken gives Auerbach and Kotlikoff's unexplained assumption of systematic underanticipation either an "old view" or a "new view" twist. Thus, the loss to old assets when the tax treatment of competing new assets is unexpectedly made more favorable is typically either regretted on unspecified equity grounds—in effect, as if it were a random thunderbolt from the sky—and/or deemed desirable on efficiency grounds as a lump-sum wealth levy.

Both sides of this ostensible tradeoff between efficiency and equity are misconceived. If people are at least implicitly betting on how future tax rules will affect supply and demand in various markets, then—for both of the bets that Lyon identifies—the "equity" problem is at best one of undesired risk bearing, posed equally, one would think, by bets about future supply and demand that depend on the course of technology or consumer taste. From an efficiency standpoint, it should be clear that investors' incentives are improved if they bear the consequences of their bets about the supply and demand effects of future tax rules. The point is one of adjustment costs when there is immobile or sunk cost investment. Just as ice cream manufacturers' incentives are improved by their bearing the risk of future changes in the level of consumer demand for ice cream, so homeowners' incentives are improved by their bearing the risk that, whether due to tax rule changes or for any other reason, future new home construction will be higher or lower than expected. For this purpose, it does not matter whether the rule change is good or bad. Recall the examples in chapter 3 of income tax lawyers anticipating the repeal of the income tax, and domestic car manufacturers anticipating the enactment of a ban on the importation of foreign cars.

In some cases, therefore, the incentive effects of anticipating a tax rule change involve a degree of offset. Thus, consider a home that, upon surprise repeal of the home mortgage interest deduction, both loses value from the effect on its own tax benefits and gains value from the effect on expected future competition. Under the analysis in this chapter, both the gain and the loss have desirable incentive effects—the former as a policy change retroactive tax, and the latter due to adjustment costs. From the perspective of each homeowner, one could think of the repeal as a two-part enactment: that pertaining to one's own asset, and that pertaining to all other potentially competing assets. As to the former, it is desirable for each homeowner to anticipate good policy. As to the latter, it is desirable for each homeowner to anticipate whatever policy actually ends up being followed.

EIGHT

ADOPTION OF CORPORATE INTEGRATION

For the last 20 years, one of the most prominent tax reform proposals in academic and practitioner circles (if not politics) has been corporate integration. This, of course, would be a tax base change, like those discussed in chapter 7. However, the complexity of both its policy and accounting elements suggest giving it a separate chapter.

A. THE CURRENT CORPORATE TAX REGIME AND HOW IT MIGHT BE CHANGED

Under the "classical" corporate tax regime that applies in the United States, corporate income (other than that of certain closely held companies) is subject to a double tax. The first tax is levied at the corporate level as taxable income accrues. The second tax is levied on shareholders upon receiving certain corporate distributions. Such distributions are treated as ordinary income if the tax law defines them as dividends. Liquidating distributions, along with those during the corporation's life that are deemed to be in exchange for stock, generally get capital gains treatment after allowance for basis recovery.

The classical regime therefore has a distinctive accounting as well as policy content. So far as accounting is concerned, the details of nominal incidence—in the sense of whether a given dollar of tax is paid by the corporation itself or its owners—may have little import given the identity of interest between the two. However, the timing details, which involve deferring a substantial portion of the overall tax until there is a shareholder-level realization event, are important to the transition analysis.

The policy content of the classical corporate tax regime involves its attaching distinctive tax consequences to choices at the following four decisional boundaries: (1) corporate versus noncorporate entity, (2) debt versus new equity financing, (3) retaining versus currently distributing corporate earnings, and (4) form of distribution of corporate earnings.

1. Distortion 1: Corporate versus Noncorporate Entity

Taxpayers may be induced either to prefer or avoid corporate as opposed to noncorporate investment, as defined for tax purposes. The prospect of a second tax upon distributing earnings to owners plainly provides a reason to avoid the corporate form. Also implicated, however, is the tax rate as taxable income accrues at the entity level. If the entity is not a corporation for tax purposes, then owners include it at their individual tax rates, rather than those determined by consulting the rate tables for corporations. If the first-tier corporate rate is sufficiently below the owners' tax rates to make up for the expected present value of the shareholder-level tax, investment in corporate form is tax advantaged rather than tax penalized. Either way, however, the classical system distorts the choice between corporate and noncorporate investment.

2. Distortion 2: Debt versus New Equity Financing

Even assuming the use of a corporate entity, the classical regime influences decisions of whether to finance investments by using debt or by issuing new equity. Debt financing is usually tax preferred, because corporations can deduct interest but not dividend payments, whereas both are typically includable by investors. In some cases, however, new equity financing may be tax preferred. Suppose, for example, that the borrower corporation is in a substantial loss position and thus is unlikely to be able to use additional deductions, whereas the prospective investor is a corporation that can exclude dividends but not interest.

3. Distortion 3: Retaining versus Currently Distributing Corporate Earnings

The classical regime also influences decisions of whether to retain corporate earnings or to distribute them currently to shareholders. Distribution is typically a realization event that may trigger the shareholder-level tax—although the extent to which this influences the present value of the tax liability is more complicated than one might initially expect.

Usually under the existing tax laws, deferring gain recognition reduces the present value of the tax liability, thus creating "lock-in," as in the standard case where one holds an appreciated asset. However, the effect of triggering the shareholder-level tax on corporate earnings is more complicated. As revealed by the "new view" of corporate distributions, a uniform tax on corporate distributions, considered in isolation, would not reward deferring shareholder distributions, or indeed have any distortive influence on the timing decision (Bradford 1981; Zodrow 1991, 497).

In illustration, suppose that all corporate earnings will eventually be paid out as dividends and at that time will be taxed to shareholders at a 40 percent rate, but that in the interim they will generate the same after-tax return no matter where held. Paying out, say, $100 of corporate earnings this year and thereby triggering an immediate $40 shareholder-level tax is no worse for the shareholders than keeping the earnings in corporate solution until they double to $200, and then, with their payout, triggering an $80 dividend tax. After all, if the expected $200 in the future has the same present value as $100 today, then an $80 tax in the future has the same present value as a $40 tax today.

Thus, assuming a uniform tax on corporate distributions, the shareholders' deferral benefit is precisely offset by the growth in the nominal amount of the dividend tax, which could have been avoided by extracting the earnings from corporate solution sooner. This is what distinguishes this case from other instances of realization taxation. When one holds an appreciated asset, triggering an immediate tax liability through sale does not permit one to avoid tax on any gain that subsequently accrues to one's investment of the sale proceeds.

The new view suggests that the decision of whether to retain or distribute corporate earnings is less distorted by the classical corporate tax regime than had previously been assumed in the literature. Nonetheless, distortion of this decision remains to the extent that the new view's stylized assumptions are either inaccurate or incomplete. In particular, distribution decisions are distorted if the corporation's tax rate differs from that of the shareholders, the present tax treatment of shareholder distributions (including the applicable tax rate) may change, or prior to distribution, shareholders may pay capital gains taxes on selling shares whose value is increased by claims to undistributed earnings.

4. Distortion 4: Form of Distribution of Corporate Earnings

Finally, the classical regime influences decisions whether to make dividend or exchange distributions to shareholders. In general, shareholders who are individuals prefer exchange treatment, so that they can receive basis recovery and possibly pay tax at the capital gains rate. Corporate shareholders may have the opposite preference, given tax rules that make their dividend receipts at least partly excludable. The tax character of a given distribution depends on corporate earnings and profits along with the degree of change in shareholders' relative ownership interests. Thus, if a corporate distribution involved redeeming the same percentage of each shareholder's stock, thereby leaving their relative interests unaffected, it would constitute a dividend for tax purposes assuming adequate earnings and profits, regardless of its status under state corporate law.

For any of these four distortions to matter economically, there must be limits to taxpayers' ability to manipulate a transaction's tax character independently of its substance. If one's tax advisors could give whatever tax labels they wanted to one's arrangements without regard to what one was "really" doing, then the classical corporate tax regime would simply create elections to choose the most tax-favored label for one's activities, with broad allocative and distributional effects but no distinctive impact on the conduct of business. Most commentators agree, however, that we are not wholly in this world of pure electability, although financial innovation and the creation of new kinds of legal entities may be moving us towards it.

Accordingly, concern about real distortions that result from the classical corporate tax regime has led to a broad academic consensus in favor of corporate integration, under which corporate income would, in substance, be taxed once. A corporate-level tax might continue to be levied, but essentially as a collection device to avoid the need to allocate corporate income directly to the shareholders. Proposed methods vary. Under an American Law Institute (ALI) study prepared by William Andrews, corporations would deduct certain dividends paid.[1] Under a subsequent ALI study prepared by Alvin Warren, shareholders would be granted a credit for the corporate tax attributable to their dividends. A recent Treasury Department study, prepared while Michael Graetz was in residence as Deputy Assistant Secretary for Tax Policy, explores the following alternatives: (1) making dividends excludable by shareholders, (2) allocating corporate taxable income directly to shareholders as it arises, or (3) adopting a "comprehensive business income tax" (CBIT), under which dividends and interest would be nondeductible by business entities generally (not just corporations) but excludable by recipients.

Each of these proposals would narrow the distortions under the present-law classical corporate tax regime. They would move towards convergence of the relative taxation of corporate and noncorporate investment as well as debt and equity, while also reducing the tax consequences of making corporate distributions to shareholders and eliminating the distinction between dividend and nondividend distributions. These are all policy changes. In addition, however, each proposal would significantly change the accounting content of corporate tax law, by moving in the direction of collecting the entire tax on corporate investment at the time when taxable income accrues at the corporate level, rather than causing so much of the tax to await shareholder-level realization.[2]

In principle (whether or not feasibly in practice), one could make only this accounting change, or only one or more of the policy changes. Thus, suppose that Congress eliminated the shareholder-level tax but held constant the expected tax burden on all corporate investment, through an offsetting increase to each corporation's tax rate (and no increase where the expected future shareholder-level tax had a present value of zero). At least with regard to distortion 1, this would maintain current policy but change accounting by shifting tax payments forward in time without changing their present value. Or suppose instead that the only change to present law was changing tax rates both at the corporate level and on shareholder distributions such that the proportion of tax paid at each stage remained the same but corporate and noncorporate investment were placed on a par. This would eliminate distortion 1 but keep accounting constant.

In practice, however, and reflecting strong considerations of administrative convenience, each of the prominent integration proposals alters both the policy and the accounting content of the corporate tax rules. This creates the potential for a variety of retroactive taxes, to which the leading proposals respond in a variety of ways. I next examine the transition content of these proposals.

B. Treatment of Transition in Leading Integration Proposals

All three of the leading integration studies discuss transition issues and advocate, or at least outline, specific responses. As it happens, the studies differ significantly in their transition recommendations. Indeed, these differences are larger than those separating their proposed steady-state implementations of corporate integration. In the steady-state realm, the studies largely share a common vision of integration's aims, albeit that their proposals differ somewhat in policy as well as accounting content. In the realm of transition, one cannot even say that their aims are similar.

Nonetheless, their discussions of transition have much in common. None distinguishes between policy and accounting changes or the potential transition consequences of each. None considers the incentive effects, either as anticipated preenactment or as remembered afterwards, of particular transition rules. Instead, they treat transition as presenting a one-shot distributional problem, to be analyzed under some incompletely specified norm such as horizontal equity or an aversion to imposing sudden wealth changes.

1. The Andrews ALI Study: Denying the Benefits of Integration to Old Corporate Equity

While proposing a dividends-paid deduction to address the classical corporate tax regime's frequent bias against corporate investment, Andrews wants to limit the benefit to new corporate equity, or that contributed after the proposal's effective date. In order to prevent old equity from benefiting, he proposes limiting deductible dividends to those that do not exceed a reasonable rate of return on new equity contributions. This eliminates the "tracing" problem of needing to determine a dividend's true source, at the cost of some inaccuracy where the actual return to new equity differs from the assumed rate.

The resulting system is in some respects quite complicated. In particular, to impede taxpayer efforts to benefit from converting old equity into new through stock purchases followed by reissuance, it includes special "converted equity" rules. Some commentators have questioned whether the plan is administratively workable (Zodrow 1991, 498). Alan Auerbach notes, however, that Andrews's basic policy aim of limiting the benefit to newly contributed corporate equity would be easy to accomplish administratively—whether or not politically—by allowing all dividends to be deducted post-enactment but charging old equity a one-time tax equal to the expected present value of these deductions. This tax could conceivably be based on corporations' accumulated earnings and profits accounts (to the extent known), since under present tax law, distributions are not dividends unless deemed made out of earnings and profits (Auerbach 1990, 115).[3]

By limiting the benefit of the dividends paid deduction to new equity, Andrews avoids policy change retroactive taxation in the form of a tax cut for old equity. He explains his opposition to the retroactive tax cut as follows:

> It is simply too late to do anything about a bias that may have existed against contributions of equity in the past. Moreover, from the standpoint of fairness, shares have traded on the general understanding that there would be a corporate income tax, with no deduction for dividends, and to change the rule on that now, for all shareholders, would produce significant shifts in

wealth but with no basis for confidence they would get to the right people. Not only is it too late to eliminate the incentive effects of biases in relation to past transactions, it is also too late to compensate the right people for distributional consequences of that bias (American Law Institute 1989, 92).

This is a pure *ex post* perspective. It does not address the retroactive tax cut's possible incentive effects, either before enactment if anticipated or afterwards if observed. It also treats the retroactive tax cut as necessarily implying a wealth shift, again without regard to anticipation. Yet suppose the adoption of corporate integration with a retroactive tax cut had been irrevocably announced decades in advance, thus inducing all investment decisions to be made in light of it. This would likely eliminate any wealth shift at the moment when the new system took effect. While, in fact, corporate integration has not been preannounced and may be considered quite unlikely, current corporate investors are at least implicitly betting that it will occur. Thus, they will lose if it does not occur, and are not necessarily the "wrong" people to win if it occurs.

Despite Andrews's stated aversion to the wealth shift that might result from a retroactive tax cut for old equity, his plan includes a proposal that would subject such equity to a retroactive tax increase. Rather than simply retain present law for old equity, the plan would eliminate the present law distinction between dividend and other distributions. In effect, all would be taxed like dividends. This proposal, by ending present law's generally more favorable treatment of nondividend distributions, would impose a wealth loss on holders of equity if underanticipated, for the same reason that unexpectedly making the tax treatment of dividends more favorable than previously would provide a gain.

Andrews offers no reconciliation between imposing a retroactive tax increase on old equity and opposing any retroactive tax cut. While the increase is a byproduct of eliminating the distortive distinction between dividend and other distributions, that goal could in principle have been met without a retroactive tax increase, at least for shareholders as a group, by using a compromise or blended rate. Thus, if one estimated that the average tax rate for all corporate distributions was about half that for dividend distributions, one could impose a tax on all distributions from old equity at half the old dividend rate.

2. The Warren ALI Study: Possible Omission of Transitional Adjustment Other than Phase-In

Alvin Warren's ALI study of corporate integration, unlike that by Andrews, takes no definite stance on transition. Warren notes that the shareholder credit method of eliminating the double tax could be limited to new equity through means such as those discussed by Andrews or Auerbach (American Law Institute 1993, 207–209). In addition, he describes how integration could be phased in (without distinguishing between new and old equity) should the enacting Congress conclude that "the gains in economic welfare from integration would have to be partially deferred, presumably for revenue reasons" (209).

Nonetheless, the study is best described as adverse to limiting the transition gain to old equity. Warren mentions only two arguments concerning the desirability of such limits, both opposed to Andrews' position. First, he notes that corporate integration will likely have a number of distinct transition effects on corporate shareholders—depending, for example, on how various international tax issues are resolved. "Some of the choices will undoubtedly create positive changes in the value of investors' assets, while others will create negative changes. The actual effect will depend on the precise combination of policies and rates imposed" (207). Hence, implicitly, why single out a particular source of transition gain for denial? Second, "basic structural change in the tax law would simply not be possible if tax legislation were always constrained to prohibit changes in the value of taxpayer assets, whether positive or negative" (208).

These are critiques that Warren has presented more fully elsewhere. For example, he has noted that pretax returns in the noncorporate sector might increase as capital left that sector in response to the newly favorable tax treatment of corporate equity. (This is another example of a betting gain on future tax rules' supply and demand effects, like those discussed at the end of chapter 7.) Why, he asks, should this transition gain be permitted while the gain to the corporate sector that Andrews addresses is denied? Moreover, he asks how, once one takes Andrews's position, one can justify changing corporate tax rates without compensation. If one claims that investors expect changes in tax rates but not in the basic corporate tax structure, "the argument turns on unarticulated assumptions as to what investors are myopic about" (Warren 1981, 757).

While these are astute critiques of the "old view" on which Andrews relies, this book's analysis advances the inquiry far beyond that point. The existence of offset between various transition gains and losses, while relevant if one views transition as a one-shot distribution problem, loses significance once one recognizes that each retroactive tax may have distinctive incentive properties. In addition, once one therefore understands that different retroactive taxes are distinguishable, arguments from analogy in the form of "why eliminate retroactive tax A when we permit retroactive tax B" cease to be germane.

3. The Treasury Integration Study: Allowing Old Corporate Equity to Benefit, but Phasing in the New Regime

The Treasury integration study rejects any limitation of the benefits of corporate integration to new equity. Rather than propose no transition relief, however, the Treasury recommends phase-in or delayed implementation (depending on the choice of integration prototype) as a device to "moderate the transition effects of integration, while avoiding the serious drawbacks of limiting integration to new equity" (U.S. Treasury 1992, 90). The latter drawbacks are said to be twofold: administrative complexity and "perpetuating the very distortions the new system seeks to eliminate" (90). Distortion would ostensibly be perpetuated because, as the Treasury study argues elsewhere, the new view of corporate distributions is false, and lock-in of undistributed corporate earnings is therefore a serious problem (224 n. 9).

This rejection of the new view reflects a failure to understand it properly (admittedly reflecting its expression in the literature). Again, the new view in its pure form simply states the undeniable arithmetic equivalence between the present value of the tax burden on current versus future corporate distributions if these distributions are subject to a uniform tax (Bradford 1981; Zodrow 1991, 497).[4] Thus, the main point of contention concerns the degree to which this stylized assumption yields valuable insights about the real world. This, however, is a dispute not at the theoretical level, but about the content of present and expected future tax rules at any given moment. The more the corporate tax system is expected to levy a uniform distributions tax, the greater the new view's descriptive accuracy. Thus, the new view, even if largely false today, may become true tomorrow simply because current or expected future tax rules have changed. Indeed, this is precisely what Andrews's proposal would do, assuming its retention to be credible, by imposing a roughly uniform tax on all distributions that relate to old equity. One cannot shed any light on the descriptive accuracy that the new view would have if Andrews's proposal were adopted by citing empirical studies that examine its accuracy today.

Corporate integration is merely a special case amongst those in which corporate distributions are not tax distorted and the new view therefore holds. Under pure integration that people expect to remain in place indefinitely, the present and assumed future tax rates on distributions are both zero. Yet it is the fact that these rates are the same, not that they are zero, that generates tax indifference as to when a distribution is made. Thus, the Treasury errs in suggesting that present law distortions will be perpetuated unless integration is extended to old equity.[5]

Given the concern expressed about perpetuating distortion, it is ironic that the Treasury's own transition proposal—unlike Andrews's—would actually do so. Phase-in or delayed implementation would deter taxable corporate distributions during the transition period. In effect, the new view would become less true than ever, given the expectation that the tax on distributions would vanish in the near future.

The Treasury's argument for nonetheless providing phase-in or delayed implementation in order to "moderate the transition effects of integration" raises issues that are best left for chapter II, where I discuss alternative mechanisms for providing transition relief. It is worth noting here, however, that transition relief (and consequent reduction of the new regime's scope of application), to the extent designed to mitigate risks of retroactive change, is in effect wasted to the extent that it applies to prospective decisions, such as those concerning new equity. Even as to old equity, however, the Treasury does not explain why the wealth effect (which, in any event, would occur only to the extent of surprise) needs to be moderated.

C. Analyzing the Transition Issues Posed by Corporate Integration

The previous section suggests the need for a fresh inquiry into the transition issues posed by corporate integration. This inquiry is complicated by the variety of decisional boundaries that the classical corporate tax regime implicates, and of forms that corporate integration could take. Nonetheless, the basic problem is well captured by asking what would happen to the four main distortions if taxpayers anticipated that, in the event corporate integration was adopted, distributions after its effective date would be tax-free. The answers are as follows:

1. Distortion 1: Corporate versus Noncorporate Entity

So far as this distortion is concerned, the prospective of a retroactive tax reduction for old corporate equity has clearly desirable features. To the extent anticipated, it reduces the classical corporate tax regime's deterrence of new equity even before integration is adopted. New equity is more attractive than otherwise if the shareholder-level tax might never be paid. Even after enactment, allowance of the retroactive tax may affect investors' views about the government's likely policy upon the repeal of dispreferences (and perhaps more generally). While made possible by the prior rules' accounting feature of deferring shareholder-level tax collection, it is a policy change retroactive tax, having desirable anticipatory effects for the same reason that the policy change is desirable.

2. Distortion 2: Debt versus New Equity Financing

This distortion, like distortion 1, is reduced by corporate integration, and for the same reasons. The tax disadvantage (in the usual case) to new equity financing is reduced by the prospect that future distributions will not generate a significant net tax liability to the parties after all, thus again involving a policy change retroactive tax.

3. Distortion 3: Retaining versus Currently Distributing Corporate Earnings

This distortion, by contrast, is worsened by the prospect that corporate integration would make post-effective-date distributions tax-free. In effect, the new view becomes less true than otherwise if tomorrow's expected distributions tax is lower than today's. Here we have an accounting change retroactive tax, which happens to create incentives that are not merely distinct from but opposite to those of the steady-state new policy. It results from the change in the nominal timing of tax collection without regard to how the overall tax burden on corporate investment changes under integration.

4. Distortion 4: Form of Distribution of Corporate Earnings

This distortion has retroactive significance only insofar as people's current investment choices affect the form of distributions that will be convenient in the future. Thus, suppose that investment A, but not investment B, would likely require future distributions that would be taxed as dividends—perhaps because investment A requires maintaining parity from a control standpoint between rival ownership interests. Present law might cause investment B to be unduly tax favored relative to A. However, the prospect that the alternative distribution taxes would be equalized, whether through corporate integration that established a zero rate for both or under a plan such as Andrews's, would reduce distortion at this decisional boundary. Here again we have a policy change retroactive tax.

Hence, the question of whether the previously expected distributions tax on old equity should be eliminated upon the adoption of corporate integration poses a dilemma. It mitigates distortions 1, 2, and 4, but worsens distortion 3. Even from a constitutional standpoint, eliminating the distributions tax on old equity both desirably imposes a policy change retroactive tax and undesirably imposes an accounting change retroactive tax. One could resolve the dilemma by revisiting the tax treatment of past years' corporate distributions to make them tax-free, but this would violate the ANR norm.

In principle, however, the two retroactive taxes could be separated, thus permitting only those resulting from the policy change to be imposed. Indeed, this might not even raise insuperable administrative problems. The most direct method would start from Auerbach's suggestion that Andrews's distributions tax on old equity be replaced by a one-time tax on earnings and profits as of integration's effective date (followed by allowance of tax-free distributions). This would eliminate the accounting change retroactive tax that would otherwise undesirably discourage pre-effective-date distributions, but at the cost of also eliminating the policy change retroactive tax that would otherwise desirably reduce discouragement of pre-effective-date contributions of new corporate equity.

The second step, however, would be to reverse the latter ill effect by giving old equity a one-time negative tax, or subsidy. Here the tax base would be pre-effective-date contributions to corporate equity.[6] If taxpayer records of past equity contributions were inadequate or unreliable, this could roughly be approximated as the tax basis of all corporate assets, minus accumulated earnings and profits.

Thus, as of the effective date, existing corporations would hypothetically both pay a tax on their earnings and profits (thus eliminating the incentive to postpone distributions until this time) and receive a subsidy with respect to prior capital contributions (thus restoring the encouragement to such contributions that would have resulted from simply eliminating the distributions tax). In principle, this proposal dominates both the Andrews-Auerbach approach (which is worse at distortions 1 and 2 while equivalent at distortions 3 and 4) and that of simply eliminating the distributions tax (which is worse at distortion 3 and equivalent at distortions 1, 2, and 4).[7]

In practice, this proposal of an offsetting one-time tax and subsidy seems unlikely to be politically feasible. At the cost of greater administrative complexity, one could try to convert both into ongoing items, such as an Andrews-type distributions tax plus a flow of deductions bearing some relationship to pre-effective-date contributed capital. If none of this is feasible, then indeed we face the dilemma of either mitigating distortions 3 and 4 at the expense of distortions 1 and 2 through the Andrews approach, or mitigating distortions 1, 2, and 4 at the expense of distortion 3 by simply eliminating the distributions tax.

The analysis in this book cannot resolve that dilemma in the abstract, but at least presents it more clearly than any prior work. My own hunch is that, if the only permitted alternatives were eliminating the tax on post-effective-date distributions or adopting Andrews's distributions tax, the former would probably be preferable on administrative grounds. Why embrace the complications of needing to defend over the long run a distinction between old and new equity for no clear net improvement in incentives? However, further permitted alternatives might muddy the administrative choice even if one could not obtain better information about the significance of the competing distortions.

NINE

Shifting between Income and Consumption Taxation

A. The Basic Policy Difference and Its Retroactive Consequences

1. Income and Consumption Taxation as Differing Solely in How They Treat the Return to Waiting

The prospect of shifting from income to consumption taxation is a perennial topic of tax policy debate, prominent in both the academic literature and leading proposals for comprehensive tax reform. From time to time, it seems on the verge of attracting serious political attention. If the shift were made, it would raise important transition issues relating to existing wealth. Yet these issues are generally poorly understood, by economists no less than policymakers.

The policy difference between the two systems—if one should even think of them as separate systems, rather than as alternative versions of the same system—is simple. The income tax reaches the return to waiting, whereas the consumption tax does not. Thus, as between two individuals or households with the same wage flow over time, the income tax imposes a higher tax burden on the later than the sooner consumer, whereas the consumption tax imposes the same tax burden, in present value terms, on each (ignoring the possible effects of changing or graduated marginal rates).

Suppose, for example, that the rate of consumption tax is a perpetual 40 percent, that I will earn an immediate $1 million subject to this tax, and that all saving earns the same "ordinary" return. Under these conditions, no matter when I, or those to whom I make tax-free gratuitous transfers, consume this wealth, it will bear a consumption tax liability with a present value of $400,000. Spending it all now would trigger a $400,000 liability. Spending it all once it had doubled through interest accrual to $2 million would trigger an $800,000 liability—still 40 percent, and having the same present value as an immediate $400,000 liability because, by hypothesis, $1 at the earlier time equals $2 at the later time. Even if I (and my heirs) never spend the money, the liability is a fixed charge to which the wealth is subject. Thus, the tax is effectively borne even without a clear due date, for the same reason that a personal balance sheet would treat the obligation to repay a perpetual bank loan at market interest as a liability.

Income tax liability has no such fixed relationship to wages, since its present value depends on the return to waiting that one earns while deferring consumption. An income tax that raised the same long-term revenue from the average million-dollar earner as the 40 percent consumption tax described above might levy taxes with a present value of, say, $420,000 on a later-consuming household, and $380,000 on one that consumed sooner.

As noted in chapter 5, this policy difference between income and consumption taxation is less important than has long been believed. The once-standard view assumed that whatever formally looks like "capital income"—including inframarginal returns, risk premia, and the returns to winning bets—is reached only by the income tax, rather than equally (if at all) by both taxes. In the tax policy literature, however, it is now widely accepted that the two systems differ only in their treatment of the risk-free return to waiting, which over the last 70 years has averaged less than 1 percent in real terms if one accepts the admittedly imperfect evidence provided by short-term government bonds.

Given this point, whenever one hears a claim about supposed differences between income and consumption taxation, it is useful to ask: What, if anything, does this have to do with whether or not we tax the return to waiting? This question can help clear away confusion not only in the transition area but also—to name a few common topics—in comparing the two systems' progressivity (which is subject to adjustment through the rate structure), administrative and political economy features, and effects on generational distribution or personal liquidity at different points during one's life span.

In all of these areas, claims about the two systems' supposed differences typically reflect either the mistaken assumption that the consumption tax exempts all "capital income," or a conflation between the basic policy difference between the systems and mere accounting differences between particular implementations of each. Surely few commentators would similarly conflate policy with accounting if the item at issue were, say, medical expenditure rather than the return to waiting. Thus, suppose that newly disallowing the exclusion for employer-provided health care might be accompanied by shifting nominal income tax liability from the employee to the employer, thus handing a transition gain to employees at the expense of employers in cases where they had agreed to long-term wage contracts that contained no adjustment provision for a shift in nominal tax incidence. Would anyone consider this transition effect pertinent to whether medical expenditure ought in principle to be included in the tax base? As it happens, however, we do not give separate names to tax bases that include or exclude medical expenditure, much less those that do so with and without imposing an accompanying accounting change, and this probably helps commentators to focus on the policy choice without regard to the effects of accounting changes that might happen to be convenient or fortuitous byproducts.

As an example of the approach that I am criticizing, consider the influential, and in many ways path breaking, work of Alan Auerbach and Laurence Kotlikoff (1987, 57–59) comparing what they call income taxes, consumption taxes, and wage taxes. Auerbach and Kotlikoff construct these tax bases through alternative combinations of three building blocks: a one-time and ostensibly lump-sum wealth tax, an ongoing capital income tax, and an ongoing wage tax. They define an income tax as a wage tax plus a capital income tax, and a consumption tax as a wage tax plus a one-time wealth tax upon its introduction. This wealth tax results from an accounting change—although they emphasize (as we will see, mistakenly) shifting the time of tax payment from when one earns to when one consumes, rather than eliminating income tax basis.

My main quarrel with Auerbach and Kotlikoff lies with their treating a wealth tax as a lump sum, notwithstanding its conditioning liability on the decision to accumulate wealth. So far as mere terminology goes, they are perhaps entitled to use whatever definitions they like. Nonetheless, their definitional choices can be criticized as too restrictive and prone to cause confusion. Why build into the definition of a consumption tax a particular accounting change and resulting retroactive tax that are analytically unrelated to the policy content of the tax laws at any time? After all, just as one could exempt the return to waiting without imposing a wealth tax, so one could impose a wealth tax without exempting the return to waiting. All this would take is an elimination of income tax basis, which in principle could be done as a stand-alone matter. One can combine their three building blocks however one likes, and there is no inherent reason why what one does with the return to waiting (their capital income tax) should have any bearing on whether one imposes the wealth tax.

The arbitrary association between building blocks in Auerbach and Kotlikoff's definitions ends up giving an odd tenor to their conclusions. They find that, due to the supposedly lump-sum wealth tax, adopting a consumption tax would yield substantial welfare gains even though its exempting the return to waiting ostensibly tends to reduce efficiency.[1] One is inclined to ask: If that is so, why not just impose the wealth tax while otherwise making no change? Only political economy concerns that they do not discuss, pertaining to a wealth tax's enactability or how the means of enacting it might affect expectations that it would recur, could make their association of it with the ongoing treatment of the return to waiting anything but a complete *non sequitur.*

2. Retroactive Consequences of Newly Exempting the Return to Waiting

Since the only fundamental difference between income and consumption taxation is how they treat the return to waiting, it is worth asking initially what would be the retroactive consequences if that return were newly exempted while all other policy and accounting remained the same. The question can be divided into two parts, reflecting that, for the owner of a given asset, exempting the return to waiting is, in effect, a two-part enactment in that it affects the taxation both of that asset and of competing assets.

a. The Policy Change Retroactive Tax

If Congress newly exempted the return to waiting, assets held on the effective date would benefit from the policy change insofar as a portion of the tax burden that they face would have been eliminated. Even before enactment, the prospect that this might happen would reduce the disincentive to saving under the income tax, except insofar as investors expected the ongoing tax on old capital to be preserved in the transition. After enactment, permitting savers to enjoy the retroactive gain would reduce the observed level of wealth taxation over time relative to taxing it away, thus presumably affecting people's estimates about future tax policy.

In the absence of any accompanying accounting change, the basic timing sequence for cost recovery would remain the same as under the income tax, although interest-type adjustments would presumably be used to provide the present value of expensing. If one's aim were to maximize the policy change retroactive tax subject to the ANR norm, this treatment would apply not only to post-effective-date investments but also to remaining cost recovery from pre-effective-date investments, thus providing expensing-equivalent treatment for the latter. Providing expensing equivalence for as yet unrecovered outlays, rather than merely continuing income-tax-style cost recovery, would give the new consumption tax the widest possible range of application, short of violating the ANR norm by directly revisiting preenactment taxable years.

Allowing existing wealth to benefit both from the increased after-tax return to waiting and from expensing-equivalent recovery for remaining cost basis is therefore the preferred approach both under my proposed constitutional norm for policy change retroactive taxes, and in a case-by-case sense if one supports exempting the return to waiting. In addition, expensing for unrecovered outlays may lessen intertemporal distortion during the immediate preenactment period by reducing the incentive to defer pending investments until the consumption tax takes effect. Thus, suppose that, in the final days of the income tax, one wanted to place in service a building that it treated as 30-year depreciable property. One would have a stronger incentive to await the arrival of the consumption tax if jumping the gun meant that expensing would be lost in full.

A final problem posed by cost recovery for pre-effective-date-assets pertains to the choice of marginal tax rate at which remaining basis should be deducted (or deemed deducted, for purposes of determining compensation). In general, new consumption tax rates, rather than old income tax rates, should be used, for "matching" reasons. Inflows from using the assets that still had cost recovery pending on the effective date will be subject to consumption tax rates, and (as discussed in chapter 6) it generally makes sense to apply the same tax rate to associated inflows and outlays.

However, a complication arises from the fact that, before the effective date, the prospect of compensation may affect investors' decisions of whether to realize gain under the income tax. Suppose that I hold an asset with a basis of $10 and a value of $50. Selling the asset and purchasing a new one with the before-tax proceeds would trigger $40 of gain under the income tax and increase by $40 the amount of recoverable basis. Here, one might like to match the tax rates on these two amounts, rather than matching inclusion and deduction rates under the future consumption tax, if the investor's marginal decision concerned whether to sell this asset rather than how much to invest. Otherwise, taxpayers would be unduly encouraged to sell assets just before the effective date when the old income tax rate was lower, and to avoid such sales when the old rate was higher.

Given the difficulty of observing which decisions taxpayers are making at the margin, this problem is hard to address. One possible mechanism (subject to the usual rational expectations critique) would be to specify an early date in the enactment process, after which the taxpayer would have to keep track of the gain reported, and its marginal effect on income tax liability, with respect to specified asset sales. The specified assets might be limited to some category such as capital assets, on the theory that their sales are generally more tax elastic than sales of items such as customer inventory. When the consumption tax took effect, compensable basis would be reduced by the amount of last-period net capital gain, and the income tax liability on the specified asset sales would be refunded (the equivalent of matching the tax rate of inclusion). In the case of a net capital loss, these adjustments would be reversed, with basis being increased and the taxpayer refunding the reduction in income tax liability.

b. Resolution of Bets Concerning Future Tax Treatment of Investment

The second part of the policy change of exempting the return to waiting—applying the consumption tax to new or post-enactment assets as well as old ones—has very different implications for the owners of old assets in their capacity as such. So long as the consumption tax increases saving relative to the income tax, it will increase the competition that old assets face from new ones, thereby driving down pretax returns and, at least in this respect, reducing the old assets' value. If the capital stock increased sufficiently rapidly in response to the enactment of a consumption tax, the wealth effect of the increased asset competition could be substantial (Lyon and Merrill 1998).

This, of course, would be a betting outcome about future tax laws' effects on asset competition, akin (though with the sign reversed) to the transition gain that homeowners would garner from reduced new home construction upon unexpected repeal of the home mortgage interest deduction. While I argued in chapter 7 that one should not generally assume investor underanticipation of a tax law change for future competing assets, here the claim of underanticipation is fairly plausible, by reason of an arbitrary limitation that heuristic biases, relating to the endowment effect, may impose on the range of politically plausible future tax law outcomes.

In principle, one could imagine the politically plausible tax rates on the return to waiting ranging from positive (as under an income tax) to negative. The latter would result if the tax system subsidized rather than taxed capital income, thus reversing the income tax's intertemporal bias by favoring deferral rather than acceleration of consumption. The rationale for such a "reverse income tax," under which work would still be burdened but saving affirmatively encouraged, would presumably be the often-heard claim that national saving is too low, perhaps due to externalities or consumers' inability to make wise intertemporal choices. Whether or not such a claim is correct, its widespread appeal might lead one to predict that the "reverse income tax" would have sufficient advocates to be amongst the politically plausible alternatives for future tax policy. And if it were, a newly enacted consumption tax that had not been certain to prevail might, in a given case, approximate the mean expected political outcome within the politically plausible range from positive to negative tax rates.

As it happens, however, the range of politically plausible tax rates on the return to waiting may, for the most part, be bounded on the low end at zero.[2] This presumably reflects the endowment effect, under which paying out a net subsidy looks fundamentally different than foregoing to collect a tax. (The same consideration impedes making, say, municipal bond interest better than exempt under the current income tax, thus requiring the value of the municipal bond preference to decline if tax rates are reduced.) To the extent that zero is an effective lower bound on taxation of the return to waiting, investors can only underanticipate, not overanticipate, the effect of a consumption tax on future asset competition. Just as a coin toss that comes out heads cannot be overanticipated unless the possibilities include "double heads," so enacting a consumption tax would, under this assumption, make the tax regime for new assets more favorable than the prior mean estimate even if enactment had been considered 99 percent probable.

Accordingly, it is plausible that holders of old assets would lose from increased future asset competition (whether or not they lost on balance) upon the enactment of a consumption tax even if they were politically quite attentive during the preenactment period. (In addition, people whose expertise in working with assets for which there now was increased demand would enjoy betting gains.) Requiring bettors to bear these losses and gains plainly has desirable incentive effects. It encourages attempting to guess the future correctly and thus to make more accurate predictions about future asset competition, thereby tending to reduce adjustment costs when the tax law changes. Such betting outcomes should therefore neither be compensated nor influence compensation decisions regarding any other retroactive gains or losses from the adoption of a consumption tax.

B. Significance for Transition of Other Policy and Accounting Changes Made by Leading Consumption Tax Prototypes

1. Key Attributes of the Leading Consumption Tax Prototypes

Under a shift from income to consumption taxation that kept policy and accounting constant except for newly exempting the return to waiting, the above discussion would be the entire transition story. As it happens, however, all prominent consumption tax proposals would make further significant policy and accounting changes, yielding further transition issues. Indeed, these changes have much in common despite the diversity in the forms that the proposals take. This can be seen by briefly examining the four leading consumption tax prototypes, each of which has guided various proposals.

a. Consumed Income Tax

The income versus consumption tax debate among academics was transformed when first Nicholas Kaldor (1958) and then William Andrews (1974) showed that consumption taxes could conveniently be collected at the individual level without requiring comprehensive records of people's consumer purchases. Individual-level tax collection (as distinct from the business-level collection of, say, a retail sales tax) was considered important because it facilitated retention of a graduated rate structure, thus providing progressivity without resort to such clumsy devices as taxing necessities (such as food) at a lower rate than luxury goods (such as yachts).

   In very broad outline, under a consumed income tax, individuals would file annual returns as under the current income tax. Cash and in-kind receipts would generally be includable as under an expanded version of the current income tax, but inclusion would also extend to loan proceeds and other dissaving (such as withdrawals from a bank account). In lieu of the present rules governing cost recovery and the retention of basis, all saving, including bank account deposits and outlays to purchase assets or repay loans, would be deductible. Cost recovery would therefore involve expensing. One prominent version, the Treasury "Blueprints" plan, would permit taxpayers in some circumstances to forego cost recovery for a given asset, and instead exempt all returns from it (Bradford and the U.S. Treasury Tax Policy Staff 1984, 101–28). The only consumed income tax that is currently prominent in Washington policy debate is the Nunn-Domenici "USA" tax, which would combine it with the next prototype that I describe.

b. Value-Added Tax (VAT) of the Consumption Type

A second consumption tax prototype, widely employed around the world although typically alongside rather than in lieu of an income tax,[3] shifts tax collection to the business level (and thus foregoes rate graduation) through the "value-added" methodology. Under a VAT, only businesses—a term of art that generally does not include individuals in their capacity as workers receiving compensation—file tax returns. In a subtraction-method VAT, businesses include all payments received for goods and services and deduct all payments to other businesses (but not to workers) for goods and services. In an invoice-and-credit VAT, businesses instead pay tax on a percentage of their payments received and receive a tax credit on a percentage of their payments to other businesses. The two methods are equivalent in the absence of tax rate differences. Expensing and its credit equivalent are what make the VAT a consumption tax; one could, in principle, have an income-style VAT by providing cost recovery with the present value of economic depreciation (Bradford 1996, 126–32).

Under either consumption-style VAT, in the absence of rate differences or timing lags in paying taxes or receiving rebates and credits, each inter-business transfer yields a net tax liability of zero, with net tax finally being collected upon the occurrence of a retail sale to a nonbusiness customer. Thus, under a 20 percent invoice-and-credit VAT, suppose the following three transactions occur: a farmer who has no supply costs sells cocoa beans and sugar to a candymaker for $10; the candymaker uses labor to turn these inputs into candy that it sells to a grocery store for $40; and the grocery store sells the candy to retail customers for $50. Assuming that all parties other than the retail customers are classified as businesses, the first transaction leads to a $2 tax payment by the farmer and a $2 tax credit to the candymaker, while the second leads to an $8 tax payment by the candymaker and an $8 tax credit to the grocery store. Only at the third stage is net tax collected, since customers cannot claim tax credits to offset the $10 tax payment by the grocery store. The common view that a VAT is collected in stages is therefore not generally correct (Bradford 1996, 127); it rests on treating nominal tax liability rather than economic incidence as the relevant consideration.

c. National Retail Sales Tax

A retail sales tax differs from a VAT in that nothing happens until the final sale to a nonbusiness customer. Interbusiness transactions prompt no cash flows between taxpayers and the government, rather than generating offsetting tax payments and credits that may net to zero. Despite this administrative difference, one should keep in mind just how similar the two systems are. Obviously, the fact that both may have zero net tax consequences until the final retail stage is evidence enough of this. Confusion may result, however, from thinking of the retail sales tax as a system that, unlike the VAT, does not involve cost recovery. While this is literally true, it has little economic significance. Eliminating the tax burden on interbusiness transactions via outright exemption is equivalent to doing so via offsetting taxes and refunds. The exemption from tax that a well-designed retail sales tax gives business purchasers is the functional equivalent of the credit or deduction that a VAT grants them to offset the tax paid by the seller, and thus should be thought of as akin to expensing.

The widespread view that retail sales taxes are inferior as a tax instrument to VATs, underlying the far greater utilization of the latter around the world, reflects an administrative difference between the exemption and deduction/credit mechanisms that they respectively employ. Even if a VAT makes net losses or credits refundable, dodging the entire tax through evasion at the retail stage may be harder if retailers must affirmatively claim deductions or credits for their purchases in excess of acknowledged sales rather than, as under the retail sales tax, simply omitting to report sales transactions.

At present, 45 states and more than 6,000 localities employ instruments that bear the name "retail sales tax," but these are generally considered poor consumption tax models given their spotty coverage, extensive rate variation between included items, and frequent application to business as well as consumer purchases (Gale 1998, 9–12). However, several recent proposals would enact fairly comprehensive national retail sales taxes, eschewing rate variations between goods or services and using business exemption certificates to avoid "cascading" tax burdens on items that are sold between businesses before the final retail sale (Gale 1998, 6–7, 21).

d. Two-Tiered Cash Flow Tax

Perhaps the most prominent consumption tax variant in current tax reform debate is the Hall-Rabushka flat tax. It is a variant of the subtraction-method VAT in which workers are in a sense treated as businesses, through the treatment of their compensation as includable by them and deductible by business payers. It typically is formally described as an integrated two-tier tax on both businesses, which pay the VAT as modified to permit wage deductions; and workers, who pay tax solely on their wages (without regard to personal saving or dissaving).

The reason for imposing a portion of the nominal tax liability on workers rather than businesses is to facilitate applying graduated rates. In the Hall-Rabushka plan, rate graduation is limited to the use of a zero-rate bracket for workers. Above the zero bracket amount, the same tax rate applies to all workers and all businesses. A variant called the X-tax, proposed by David Bradford (1988, 384–86), would impose progressive positive tax rates on workers, with the top rate being the same as that for businesses.

2. Main Transition Issues That Would Be Posed by Enacting the Leading Consumption Tax Prototypes

Each of the above-described consumption tax prototypes would make either one or two key policy changes apart from exempting the return to waiting, and two to four key accounting changes. These changes, and the transition issues they raise, are discussed in the paragraphs that follow.

a. Policy Change 1: Eliminating Inter-Asset Distortions

Each prototype would largely eliminate inter-asset distortions under the current income tax, such as those resulting from various special exclusions and deferrals or from dispreferences pertaining to inflation and corporate equity investment. For this reason, as William Gentry and Glenn Hubbard (1996, 1) have observed, one could aptly describe their implementation as a two-stage process, in which first the current income tax is replaced by a comprehensive income tax through the wholesale elimination of preferences and dispreferences, and then the tax on the return to waiting is eliminated. Gentry and Hubbard note that eliminating inter-asset distortions is by far the more significant of the two changes.

Absent transition relief, the resulting policy change retroactive tax would tend to reduce the incentive effects of provisions that create preferences and dispreferences in the current income tax. For example, the home mortgage interest deduction and municipal bond exemption are somewhat reduced in scope (all else equal) by the prospect of their repeal in the course of adopting a uniform consumption tax. These incentive effects of repeal are desirable both under the CTB norm and under my proposed norm supporting the imposition of policy change retroactive taxes. This suggests that transition relief reducing the retroactive impact is undesirable, problems of transition risk aside.

b. Policy Change 2: Reducing Rate Progressivity and Tax Rates

Many, although not all, of the prominent consumption tax proposals would substantially reduce the current tax system's rate progressivity, moving at least part of the way towards a flat rate structure. This, too, may be considerably more significant than eliminating the tax on the return to waiting. The transition effects, as with rate changes generally (as discussed in chapter 6), would include the following:

1. To the extent that the pre- and post-enactment tax systems succeeded in measuring endowment, the reduction in progressivity would redistribute wealth from low-endowment to high-endowment individuals. This is a transition effect not involving retroactivity since it is conditioned on people's attributes rather than their decisions. Whether it is good or bad depends on one's distributional views and assessment of the tradeoff between distribution and efficiency.

2. Anticipation and observation of the reduced progressivity would lessen disincentives to human capital investment by potential high-earners whose expected marginal tax rates declined, but increase such disincentives for potential low-earners whose expected tax rates increased. Here, where decisions are involved, we have a policy change retroactive tax, the merits of which are likely to be the same retroactively as prospectively.

3. People whose marginal tax rates declined upon adoption of the consumption tax would be induced to shift deductions to preenactment, high-rate years, and inclusions to post-enactment, low-rate years (with the opposite holding where marginal rates increased). As discussed in chapter 6, such intertemporal distortion is undesirable but hard to prevent, although the use of an early effective date may help, at least in the short run, assuming surprise.

4. Again reflecting nonapplication of the new rates to pre-effective-date taxable years, taxpayers who under the prior income tax had received up-front cost recovery (an accounting feature, although typically linked to preferentiality) would potentially benefit from the arbitrage between high-rate deduction and low-rate inclusion. This is the matching problem that

the 1985 Treasury II tax reform plan unsuccessfully proposed addressing through depreciation recapture. Similar adjustments might be desirable here, if politically and administratively feasible.

c. Accounting Change 1: Timing Change from Deferred to Immediate Cost Recovery

Each of the consumption tax prototypes would eliminate the use of deferred cost recovery that is a central accounting hallmark of the current income tax. Under the prototypes that would still have explicit cost recovery, expensing would replace economic depreciation and similarly deferred methods. This, of course, is partly a policy change since it increases the present value of cost recovery, but it is also an accounting change because it changes nominal timing. The retail sales tax differs only in form, since business exemption is functionally equivalent to allowing the seller a deduction or credit.

David Bradford (1996, 134; 1998, 157–59) neatly captures the potential retroactive consequences of this timing change through a hypothetical in which an income-type VAT is replaced by a consumption-type VAT, with adverse consequences on a grocer who had the ill fortune to purchase a stock of canned tomato juice for $10,000 on the last day the income tax was in force—say, December 31—and then to sell it for $10,000 the next day—January 1—after the consumption tax had taken effect. The grocer would never get to deduct his inventory cost, since, in effect, the income tax auditors would say "deduct it next year," while the consumption tax auditors would say "it should have been deducted last year." He thus would pay whatever positive tax liability resulted from applying the consumption tax rate to $10,000, turning a break-even transaction before tax into a source of substantial tax liability.

While stated in terms of the VAT, this scenario applies equally to the other three main consumption tax prototypes. This may be clearest under the two-tiered cash flow tax, which after all *is* a VAT apart from its distinctive treatment of compensation paid to workers. However, under the consumed income tax, suppose an individual bought a financial asset for $10,000 on the last day of the income tax and then sold it for $10,000 on the first day of the new system. This break-even transaction would generate a substantial net tax liability if the asset's income tax basis disappeared without compensation and the new system's provision of expensing (or yield exemption) was denied to pre-effective-date investments.

Finally, under the retail sales tax, despite the lack of explicit cost recovery deductions, the logic is precisely the same as under the VAT. After all, the tomato juice example would not change if the identical tax liability on January 1 resulted from a retail sales tax rather than a VAT. The sense in which there is an accounting change here is that the income tax deduction for cost recovery was deferred and now is lost, notwithstanding that the seller in the December 31 transaction presumably included its receipt in gross income. Had the retail sales tax been in place on December 31, it would have provided an expensing equivalent, in nominal timing as well as present value terms, through the tax exemption for business purchases (thus eliminating the seller's inclusion).

In sum, all of the major consumption tax prototypes would impose a major accounting change, going to timing as distinct from time value. The same accounting change would arise if we retained the policy content of the current income tax but changed its accounting content to move all cost recovery up front, discounted to hold constant its present value. And the accounting change could be avoided despite shifting to a consumption tax if the new system retained the current income tax's timing conventions but achieved expensing equivalence by allowing interest on unrecovered basis.

The potential basis wipeout from this accounting change is the big transition effect that has attracted substantial attention in the literature. As an accounting change retroactive tax, it is presumed undesirable under my constitutional norms. Even in a case-by-case sense, one is hard pressed to see why it would have the lump-sum character that is so often attributed to it. The fact that it might to some extent catch investors by surprise is hardly dispositive under a rational expectations view. Its adoption would provide information regarding outcomes under our political system, and thus have predictive value regarding future tax policy—and all the more so if the basis wipeout played a significant political role in motivating adoption of the consumption tax.

Auerbach and Kotlikoff look only at *ex ante* anticipation, without regard to *ex post* observation. They argue: "Individuals who have already accumulated wealth at the time the consumption tax is unexpectedly introduced have no way of avoiding paying consumption tax when they spend this wealth. Since their consumption out of wealth is a perfectly inelastic form of behavior, taxing this behavior is nondistortionary" (1987, 79). The problem with this argument is that the timing of when people spend their wealth is *not* perfectly inelastic. Any subsequent delay in spending their wealth subjects them to a repeat performance. After all, so long as the tax that they expect at any time falls short of full expropriation, the Auerbach-Kotlikoff argument is infinitely repeatable. Surely, when the government enacts a significant *ex post* wealth tax, even with the solemn promise never to do so again, it shows a propensity to tax wealth *ex post,* which people may observe with consequences for their subsequent behavior.

If Auerbach and Kotlikoff are correct, then repudiating the national debt is unambiguously in the long-term fiscal interest of American taxpayers. After all, the money has already been lent, and waiting for it to be repaid is inelastic absent an ability to compel repayment. Why worry about the possible effect on the interest rate the next time the government wants to borrow? And if they are correct, then perhaps all preannounced taxes should be eliminated, with the government instead relying on "surprise" levies that it announces on what it promises is a one-time basis each December 31.

To be sure, in the case of a repeated, and hence utterly predictable, December 31 levy, it is easy to see that people would come to discern the real policy, as distinct from the preannounced policy that was on the books for 364 days out of each year. Those who believe that the basis wipeout has elements of a lump-sum tax may like to think that, so long as the government really plans to do it just once (although why stop there, given the repeatability of the argument?), it can persuade people that this is its intent. However, even if the government could be said to have such a meaningful intent (notwithstanding political turnover), it might have difficulty persuading others of this, and all the more so after imposing a big surprise. After all, the same asymmetric information that permits surprise impedes credible commitment against recurrence. Thus, the rational expectations benchmark should prevail, absent good arguments to the contrary, because if the wealth tax truly is a one-time event, its *ex ante* underanticipation is likely to be succeeded by *ex post* overanticipation as people mistakenly anticipate its recurrence.[4]

So much, then, for the claim that the accounting change retroactive tax from eliminating income tax basis is lump sum in character. How does it fare in a case-by-case analysis if we treat it, for simplicity, as fully anticipated? In some respects, this makes it comparable to such preannounced wealth taxes as the income tax's levy on the return to waiting. Thus, consumption tax advocates presumably should oppose it here just as they oppose wealth taxes elsewhere (as noted by Kaplow 1995, 1114; and Bradford 1996, 146–47), while income tax advocates should consider supporting it. However, this particular wealth tax has four distinctive features that make it possibly worse, and certainly different, than a preannounced, ongoing wealth tax.

First, the tax is levied on income tax basis rather than net wealth at the time of its imposition. Thus, if on the effective date a taxpayer holds an asset with a basis of zero and value of $1 million, the accounting change has no effect. Likewise, if a taxpayer's portfolio consists of two items, an asset with basis and value of $1 million and a $1 million liability, then the taxpayer has zero net worth and yet loses basis—ignoring possible offsetting transition consequences pertaining to the loan under the consumed income tax.

Second, transition risk is likely to be greater if the actual wealth tax remains unknown while people make work and savings decisions. This risk may be systematic rather than diversifiable (other than by internationalizing one's tax exposure), and thus widely undesired yet difficult to avoid.

Third, *ex post* wealth levies may have distinctive political economy attributes, thus causing their increased use to affect the level of wealth taxation that we should expect over time. Among the possible equilibria is *reduced* wealth taxation—for example, if the imposition of an ex post levy encourages the later adoption of *ex post* wealth subsidies, or else is approved in the political arena in exchange for abandoning preannounced wealth taxation. Another possible equilibrium—common around the world, although perhaps not likely in the present United States—is one in which investment is catastrophically deterred because the expected policy becomes one of expropriation. The actual long-term political economy effect of adopting this particular *ex post* wealth tax is hard to assess.

Fourth, the fact that this particular wealth tax, whether preannounced or not, is levied at a particular time—the effective date when income tax basis is lost and subsequent outlays become expensible—means that it may induce significant intertemporal distortion. Unless adoption was overnight and substantially underanticipated at the time, it would create strong incentives to defer saving until the effective date had passed, and indeed to "dip into previous savings to go on consumption binges" (Kaplow 1995, 1116). It would also tend to increase the preenactment "lock-in" of unrealized asset appreciation, given the possible disappearance of any extra basis acquired through taxable sale and reinvestment.

To avoid these particular retroactive effects, one would have to allow taxpayers to recover income tax basis that remained as of the effective date. Ignoring for the moment important accounting changes that certain of the consumption tax prototypes would make to *who* is a taxpayer—accounting change 3, discussed below—this response would apply to any and all property with basis that would be implicitly or literally recoverable if the income tax remained in place. For example, under a consumed income tax in which saving is deducted and dissaving included, the logic applies no less to cash in a bank account on the effective date than to tomato juice inventory—although one could exempt the subsequent expenditure of such cash, in lieu of providing an up-front deduction to offset later inclusion (Bradford and the U.S. Treasury Tax Policy Staff 1984, 183).

No cost recovery would be needed, however, for basis not associated with a subsequent inclusion. Thus, for a durable consumer asset such as a home or personal car, basis recovery would not be needed or appropriate if the new consumption tax would not subsequently be including imputed rental income from using the item or the proceeds from selling it. (The Treasury "Blueprints" plan proposes nondeductability for purchases of durable consumer assets along with noninclusion of the sale proceeds.)

The proper marginal tax rate for cost recovery would reflect new consumption tax rather than old income tax marginal rates, so as to match the tax rate on future income. If only this accounting change were being made, one presumably would leave unchanged the present value of income tax cost recovery. As noted above, however, the aim of increasing the basic policy change retroactive tax from switching to consumption taxation might induce one to provide expensing-equivalent treatment for remaining basis.

One might, however, want to consider denying any recovery for income tax basis that, rather than reflecting taxpayer outlays, arose through the tax-free step-up to fair market value in the basis of property at death (IRC section 1014). Thus, suppose I inherited property with a value of $100 and a basis to the decedent of 0. Under the current income tax, I would hold the property with a basis of $100 despite the absence of unrecovered outlays in the chain of ownership. Denying cost recovery for basis that arose through section 1014 would impose a policy change rather than an accounting change retroactive tax, arguably supportable on the ground that section 1014 is bad policy. Such denial, to the extent anticipated, would limit the distortions caused by section 1014 (such as deciding whether to sell an appreciated asset).

There is, however, a practical difficulty with attempting to deny transition relief for section 1014 basis under a newly enacted consumption tax. Taxpayers who anticipated such a rule might try to expunge the "tainted" basis of their current assets through preenactment sales. In the above example, this might involve my selling the inherited property for its basis and value of $100, thus incurring no income tax liability, and using the proceeds to purchase a new asset that would have cost basis of $100. Such transactions might be hard to defeat without administrative complexity and perhaps something verging on indirect nominal retroactivity, although (assuming surprise) one might consider determining the amount of each taxpayer's tainted basis, for which there would be no recovery under the consumption tax, as of an early effective date.

d. Accounting Change 2: Timing Change from Current to Deferred Taxation of Gains

Just as the various consumption tax prototypes would generally accelerate cost recovery relative to the current income tax by providing expensing in lieu of economic depreciation, so they would in certain cases defer accruing tax on gain. It may be helpful to explain the basic accounting change before considering its significance to transition.

Under the current income tax, when yield-to-maturity rather than wait-and-see or realization accounting is employed, gain is taxed as it accrues without awaiting any such event as a sale. This is partly an accounting rule that goes to timing, but (as with OID bonds) it generally correlates with an income tax CTB policy content, whereas deferral generally correlates with income tax preferentiality given the lack of interest adjustment.

The consumption tax prototypes generally use wait-and-see accounting. For example, under a consumed income tax, an individual who holds an appreciated asset is typically taxed upon selling the asset and using the proceeds to finance consumption. Likewise, under a VAT, appreciation of inventory—or the fact that a company with modest initial capital has turned into Microsoft—generates net tax liability as goods are sold to consumers. In principle, however, one could use yield-to-maturity accounting in a consumption tax. For example, if what was otherwise a mark-to-market Haig-Simons income tax exempted the return to waiting (with gain and loss relative to this benchmark being included and deducted currently), it would be a yield-to-maturity consumption tax.

In cases where the current income tax already uses wait-and-see accounting, adopting any of the consumption tax prototypes would not in this respect change accounting. This is why no general transition adjustment is needed for unrealized appreciation (or similarly, unrealized losses). If, for example, I hold an asset with a basis of zero and a value of $100 when the current income tax is replaced by a consumed income tax, elimination of the deferred income tax liability does not really benefit me—ignoring any rate change—given that I now face a deferred consumption tax liability that will be due when I sell the asset and consume the proceeds. Or to make the same point a different way, taxing my deferred $100 gain upon eliminating the income tax would have no net impact on me if the resulting $100 increase in my income tax basis triggered an offsetting deduction at the same marginal tax rate.

In cases where the current income tax uses yield-to-maturity accounting, adoption of any of the consumption tax prototypes would involve an accounting change, but of relatively limited retroactive significance. Insofar as the basis of an asset subject to such accounting under the income tax equaled its value at the moment of transition, and assuming expensing-equivalent cost recovery for income tax basis generally, its deferred tax burden would remain zero. Expensing of the basis would compensate in present value terms for the expected future inclusion of the value.

In such a case, the main long-run significance of the income tax's having used yield-to-maturity accounting, rather than a policy-equivalent version of wait-and-see taxation, is a "boundary" effect. Despite the switch to consumption taxation, the repealed income tax ends up reaching returns to waiting that accrued and were taxed while it was in force. Expensing basis at the moment of transition does not fully offset the prior imposition of this tax, given the uncompensated deferral of the deduction relative to the earlier inclusion. And the ANR norm presumably bars looking back to the pre-effective-date period to determine (for purposes of offset) what income tax was actually imposed on the return to waiting.

However, the analysis would change if income tax basis were eliminated without compensation upon adoption of the consumption tax. Now, yield-to-maturity assets would suffer a further disadvantage: The extra basis they had acquired by incurring accelerated income tax liability would disappear, rather than merely being offset later than it was included. Accordingly, given the structure of the current income tax, the retroactive consequences of a transitional basis wipeout would include increasing the tax advantage generally enjoyed by wait-and-see assets relative to yield-to-maturity assets.

e. Accounting Change 3: Changes in Who Is a Taxpayer

A third major accounting change that might result from adopting a consumption tax goes to who is a taxpayer. Three of the major prototypes—all but the consumed income tax—shift tax collection from the individual level to the business level. Under the VAT and the retail sales tax, individuals cease to be taxpayers under the new system. Under the two-tiered cash flow tax, while individuals remain taxpayers with respect to their wages, they cease to report any nonwage gains and losses, or saving and dissaving. These changes have significant retroactive consequences despite their pertaining, in a steady-state sense, only to nominal rather than real economic incidence.

The issues raised can be illustrated by adapting Bradford's tomato juice example to pertain to a financial asset that an individual purchases for $10,000 on December 31, when the current income tax is in force, and sells on January 1 for $10,000 after the switch to a VAT, retail sales tax, or two-tiered cash flow tax. Here, if the income tax had been retained, he would have both included and deducted $10,000 on January 1. Now, absent a specific transitional adjustment, he would do neither. Accordingly, the taxpayer remains whole even without basis recovery, and such recovery should not be provided. To state the point more generally, upon adoption of a VAT, retail sales tax, or two-tiered cash flow tax, basis recovery should be limited to business assets as defined for purposes of determining what receipts are subsequently includable.[5]

Suppose instead, however, that the financial asset has appreciated or declined in value before repeal of the current income tax, without tax consequences because it is a wait-and-see rather than a yield-to-maturity asset. Thus, say we modify the above example so that an asset purchased for $10,000 some time before is worth $50,000 on December 31, and is sold for that amount on January 1. Here, the two deferred tax consequences that the accounting change away from individual-level taxation has eliminated are not precisely offsetting. Instead, on balance, an expected tax on $40,000 (which would have been reached by a consumed income tax that provided transitional basis recovery) has been eliminated.

The prospect of incurring this accounting change retroactive tax would have two main incentive effects under the current income tax: favoring wait-and-see assets relative to yield-to-maturity assets, and increasing the lock-in effect with respect to wait-and-see assets. However, one could eliminate these effects by giving tax consequences to the (positive or negative) difference between assets' basis and value when the tax significance of this difference disappeared due to the shift to a business-level tax.

If one's sole aim were to eliminate the retroactive consequences of the accounting change, one presumably would levy a tax equal to the expected value of the deferred income tax liability absent repeal. Policy changes are also implicated, however. The aim of mitigating inter-asset distortions and lock-in under the prior income tax would imply treating repeal as a realization event that triggered immediate full taxation of the gain (assuming this to be the upper bound on permissible retroactive tax consequences under the ANR norm). On the other hand, the aim of maximizing the reach of the new consumption tax policy of exempting the return to waiting might suggest levying no tax on the unrealized gain, even to the extent of the deferred liability's expected value.

The interaction of these conflicting goals presents a dilemma. In principle, if one wanted to maximize the policy change retroactive taxes (subject to the ANR norm) while eliminating the accounting change retroactive tax, one would treat repeal of the current income tax as an immediate realization event, but reverse the effect on the return to waiting through a one-time subsidy to capital generally.[6] Since this is unlikely to be politically or administratively practical, however, how best to resolve the dilemma is unclear.

f. Accounting Change 4: Eliminating Wages' Deductibility and Includability, with Possible Price Level Effects

A final transition issue presented by the enactment of a consumption tax lies in the possibility that it would cause a one-time price level increase throughout the economy, as distinct from any effects on relative asset prices. However, both the reasons why enacting a consumption tax might induce a price level increase and the significance of such an increase for transition policy have been widely misunderstood in the literature—at least, until David Bradford's (1996) path-breaking analysis.

The usually assumed mechanism for the price level increase is as follows. Suppose that I earn a wage at time 1 but do not consume until retirement at time 2. At time 1, under our current income tax, taxes are levied as people earn wages. At time 2, with the enactment of a consumption tax, the collection point shifts from when people earn to when they consume. This accounting change in the timing of taxation, while unrelated to whether we tax the return to waiting, seems to result in my being taxed twice—first when I earn and then again when I consume (Graetz 1979, 1653; Auerbach and Kotlikoff 1987, 59). To Auerbach and Kotlikoff, among others, this is the source of the supposedly lump-sum wealth tax from enacting a consumption tax.

This view, however, is mistaken in three key respects. The above accounting change should have no price level effects; any price level effects from enacting a consumption tax would result instead from a distinct accounting change that only some of the leading prototypes would make; and a price level increase is less a wealth tax than a tax on holding certain types of financial positions.

An initial point worth clarifying, since it is typically left unstated in expositions of the standard (pre-Bradford) view, is that—other than under the consumed income tax, with its disappearing-basis problem for personal saving—one must posit a price level increase at time 2 for the story even to get off the ground. Why should I care that retailers now remit a portion of what I pay them to the tax authorities if the prices they charge me remain the same? Perhaps the expositors of the standard view think it obvious that the retailers will pass on a newly imposed cost of doing business. However, this ignores the fact that the tax on their workers has been eliminated.

Once we look at both sides of the affected transactions, the ostensible timing distinction between levying a tax when people earn and when they consume becomes a distinction without a difference. After all, a typical consumption transaction involves consumers on one side and workers on the other side. Accordingly, to provide that the tax on consumption transactions will henceforth officially fall on consumers rather than workers is not a timing change. Even as a nominal incidence change, it carries no implication of a price level increase. Holding the tax level constant, all that it does at the retail level is relabel the tax that the retailer must collect from the consumer as one that nominally falls on the consumer rather than the worker. The standard view therefore provides no basis for expecting preenactment savers to bear a price level increase and consequent double tax at the transition.

There nonetheless is a reason why enacting a consumption tax might induce a price level increase. However, it not only relates to nominal incidence rather than nominal timing, it does so in a very particular way. Thus, while all four consumption tax prototypes nominally tax consumption rather than work—and, with greater pertinence, generally use the same timing conventions (immediate cost recovery for outlays and deferred taxation of gains)—only under the VAT and retail sales tax, which most sweepingly shift nominal incidence from the individual to the business level, is there any reason to expect a price level increase upon enactment.

The key nominal incidence change that the VAT and retail sales tax—but not the consumed income or two-tiered cash flow tax—would implement is making wages nondeductible by businesses and nonincludable by workers. The retroactive consequences can be illustrated by revising the tomato juice example in two respects. First, suppose that the grocer's purchase and sale of the juice, along with all prior transactions in the production network, occur under the same tax regime—be it the current income tax or any consumption tax prototype—rather than straddling the boundary between December 31 and January 1. Second, suppose that the grocer's entire $10,000 outlay is paid to workers, defined as anyone not qualifying as a business for VAT deduction or credit purposes.

Under the current income tax, the grocer incurs no tax liability by both spending and receiving $10,000. The workers clear $10,000 minus the tax on their wages—leaving them with $8,000 if the income tax rate is 20 percent. All this would continue unchanged if the income tax were replaced by a 20 percent consumed income tax or two-tiered cash flow tax (except that, under the former, workers who saved would defer the tax without reducing its present value). There thus is no reason to expect a price level change if either of these prototypes is enacted.

Suppose instead, however, that a VAT or retail sales tax is enacted, again with a 20 percent rate. Now, if all wages and prices remain the same, the grocer will have to pay $2,000 of tax even though his inflows equal his outlays. Moreover, his workers will suddenly be taking home $10,000 after tax, instead of only $8,000. Even before the grocer goes bankrupt, these outcomes are unsustainable. Since, so far as we know, supply and demand in the markets for being a grocer and working for a grocer remain unchanged, the conditions for equilibrium in these markets are being violated by changes in after-tax return that result from a mere shift in nominal tax incidence.

To restore equilibrium, there must be some change in the price that the grocer receives from customers or the wages he pays his workers. Treating these as polar outcomes for simplicity, he will either increase the price of tomato juice from $10,000 to $12,500 and pay $2,500 of tax, or else reduce wages from $10,000 to $8,000 and pay $2,000 of tax. Once generalized throughout the economy, the former outcome involves a 25 percent price level increase, while the latter involves no change to the price level. Yet they are identical in their real marginal effects on workers, consumers, and the Treasury. After all, each dollar is worth 25 percent less in a world where the price level has increased by 25 percent than in one where it has not changed.

To what extent would each of the alternative outcomes prevail upon introduction of a VAT or retail sales tax? Bradford (1996, 135) notes that this "is not a matter that is settled by well-developed theory. . . . It will depend on the institutions of wage and price setting and on monetary policy." However, he provides two reasons why economists generally agree that, in the main, consumer prices would increase rather than nominal wages decline. First, as has been noted since Keynes, nominal wages tend to be "sticky" in the short run, due both to long-term labor contracts and workers' preferences. Nominal consumer prices are thought typically to be more flexible. Second, the monetary authorities at the Federal Reserve Board are considered likely to facilitate a price level change through an accommodating monetary policy. Their presumed motivation would be to ease financial distress—or more specifically, the transactions costs incident to default—in situations where highly leveraged businesses faced unexpected tax liabilities (whether due to the basis wipeout or sticky wages) that affected their ability to continue servicing their debts.

This brings us to the question of what significance a price level increase would have. Again, under the standard view, it imposes a wealth tax: My time 2 savings will buy me less consumption opportunities if a dollar buys less than it used to. Yet this ignores the possibility that I may hold assets whose value changes with the price level. In general, all assets do this except for cash and expectations of future cash (such as from repayment of a loan) that happen not to be indexed for inflation.

This suggests that a price level increase is less a wealth tax than a betting victory for holders of "short" financial positions that are not indexed for inflation, at the expense of holders of unindexed, "long" financial positions. For this purpose, the term "financial position" should be interpreted to embrace anything potentially involving cash. Explicit loans, where the lender is long and the borrower is short, provide only one example. If I expect future Social Security benefits from the government, then again I am long, since the payments will be in cash rather than in-kind. Whether I am indexed depends on how Social Security payments are likely to change (given both present law and the alignment of political forces) in the face of inflation.

As it happens, the federal government has an overall betting position on inflation that presumably is borne in large part by taxpayers in their capacity as such. Unindexed government bonds would lose real value in the event of inflation, thus benefiting the government financially in the same sense as would explicit partial default. This betting gain could conceivably permit the government to lower various distortive taxes. The problem, however, is the usual one. An underanticipated inflationary event that devalues government bonds and was perhaps, in part, deliberately chosen for that reason should not be viewed as lump sum. Rather, it may influence expectations, such as by increasing the perceived likelihood that the government will deliberately use inflation again. This might result in increased interest rates on government bonds, thus triggering an offsetting increase in the distortive taxes needed to pay the interest. The overall effect on distortive taxes is hard to determine in the abstract (the core reason for a rational expectations benchmark).

From the standpoint of normative transition policy, a price level increase simply layers a further retroactive tax on top of all the other retroactive taxes that I have identified. Each of the other retroactive outcomes, such as the basis wipeout if imposed, continues to occur. Moreover, all remain relevant to incentives even if particular individuals' losses from one area happen to be more or less offset by gains from another.

In illustration, recall the initial example of the grocer who purchased $10,000 of tomato juice on December 31, but with the added fact that the purchase was entirely financed by unindexed debt. Suppose further that on January 1 a 20 percent VAT is enacted, inducing a 25 percent price level increase. The grocer therefore sells the tomato juice for $12,500, pays $2,500 of tax to the government, and uses the remaining $10,000 to settle the debt, thus shifting the net transition loss to the lender, whose money has lost 25 percent of its purchasing power (Bradford 1996, 135). Even though the grocer ends up breaking even, the incentive effects are still best captured by saying that he lost from the basis wipeout *and* gained from the price level increase. After all, he presumably could have bought tomato juice without acquiring an unindexed short position, or acquired such a position without buying tomato juice. Only if one misunderstood transition issues as posing a one-shot distributional problem, rather than as raising incentive issues given their possible recurrence, would one think that information about people's overall gains and losses from the transition was most pertinent.

Since the price level increase results from an accounting change from individual-level to business-level tax collection, it is an accounting change retroactive tax, albeit one that happens to be influenced by the details of monetary policy and relative price and wage stickiness. As such a tax, it is presumed undesirable under my constitutional norms. Under a case-by-case analysis, it fares poorly as well. Its main incentive effect is to burden holding unindexed long positions (such as cash) and encourage holding unindexed short positions. This presumably generates undesirable excess burden. The transition risk analysis is more ambiguous. Insofar as people use financial positions to make the bets they like on future price levels, the risk effects should not be a concern even if the incentive effects are. However, if unindexed financial positions are costly to avoid, then the prospect of a price level change may induce undesired risk bearing.

Transition relief from the effects of a price level change might therefore be desirable, but I will not pursue that possibility here given its evident political and perhaps administrative impracticality. A second possible implication of the above analysis is that the monetary authorities should not be quite so willing to accommodate the pressure for a price level increase through an expansionary monetary policy as has typically been assumed. However, it is unclear how to weigh the benefit of reducing the accounting change retroactive tax from a price level change against the detriment of increasing transactions costs incident to default on unindexed financial instruments.

C. RATE CHANGES UNDER THE CONSUMPTION TAX

The discussion thus far has considered only the initial enactment of a consumption tax. However, two of the accounting changes that the leading prototypes would make—shifting from deferred to immediate cost recovery and from current to deferred taxation of gains—would have further retroactive consequences whenever tax rates changed under the new consumption tax. Each is worth examining in turn.

1. Rate Changes and the Shift from Deferred to Immediate Cost Recovery

The transition problem raised by the accounting shift from deferred to immediate cost recovery can be illustrated by returning to the tomato juice example. Suppose that, under a consumption tax fitting one of the four prototypes, a grocer buys $10,000 worth of tomato juice on December 31 when the tax rate is 30 percent, and then sells the goods for $10,000 on January 1 when the tax rate has changed to either 20 percent or 40 percent. Given the bar on nominally retroactive application of the new tax rate, and assuming the unavailability of Treasury II depreciation recapture-style adjustments, this otherwise break-even transaction ends up generating a net tax liability of either positive or negative $1,000, depending on the direction of the rate change. Such a retroactive tax has clearly undesirable incentive effects.

Rate changes would not cause this problem under a system, such as a typical income tax, that matched outlays with related inflows so that both were taken into account in the same taxable year. Likewise, it would be avoided under a Haig-Simons income tax that dispensed with accounting for specific cash flows and relied instead on simply measuring year-end net worth. However, it is these systems' accounting content, rather than their treatment of the return to waiting, that makes them rate-change-proof in this respect. Thus, David Bradford (1998) has proposed revising consumption tax prototypes to use the timing conventions (such as economic depreciation) of a typical income tax, with expensing equivalence resulting from the allowance of interest on unrecovered basis. Similarly, one could in principle adapt the Haig-Simons methodology to exempt the return to waiting and thus levy a consumption tax that avoided taxable year mismatches.

The rate change problem provides a reason for preferring a cost-recovery method that matches outlays with related inflows rather than allowing deductions up front. Yet there may be competing considerations. As discussed at the end of chapter 6 (concerning Treasury II-style depreciation recapture), deferring deductions makes their value more inflation sensitive if the tax system is unindexed, may reduce the tax system's transparency if the choice of interest rate is manipulable, and keeps open for longer Congress's power to revise the tax treatment of a particular outlay without violating the ANR norm.

2. Rate Changes and the Use of Deferred Accounting for Gains

A second rate change problem caused by deferred accounting pertains to the tax rate on gains, considered without regard to the relative treatment of outlays and inflows. Even under a consumption tax that used deferred cost recovery, suppose I held inventory that had appreciated by more than the return to waiting (for example, because tomato juice prices had increased). I would have an incentive to rush to market before the tax rate increased, or else postpone going to market until the tax rate declined. Similarly, under a consumed income tax, I would have an incentive to dissave, and thus trigger personal tax liability, in low-rate rather than high-rate taxable years.

This problem already exists under the current income tax wherever there is deferred accounting for gain. Consider the incentive to sell appreciated capital assets in tax years when the capital gains rate is relatively low, or to supply labor in low-rate years (reflecting the lack of Haig-Simons-like taxation of appreciation to human capital, as noted by Kaplow 1994(a)). The consumption tax prototypes would extend the range of settings where the problem arises, however, by eliminating yield-to-maturity accounting where currently used by the income tax.

The most direct response would be to adopt mark-to-market accounting for gain (in principle, including that from human capital), adjusted under the consumption tax to exempt the return to waiting. Or to mitigate the problem without requiring ongoing valuations, one could treat gain triggered by the sale of an asset as having accrued ratably over the taxpayer's holding period for the asset, for purposes of determining the applicable tax rate.[7] Even this, however, is presumably quite impractical. Accordingly, one perhaps cannot much improve on the current transition policy of using early effective dates when taxpayers seem likely to have underanticipated the direction of a particular rate change.

TEN

SOCIAL SECURITY REFORM

A. THE CURRENT "SOCIAL SECURITY SYSTEM" AND ITS LONG-TERM FISCAL CRISIS

What we call the "Social Security system" is to some extent in the eye of the beholder. Its administrative details aside, it embraces two main sets of tax and transfer rules under present law. The tax side is an arbitrarily defined portion of overall payroll taxes levied: 11.5 percent of the 14.2 percent payroll tax[1] on annual wages up to an inflation-adjusted threshold that exceeds $70,000. On the transfer side, the Social Security system mainly embraces certain payments to retirees that are determined by applying formulas based on earnings during a portion of the recipient's (or spouse's) career.

The only sense in which the scope of the "Social Security system" matters is that this system has been described and widely accepted politically as a self-financing package. Social Security taxes (plus whatever are deemed the returns from investing them before disbursement) are supposed to pay over time for Social Security benefits (plus related administrative costs), and for nothing else. This, in turn, is a prediction, expectation, or policy that Social Security taxes and benefits will be adjusted over time to ensure that the preferred arithmetical relationship between them holds.

While the term "Social Security system" may describe a woolly political understanding about expected long-term relationships between certain revenues and outlays, it has no well-defined economic content. For example, does it properly include the income tax revenues from taxing a portion of Social Security benefits? As it happens, these are officially credited to the Social Security Trust Fund (a bookkeeping device for keeping historical track of the relationship between the system's counted inflows and outlays). Should the Trust Fund also be credited with income tax revenues from including the employee share of the Social Security tax in taxable income—or, perhaps, debited with the income tax revenue loss from not including the employer share? Such adjustments are not made. If cash credited to the Trust Fund is invested in the stock market, should the Trust Fund be credited not only with the after-tax profits but also with corporate and property taxes paid on the underlying investments? Martin Feldstein and Andrew Samwick (1998, 221) assert this would be "reasonable and fair" under a privatized Social Security system, but a similar argument could presumably be made in the event of such investment today.[2]

Nonetheless, one can meaningfully characterize the specific tax and benefit rules that are the system's main building blocks. What these two sets of rules do in combination is levy a wage tax during one's working years that is succeeded by a retrospective wage subsidy during one's retirement years. (Here, in contrast to the current income tax as discussed in chapter 9, the accounting content of having the tax precede the subsidy is crucial to the system's presumed policy aim of inducing retirement saving.) The tax and subsidy offset each other, resulting in no net tax or subsidy if they happen to have the same present value to the worker. However, the relationship between them varies greatly with the individual—depending, for example, on one's year of birth, wage history, and receipt of spousal benefits. Thus, in practice, the system imposes net wage taxes on some workers and provides net wage subsidies to others (Feldstein and Samwick 1992).

The fact that, for any given worker, the tax precedes the subsidy creates a potential for retroactivity going beyond that inherent to any long-term government rule. As under the present income tax, which provides for future cost recovery through the mechanism of basis, present Social Security rules express a government plan to make payments in the future. Until the payments are made, however, the government has the practical opportunity to change its rules and forego making them without nominal retroactivity.

As it happens, the current relationship between Social Security taxes and benefits is generally recognized as unsustainable, because by early in the twenty-first century, the latter will greatly exceed the former. Recent projections suggest that by 2030, bookkeeping entries for the Trust Fund will show the elimination of its positive balance, leading to a violation of the self-financing principle as Social Security benefits continue substantially to exceed Social Security taxes. This shortfall has two main causes. First, the system was never fully funded in a long-term sense, reflecting both "pay-as-you-go" financing and the political aim of showering benefits on current retirees in excess of the value of their contributions. Then adverse demographic and economic trends—the relative size of the post–World War II "Baby Boom" generation and the slowdown in productivity growth beginning in the early 1970s—administered the coup de grace to hopes of meeting the self-financing aim without significant adjustment.

Given the artificiality of the distinction between the "Social Security system" and other government tax and transfer programs, this financing problem might not matter so much were it not embedded within a broader "tax lag" problem for the federal government generally (Shaviro 1997). Despite recent budget surpluses, overall federal government revenues are expected to fall increasingly short of projected government spending, due in good part to obligations that would arise under present Social Security and Medicare rules. Thus, it is generally agreed that, within the Social Security system (and also outside it), there is a long-term need for some combination of reducing benefits, increasing taxes, and otherwise increasing the funds that are available.

The long-term financing problem has prompted a variety of Social Security reform proposals that often have two main components. One is a proposed set of changes to the system's real (however arbitrarily demarcated) content—that is, its 11.5 percent share of the payroll tax and its benefit formulas. The other is the identification of a supposed money machine that can be activated and have its proceeds dedicated to the Social Security system.

Proponents may intend that the system's use of a given money machine be conditioned on the adoption of other proposed changes. This is not, however, a condition that anyone need accept. Any money machine that would actually work as claimed—producing substantial revenue at little or no social cost—should presumably be adopted in any event. In this sense, the proposed money machines have no necessary relationship to Social Security as such. They could just as well be used to pay for a defense build-up or spending on education, as for what are called Social Security benefits. Nonetheless, the money machines are worth discussing here briefly, before we turn to proposed program changes and the resulting transition issues, due to their prominence in the ongoing debate about Social Security reform.

1. Investing Trust Fund Monies in the Stock Market

At present, monies credited to the Trust Fund are exclusively invested in government bonds that earn a low, albeit secure, return. Some advocates of keeping the Social Security system relatively unchanged have suggested that some of these monies could instead be used to purchase publicly traded stocks and other high-yielding securities. This would permit the Trust Fund to grow faster than otherwise (assuming continuation of historical rates of return), reducing the extent to which taxes would have to increase or benefits decline to meet the self-financing aim.

If this is a good idea—notwithstanding the specter of politically motivated government investment decisions that might impair market efficiency[3]—then the government could do it at any time, without regard to the Trust Fund or Social Security as such, by selling bonds to the general public and using the proceeds to buy stock. The real economic significance of such a step is open to question, however. Some investors, noticing that their implicit investment portfolios via Social Security (or as taxpayers) now included more stock and less government bonds, might respond by making opposing swaps in their personal investment portfolios. Even to the extent this did not happen, the asset switch would simply alter relative prices on different financial instruments, perhaps to little effect as a matter of economic substance, but requiring the government—outside the Social Security system—to increase the interest rates on its bonds so that it could still sell them all. Thus, the system's formally determined revenue gain would exceed that of the entire government, even ignoring the question of whether there is any real point to swapping one set of assets for another that the market views as of equal value.

2. Imposing a "One-Time" Wealth Levy through the Introduction of a Consumption Tax

Laurence Kotlikoff has inserted in the Social Security debate his long-standing claim that a newly introduced consumption tax would include an efficient lump-sum tax on existing wealth (Kotlikoff 1998, 294). As we saw in chapter 9, this claim requires persuading savers that the decision to impose an odd form of capital levy has zero probative value regarding the likelihood that any such levy will ever be imposed again. The decision to impose a wealth levy also, as Kotlikoff recognizes, has no conceptual link to Social Security's financing problems. Thus, if feasible, it presumably would be worth doing in any event, and the proceeds could be used on anything.

3. Increasing Saving

Martin Feldstein, a longtime advocate of increasing saving, has returned to this theme in recent studies of Social Security privatization. His central claim is that, at the margin, while increased saving generates a 9 percent real return (Feldstein and Samwick 1998, 218), future cash flows to individuals should be discounted at only 3 percent (241). This is in some tension with conventional economic reasoning, which typically deduces preferences (such as discount rates) from behavior, and thus might suggest that nonsavers are optimizing as things stand.[4] Arithmetic computations in his work suggest that the money machine from earning at 9 percent and, in effect, paying at only 3 percent is sufficiently powerful to pay for cutting taxes, increasing benefits, and eliminating Social Security's fiscal imbalance all at a single stroke.

In substance, however, the argument remains one for increasing saving —presumably, far beyond the level needed to fund Social Security, since the money machine does not run out until the rate of return ceases to exceed the discount rate at the margin. Thus, while Feldstein shows (if one believes him) that paying off all existing unfunded claims to Social Security benefits would be surprisingly painless, he does not illuminate whether that is a desirable course. That would require a broader policy assessment of the relevant retroactivity issues. Before assessing these issues, however, it is worth examining briefly how steady-state Social Security policy might change in the course of restoring its internal fiscal balance.

B. Marginal Adjustment to Social Security Rules versus Privatization, and the "Transition Path" Problem

Proposed money machines notwithstanding, participants in the Social Security debate generally agree that the system's tax and transfer rules must change to some extent. On balance, if one takes account of expected future benefits, the system has to date provided a net wage subsidy since its introduction. This suggests the likely need to impose a net wage tax through the system from now on, presumably via changes in the tax and benefit rules given current projections.

Some participants in the Social Security debate argue that only modest changes to the tax and benefit rules are desirable or necessary. Projected balance can in fact be restored by such devices as increasing the Social Security tax, raising the retirement age for receiving benefits, and modifying benefit formulas to include more low-wage years in relevant career earnings. This was the course proposed by 6 of the 13 members of an Advisory Council on Social Security that issued a widely noted public report in January 1997. However, in the "Maintenance of Benefits" (MB) plan that these six members set forth, they proved too leery of near-term tax and benefit changes to restore system balance without also using the ostensible money machine of investing Trust Fund monies in the stock market, and proposing a payroll tax increase that would not take effect until 2045(!).[5]

To others, the financing problem presents an argument or opportunity for more significantly changing the relationship between Social Security taxes and benefits. The proposed new approach is commonly called privatization. If fully implemented, it would involve replacing the entire present system with mandatory individual retirement accounts that might be government administered but would provide contributors with a wide choice of investment vehicles. One could, for example, elect greater, lesser, or no participation in the stock market. Proceeds from one's account would be disbursed in the form of a retirement annuity, the value of which would depend on what the account had earned. At present, Martin Feldstein is perhaps the leading advocate of this approach, but the other 7 of the 13 members of the recent Advisory Council endorsed at least some movement in this direction, as did a bipartisan commission chaired by prominent Senators Kerrey and Danforth that prompted the introduction of proposed legislation.

Under a fully privatized system, for each worker the wage tax would equal the wage subsidy in *ex ante* present value terms except for the lost utility from forced saving (presumably justified on grounds of paternalism or positive externalities to retirement saving). Thus, no one would face a net wage tax or subsidy from Social Security, the forced saving element aside. Important though this change might be in practice, its structural consistency with the existing Social Security system is worth noting. The net wage tax within the system is already supposed to be zero overall under the self-financing principle, subject to the vagaries of what returns to saving one credits to the system.

Privatization would thus combine three analytically distinct changes, which in principle could be adopted or not in any combination (although the literature tends to present it as a unitary package). First, it would be fully funded, implying greater saving overall to the extent that saving outside the system did not correspondingly decline. Second, it would increase investment choice within the system, permitting beneficiaries who so preferred to achieve higher and riskier returns overall to the extent that Social Security had previously locked them into an unduly low-risk, low-return position despite the at least theoretical availability of offsetting adjustments to their portfolios. Third, it would eliminate redistribution within Social Security, both between age cohorts and progressively within age cohorts, with the overall effect again depending on what offsetting adjustments, if any, were made outside the system.

Advocates of privatization generally agree that they face what Feldstein calls a "transition path" problem. How does one get from the present system, in which current payroll tax collections pay for benefits to today's retirees, to a system in which the same funds pay for the future retirement benefits of today's workers (Feldstein and Samwick 1998, 216)? While this way of putting the problem may accurately describe a political obstacle to the adoption of privatization, it is flawed as a substantive description by its overlooking the fungibility of money—potentially to the end result of obscuring real policy choices that we face. Who cares (or at least should care) which dollar bills are used on which expenditures? The formulation is thus akin to saying that one faces a "transition path" problem in paying for a new missile system given present income tax levels, past statements about future defense spending (which are assumed without explanation to be binding), and the explicit national debt to which past defense spending contributed. Still, since the overall financing issue is real enough and the politics not necessarily immutable, the problem is simply that one ought at some stage to evaluate normative transition policy, not just assume grandfathering.

C. Transition in Social Security Reform and the Choice between High Wage Taxes in Different Periods

The potential retroactive effects of changing the Social Security rules extend to a wide range of past decisions concerning how much to work, how much to save, and how much earning potential to develop. Thus, suppose one developed one's labor market skills in order to have a low earning ability rather than none at all, only to come up against the elimination, through privatization, of the net wage subsidy that Social Security (in contrast to the tax-transfer system as a whole) currently may offer a low-earner. The result would be a retroactive tax increase even if one had not yet accrued any benefits.

As an effective political matter, however, the relevant transition issue posed by Social Security reform is considerably narrower. It concerns what to do about benefits that one accrued under the present rules by working prior to any new rules' adoption. Complete grandfathering would involve providing these benefits in full—and perhaps even enhancing their current legal status by issuing formal debt obligations to make them unrenounceable (Feldstein 1998, 16). A complete "cold turkey" approach to the transition would instead eliminate all benefits that had accrued under the old rules, and apply the new benefit rules solely to post-effective-date earnings (Kotlikoff 1998, 280).

The question proposed by this transition choice is whether to enact a retroactive net wage tax increase for past work. A similar choice would be presented within the income tax if, say, past years' income taxes had been collected under a law stating that a given percentage of the collections would ultimately be refunded, and then the question arose of whether to honor this statement. In either case, if retroactivity is like prospectivity (*ex ante* variance aside), the result is increased distortion of work-leisure choices, but this distortion is potentially offset (as under a wage tax generally) by desired distributional effects.

Particularly for Social Security, given the self-financing principle, the likely alternative to retroactively increasing the net wage tax on past work is to, at some point, enact a tax increase, whether retroactively or prospectively, for future work. Thus, in a sense, the question of whether to grandfather Social Security benefits amounts to asking for which period the tax rate should be increased in response to the system financing and broader tax lag problem.

This question is inherently difficult to analyze. In general, throughout this book, my premise has been that even insofar as distortive taxes are inevitable given distributional aims, those that are less distortive, such as an income or consumption tax CTB, should be preferred to those that are more distortive. Here, however, the base for the retroactive tax is essentially the same as that for its assumed alternative, and efficiency conclusions therefore cannot be drawn without additional information. In addition, I have mainly avoided difficult and controversial issues of distribution both by arguing that they are best handled through tax rates, and by not trying to determine what rates are best. Here, however, rate specification for different periods is the very question presented.

I therefore do not attempt to provide definite answers here akin to those suggested in earlier chapters. Instead, the remainder of this chapter explores various considerations and alternative approaches that might be used in a more definite and extended treatment of the Social Security transition issue.

D. SOME POSSIBLE APPROACHES TO THE QUESTION OF WHETHER TO GRANDFATHER ACCRUED SOCIAL SECURITY BENEFITS

1. Policy Change versus Accounting Change in Social Security Transition

An initial question of possible interest is how the treatment of accrued Social Security benefits might relate to whatever policy change was being adopted. Here an analogy is useful. Suppose the income tax was collected at a 40 percent rate but had an announced rate of 30 percent, since 10 percent was stated to be ultimately refundable (and in practice was refunded) with interest. To renege on as yet unpaid refunds for past years in connection with shifting to a system where the collection rate, like the announced rate, was 30 percent would be to impose an accounting change retroactive tax. The same would hold if Congress simply reenacted the Internal Revenue Code with no substantive change, but announced that no refunds would be offered under the new Code for excess payments under the old Code. This would be akin to wiping out the value of green dollar bills upon a shift to the use of red dollar bills, rather than letting the old currency be traded for the new.

Suppose instead, however, that Congress increased the announced income tax rate to 32 percent. The way to extend the new policy to past taxable years—that is, to impose the maximum policy change retroactive tax that was consistent with avoiding nominal retroactivity—would be to refund only 8 percent rather than 10 percent for all past years for which refunds remained outstanding. Indeed, even if Congress not only changed the announced rate to 32 percent but also equalized the collection rate with the announced rate and reneged on all refunds for past years, an intent-free account of the effects of what it had done might reasonably attribute only 8 percent of the renounced refund to the accounting change, and attribute the overdetermined 2 percent to the policy change that the renunciation effectively extended.

Returning to Social Security, the implications are as follows. To wipe out accrued benefits simply because one is creating a "new" Social Security system would have at least a large element of accounting change retroactive taxation. In the pure case where one only renounced past benefits while otherwise keeping the system unchanged, this would be the entire story. If one also enacted substantive changes, however, then some benefit wipeouts— those that would have resulted from changing the system for all past years and imposing the changes retroactively insofar as benefits had not yet been paid—might be consistent with policy change retroactive taxation.

This distinction matters for two main reasons. First, it might inform advocates (and opponents) of the policy change as to what degree of grand-fathering was consistent with its prospective policy content. A supporter of privatization, for example, might want to give this policy retroactive effect while otherwise having no reason to favor benefit wipeouts. Second, identification of the accounting change element may be of interest insofar as one believes that a particular constitutional norm for such changes should apply in the Social Security or retirement policy realm, or indeed more generally. In this book, however, I have argued that such norms should depend on the political economy features of particular policy areas. Thus, one might oppose accounting change retroactive taxation under the income tax, yet believe that it tends to improve political outcomes with respect to, say, pollution permits (as suggested in chapter 4). I discuss the political economy aspects of Social Security policy later in this chapter.

In the case of privatization, elimination of accrued benefits that would create or increase a net wage subsidy to the recipient through Social Security, rather than push the recipient's net wage tax from the system towards zero, would extend the policy change. In practice, precise implementation of such a transition rule would be impossible, since it would require determining rates of return on past Social Security tax payments that depended on investment choices that the taxpayer had never been asked to make. Nonetheless, one could imagine such a transition rule's being approximated by a variety of means. One possibility would be to eliminate all benefit payments under the old rules, but to determine each participant's net wage tax (if any) to date under some set of assumptions regarding rates of return, and then treat this amount as deposited in the recipient's mandatory individual retirement account, where it would generally be treated like any post-effective-date contribution. One effect of such a method would be to increase rather than reduce some recipients' Social Security benefits with respect to pre-effective-date work—consistently, however, with the new policy.

The main motivation for doing this, presumably, would be that one supported privatization's policy of eliminating net wage taxes and subsidies from within the Social Security system except insofar as the element of forced saving imposes a tax. Yet this policy is not self-evidently correct. Perhaps its main virtue is that it minimizes distortion of work choices by Social Security. Obviously, however, what really matters is overall distortion, given the entire United States fiscal system and much else besides, without regard to Social Security's formal boundaries. In this regard, it is worth noting that low-wage workers whom the current Social Security system tends to subsidize (Feldstein and Samwick 1992) may in other respects face the highest marginal tax rates of anyone, given phaseouts of multiple income-conditioned transfers (see Shaviro 1999). However, even if privatization reduces overall distortion of work decisions, no definite conclusion about its prospective or retroactive merits follows. Anyone who supports the use of *any* work-conditioned tax base, such as income or consumption, to allocate tax burdens is evidently willing to distort work choices to some extent for distributional reasons. Thus, anyone who favors such a tax base need not be predisposed, before further inquiry, to favor privatization's degree of emphasis on incentive over distributional considerations—except, perhaps, on administrative or political economy grounds relating to which parts of the tax-transfer system are best used in distribution policy.[6]

Under a more traditional approach to Social Security's financing problems, the degree to which a benefit wipeout would advance the new policy might be ambiguous, given the difficulty of describing the steady-state policy either before or after the adoption of particular tax and benefit changes. During Social Security's history, taxes and benefits have repeatedly been adjusted on an *ad hoc* basis to implement something approaching "pay-as-you-go" financing, under which tax receipts would equal benefit payments each year, but subject to permitting some degree of positive Trust Fund accrual as a nod in the direction of long-term internal financing. Thus, tax and benefit changes have typically been enacted not on the theory that, like a CTB to its adherents, they implement some notion of optimal design, but to have specified distributional effects (chosen in light of financing considerations) on particular age cohorts given where these cohorts currently stand in their life cycles. An example would be increasing both taxes and benefits to aid current retirees, who are past having to pay the taxes.

Insofar as traditional Social Security has had a consistent underlying policy beyond simply providing a decent but unspecified level of retirement support, this policy can only be inferred from the idea of pay-as-you-go financing, under which current workers are thought of as supporting current retirees. For an age cohort as a whole (ignoring redistribution within it), this implies that the rate of return one could compute by comparing its taxes paid to its benefits received depends on two main things: productivity growth (which presumably determines wage growth, with implications for taxes paid per worker), and whatever demographic and other fortuities determine life spans and the ratio of current to retired workers at any time. However, there appears to be no consistent philosophy for dealing with the latter fortuities. From the 1930s through the 1970s, large worker cohorts were tapped to finance benefit expansion to small retiree cohorts, but offsetting benefit contraction when retiree cohorts grow in relative size may be thought to contradict the premises (also considered part of the system) of always providing decent retirement support without sending payroll taxes through the roof and of being slow to reduce promised benefit levels.

Murky though the current system's policy content may be, it does have implications for Social Security transition that form an interesting contrast to the stance taken by Martin Feldstein in advocating privatization. Whereas Feldstein (1998, 16; Feldstein and Samwick 1998, 216–17) proposes full grandfathering, the advocates of the MB plan agreed that "it is fair to ask present beneficiaries to help bring Social Security into long-term balance" (Advisory Council on Social Security 1997, 78). A practice of thinking mainly in terms of *ad hoc* distributional adjustments between age cohorts may help to discourage thinking of accrued benefits under the current rules as sacrosanct, even if it induces giving current retirees' interests greater weight than those of younger and unborn individuals.

2. Rate Smoothing between Calendar Years

A second way to approach the question of eliminating Social Security's financing shortfall is to treat the need for a wage tax increase as an opportunity to move in the direction of equalizing net wage taxes in different years across the potentially affected period. In illustration, suppose that, for all workers, the annual net wage tax would be 30 percent for all years before privatization and an expected 40 percent for all years afterwards if all accrued benefits were paid, but 35 percent throughout if no accrued benefits were paid. Under these circumstances, and applying as well the simplifying assumption of full anticipation (in part because the decision would shed light on how future rate changes were likely to be handled), the latter option would have two efficiency advantages over the former. First, by showing a policy of "smoothing" rates across time, it would tend to reduce the intertemporal distortion that results when people shift their work from high-rate years to low-rate years. Second, even without regard to such intertemporal shifts, it would tend to reduce overall work deterrence by the tax-transfer system. It is a truism in economics that the distortion caused by a tax rises more than proportionately with the marginal tax rate

(Rosen 1995, 314). Thus, reducing high rates tends to reduce distortion more than comparably increasing low rates increases it.

Unfortunately, the implications of this approach for Social Security transition are hard to determine. One would need a great deal of information regarding both past and future net wage tax rates (in light of the entire tax-transfer system) under alternative treatments of the accrued benefits in order to determine how rate smoothing was best advanced. In addition, rate smoothing is not necessarily the best approach when one considers the implications for intergenerational distribution of how one treats accrued Social Security benefits. Conceivably, despite the aim of minimizing overall distortion of work decisions, one would want people who were born at different times, and thus had different lifetime consumption opportunities, to face different lifetime (and thus annual) wage tax rates. Any added distortionary cost would simply be the price of achieving desired progressive redistribution between members of different age cohorts. Accordingly, even if it were clear what treatment of accrued benefits would maximize rate smoothing between different years across time, that treatment might require adjustment on distributional grounds and thus would lack clear implications for transition policy.

3. Increasing Saving through Social Security Transition Policy

A very different approach to Social Security transition might be suggested if one agreed with Martin Feldstein that the present level of saving is suboptimal. This view, again, departs from a conventional economic framework for analyzing life-cycle consumer choice, and instead treats current consumption as in a sense like pollution, except that, if the underlying theory is paternalistic, the undervalued harm is to oneself rather than to others. Income effects that alter people's saving decisions therefore end up having claimed efficiency consequences. While I myself do not find this view compelling (see Shaviro 1997, 164–85 on the difficulty of determining the optimal rate of saving), many others do, and its implications are thus worth considering.

From such a perspective, while forcing people to save for their retirement is better than letting them decide not to save, it has the disadvantage of reducing their voluntary saving on the side by at least partly taking care of their retirement needs. If one could instead somehow cause some of their wages to be saved and productively invested without directly funding their own retirements, then while their work incentives would be impaired, they presumably would do more retirement saving on their own. Taking money away from them and saving it is thus the best policy of all from this perspective, leaving aside the political economy question of how to ensure that it is invested productively.

The relationship of such concerns to Social Security policy is one that Feldstein noticed at an early point. Since the 1970s, he has emphasized the present Social Security system's negative impact on saving through the "asset substitution effect" (Feldstein 1974, 908), under which the prospect of receiving a net wage subsidy at retirement (as was common in the system's first few decades of operation) reduced people's direct retirement saving for the same reason that one would save less if one anticipated winning the lottery at age 70. Yet the argument on this ground against a net wage subsidy logically extends to an argument in favor of imposing a net wage tax. Even the political economy questions are similar. Just as one might question the benefit of imposing a net wage tax by asking how productively Congress would invest the proceeds, so one might question whether the net wage subsidy really did any harm, by asking what Congress would alternatively have done with the funds that would have been freed up by not providing it.

The point that one may increase private saving by imposing a net wage tax through Social Security has implications for retroactive no less than prospective policy. It suggests that taking away accrued Social Security benefits would have observation effects that are desirable if one wants to encourage saving. People counting on government rules that offer future benefits presumably would draw the inference that these benefits are not entirely to be counted on and would respond to some extent by increasing their own direct saving. Better still, this income effect—unlike that from, say, anticipating a wipeout of income tax basis—would not have an offsetting substitution effect that was adverse to saving, because people's own private saving efforts would not have been what the retroactive tax targeted. Thus, as a matter of basic intellectual consistency, one might expect people who share Feldstein's view of saving (and his consequent dismay about the current system's income effects on workers in past decades) to find a benefit wipeout potentially attractive.

4. Responding to Misunderstanding of Current Social Security Benefit Formulas

Laurence Kotlikoff (1998, 272) suggests that, due to the complexity of Social Security benefit formulas, workers may generally underestimate the link between earnings and benefits, and thus the extent to which the system imposes a net wage tax. Such a mistake by workers would tend to increase work deterrence by the current system. In noting this possibility (unlike in discussing income to consumption tax transition), Kotlikoff in no way contradicts this book's advocacy of a rational expectations benchmark. He offers a specific claim of systematic error, rather than overlooking the issue, in a setting where the claim has at least *prima facie* plausibility. Consider that many low-wage people to whom the system may conceivably offer net wage subsidies (at least under the present rules), seem quite willing to avoid legally mandated participation in it.

The main conclusion Kotlikoff draws from the possibility that people make this systematic error is that privatization might reduce work deterrence simply by making the link between earnings and benefits more transparent. In this regard, it is worth noting that the perceptual error is not directly linked to the policy differences between the current and a privatized system, and thus that one could, in principle, address it by different means. For example, the government could better publicize the link between earnings and benefits under present law, or implement a system that was more transparent but continued to engage in redistribution from high-wage to low-wage workers.

In the transition setting, whether privatization is adopted or not, Kotlikoff's systematic error claim might strengthen the case for not fully grandfathering accrued benefits. If workers mistakenly view current benefits as lump-sum transfers rather than as work-conditioned transfers, then, conceivably, they might view repeal as lump sum, rather than as showing an inclination to raise wage taxes retroactively. The problem with such a claim, however, is that erroneous beliefs are subject to revision. Thus, suppose that a cold-turkey transition prompted public debate that drew attention to the benefits' relation to past wages or otherwise undermined confidence in the new system's more transparent wage subsidies. If this were to happen, then taking away accrued benefits, while not necessarily worse than raising future wage taxes, would cease to have the advantage (from an incentive standpoint) of being a hidden wage tax.

5. The Political Economy of Whether to Grandfather Accrued Social Security Benefits

The discussion thus far has ignored the widespread view that accrued Social Security benefits ought to be provided because they were specifically promised when workers paid Social Security taxes. In effect, the claim underlying this view is that the benefits are like debt. To this there is a simple answer: They were not, in fact, debt. No binding legal obligations were issued, and the tax payments were legally mandated from workers and employers, rather than being provided in a distinct voluntary transaction like a loan. One never hears the claim that, say, welfare recipients were entitled to all the future benefits they would have received in the absence of 1996 welfare reform, or that paying income taxes triggers an entitlement to have specific spending programs retained.

Nonetheless, there is more to be said about the claim that accrued Social Security benefits are relevantly like debt. After all, the claim is not that they *are* debt (and thus to be honored, as discussed in chapter 3, so that the government can preserve its ability to make credible commitments), but simply that they resemble it in the sense of meriting guaranteed status. This claim can take either of two main forms. The first concerns the insurance function that a system for providing retirement benefits may be designed to serve. The second is a political economy claim to the effect that treating accrued benefits like debt tends to offset political distortions in operating a government retirement program.

The first of these two arguments—that a government retirement program can better serve its insurance function if it offers debt-like benefit guarantees—is easily disposed of under the current system. An initial point is that the desirable level of insurance depends in part on incentive and other relevant behavioral effects (including the income effect on saving if one believes that saving ought to be encouraged). More fundamentally, however, protecting accrued benefits on insurance grounds is questionable when, as Robert Shiller (1998) has noted, the current Social Security system is less a true insurance or risk-spreading device than a distributional device for assigning given risks to one age cohort rather than another. Thus, suppose current benefits are premised on a set of assumptions about productivity growth and the relative size of present and future age cohorts of workers. To treat these benefits as guaranteed is to create a one-way ratchet, such that they can increase if economic and demographic circumstances improve but cannot be reduced if circumstances worsen. This simply assigns the downside risk relating to these circumstances to future generations, rather than spreading it between generations like a true insurance scheme.

The political economy argument for guaranteeing benefits faces difficulties as well. Suppose initially that Congress, for reasons of short-term fiscal convenience, was strongly predisposed to renege on promises of retirement support, thus making a Social Security-type program politically unsustainable. If such a program is a good idea to begin with, a norm of treating accrued benefits as guaranteed may tend to offset this political distortion and make a decent-sized program more politically feasible, just as one may (as discussed in chapter 4) reduce overbuilding by the highway authority by requiring it to compensate owners whose land it seizes. In fact, however, there is little reason to think that Congress leans unduly against protecting Social Security benefits. Not only are legislatures often prone to favor grandfathering so as not to impose concentrated costs, but the current elderly typically have strong interest group advantages over the members of younger age cohorts (Shaviro 1997, 142). This is why "saving Social Security" has long proved such a potent political slogan, and why the American Association of Retired Persons (AARP) is so feared and conciliated as a lobbying group.

The fact that the dominant political bias in intergenerational distribution policy seems, if anything, to favor the elderly may seem to indicate that accrued Social Security benefits instead ought definitely *not* to be treated as guaranteed. Even this is not entirely clear, however. The problem arises from the difficulty of determining, as things stand and even given the AARP-type political bias, whether the current elderly are doing too well or not well enough relative to members of younger age cohorts. That depends on future economic, technological, environmental, and other such developments that are extremely hard to forecast with any confidence. It is clear that, for some centuries, living standards in Western societies have for the most part steadily improved. If this continues, the political bias in favor of older generations may turn it out in retrospect, from the standpoint of optimizing overall distribution, to have been too small, rather than too great (Shaviro 1997, 176–85). Thus, it is hard to say with confidence whether treating accrued retirement benefits as guaranteed would worsen or improve overall intergenerational distribution.

6. A Limited Distributional Analysis

A final perspective on Social Security transition would emphasize the specific intergenerational distribution question that is posed by needing to increase net wage taxes in response to the long-term financing problem. As noted previously, since the retroactive and prospective wage tax bases are largely the same and the overall level of net wage taxation over time may not be greatly affected by the decision of whether or not to grandfather, distribution issues should be prominent in making this decision. These include issues of progressivity within an age cohort, but they are largely intergenerational given that, for life cycle reasons, currently accrued benefits mainly pertain to older workers and retirees.

From an intergenerational standpoint, while what really matters is overall distribution given all the many factors that affect it, one could argue that the difficulty of making such a broad assessment suggests casting one's net more narrowly. One might, accordingly, want to consider how the burden created specifically by Social Security's current financing problems (and "tax lag" more generally) would optimally be distributed if intergenerational distribution were otherwise appropriate, or at least if one could not tell in what direction it erred. The answer, in general, would be to distribute the burden widely, rather than concentrating it on any particular groups—thus, unlike the current Social Security system, spreading rather than merely shifting risks that relate to productivity growth trends and differences in the numbers of workers in different age cohorts.

This, in turn, suggests that all age cohorts should share to some extent in the burden of eliminating the financing shortfall. Under such a goal, full grandfathering would clearly be inappropriate, since it would exempt retirees from bearing any share of the burden. Only through some reduction in accrued benefits (alongside fully prospective net benefits) can the wage tax increase that is needed to restore Social Security's fiscal balance be dispersed among the members of all living and future generations.

ELEVEN

ALTERNATIVE INSTRUMENTS
FOR PROVIDING TRANSITION RELIEF

A. The Chief Transition Instruments

When the government decides to provide transitional adjustment limiting the post-enactment reach of a new rule, a number of different mechanisms are available. In particular, it can provide or extract compensation; use grandfathering to preserve the post-enactment application of the old rule in specified cases; or delay full implementation across the board, with or without a gradual phase-in, for a period of time after the date of enactment. A further alternative is to scale down the degree of change made by the new rule but to implement immediately the change that is made (Zodrow 1981). I henceforth call these the transition instruments of compensation, grandfathering, delay, and partial immediate implementation.

So far in this book, I have mainly assumed that grandfathering would be the transition instrument of choice, although in some cases I have mentioned compensation or delay. (In addition, chapters 6 and 7 discuss the use of a preenactment effective date, generally limited by the ANR norm to the year of enactment.) A fuller comparison of the alternative instruments is needed, however, focusing in particular on grandfathering and delay, since they are typically the most prominent alternatives. Compensation is often politically unfeasible (Zodrow 1985, 211 n. 1), and perhaps rightly so for reasons of political economy. It tends to lack natural boundaries, since any one-time tax or transfer could be called compensation for some rule change, and it may undermine such constraints as the ANR norm and the constitutional bans on takings and bills of attainder. Partial immediate implementation sufficiently resembles delay to be treated, for convenience, as a variant to it rather than as a completely distinctive instrument. I therefore defer discussing it until the end of this chapter.

While both grandfathering and delay are commonly used, grandfathering is the traditional favorite in reliance-based "old view" style advocacy of transition relief, because it can address retroactivity by distinguishing between pre- and post-enactment behavior. Michael Graetz (1977, 87), however, has prominently argued that delay should generally be the preferred instrument when, contrary to the main tenor of his "new view" arguments, transition relief is provided. This in part reflects his emphasizing the "magnitude" of transitional wealth changes, without regard to incentive effects. His arguments need not be directly addressed here, since they proceed from such a different (and less specified) framework, but they help to show that the relative advantages of grandfathering and delay remain a live issue in current debate.

In comparing grandfathering to delay, the distinction between policy changes and accounting changes is critical. Policy changes present the transition question of which policy should apply in a given case, and either instrument can affect this in ways that one likes or dislikes. By contrast, accounting changes present the transition question of whether a rule change in the middle of a single or related set of transactions should have consequences that neither the old nor the new rule, if applied consistently, would have had. Grandfathering can be used to target this problem in a way that delay cannot. I start with policy changes.

B. Choosing between Grandfathering and Delay to Address Policy Change Retroactive Taxes

1. Effects of Instrument Choice on Accommodation of the Old Rule

Due to the ANR norm, all policy changes in a sense have delayed implementation. They cannot apply to tax computations for the period prior to the calendar year of their enactment, even though they may have been anticipated. Hence, behavior over time ends up being divided into that which is taxed under the old policy, and under the new. Transition instruments help determine the precise location of the boundary between the old and new policies' range of application. For convenience, one can describe a transition instrument as "accommodating" insofar as it expands the old policy's range of application relative to that which would have resulted from immediate full implementation of the new policy upon enactment. An initial question of possible interest is how the choice between grandfathering and delay affects the extent to which transition policy is accommodating.

Not surprisingly, neither grandfathering nor delay past the date of enactment is uniformly more accommodating. In part, this depends on how they are fine-tuned, as through the choice between 1 and 10 years' delay in implementation, or grandfathering 50 percent versus 100 percent of an item's unrecovered income tax basis. In addition, however, the accounting features of the old rule largely control the extent to which grandfathering can be accommodating. These accounting features determine what portion of the old rule's application to past transactions can still be changed without nominal retroactivity, and thus would be altered in the absence of grandfathering.

This can be illustrated by considering repeal of the municipal bond preference, defined solely by its policy content of effectively exempting municipal bond interest without requiring a particular (such as the actual) accounting implementation. Suppose initially that the old rule provided expensing for the purchase price of a municipal bond and then required inclusion of all subsequent receipts (yielding an effective tax rate of zero under standard assumptions). Here, grandfathering would offer no opportunity to be more accommodating than immediate full implementation of repeal, because all of the preferential deductions would already have been taken in prior taxable years (and thus be protected by the ANR norm). By contrast, delay would be more accommodating than immediate full implementation.

Now, suppose instead that municipal bond exemption was provided entirely at the back end, by including bond interest in taxable income and then refunding all resulting tax liability with interest when the bonds were redeemed by the issuer. Under this accounting implementation, grandfathering would be extremely accommodating, since without it all previously issued bonds that were still outstanding on the repeal date would lose the preference. Delay would be less accommodating than grandfathering with respect to old bonds, since they would still lose the benefit of the preference to the extent that the new rule was implemented before they were redeemed. However, it would be more accommodating than grandfathering with respect to bonds issued after enactment.

Finally, suppose that what is repealed is the actual municipal bond preference under present law, with its annual exemption for municipal bond interest. Here, grandfathering is less accommodating than in the case where the preference used back-end accounting, since more of the benefit to old bonds is protected in any event by the ANR norm. One still has the same basic tradeoff, however: The more accommodating instrument for old bonds is grandfathering; for new bonds, it is delay.

Accordingly, the choice of transition instrument involves a choice of how to direct the accommodation provided as between preenactment and post-enactment decisions. Grandfathering can be devised in such a manner as to accommodate only the former, while delay shifts some of the overall accommodation that is provided to the latter. Thus, holding overall accommodation constant, the choice between the instruments depends on which decisions one wants to accommodate.

However, the level of overall accommodation is not entirely exogenous to the choice of instrument. Delay is unavoidably more accommodating than grandfathering if the old policy used completely front-loaded accounting. Even in other cases, delay gives the level of possible accommodation a higher ceiling. After all, at the limit, delay would be infinite, meaning that the new rule never took effect and thus applied to no cases, whereas under grandfathering, the new rule takes effect immediately as to post-enactment decisions.

On the other hand, the political economy of grandfathering can perhaps lead it in practice to be more accommodating, at least in forestalling transition loss. A taxpayer who has already acted may be more inclined to demand favorable transition treatment than one who can still mitigate the loss by changing subsequent decisions. In addition, if reliance is an influential norm, then emphasizing past decisions may increase the likelihood of a sympathetic hearing.

2. Tradeoffs Presented by Grandfathering versus Delay

In cases where the choice between grandfathering and delay will affect the extent to which transition policy is accommodating, this difference may provide a reason for preferring one or the other. For example, suppose that one supports imposing policy change retroactive taxes and thus would like to provide zero accommodation. If this choice is unavailable, one may prefer, all else equal, the instrument that is likely in practice to prove less accommodating.[1] Opposition to a policy change retroactive tax may induce the opposite preference.

Also potentially significant is how transition policy allocates accommodation between preenactment and post-enactment decisions. However, in evaluating this choice, it is useful to start by noting how a rational expectations viewpoint affects its significance. If incentive effects are best captured by the simplifying assumption that, on average, policy is in effect accurately anticipated (taking account of *ex post* observation), then the timing of announcement relative to when decisions are made matters less than one might otherwise have thought. One is driven towards the view that, so far as incentive effects are concerned, all policy decisions should at a first approximation be treated as if they had been preannounced. Thus, retroactivity, or applying a new rule to past decisions, is distinctive only insofar as it affects transition risk.

Nonetheless, even within a general rational expectations framework, the choice between accommodating past and future taxpayer decisions upon adopting a policy change matters in the following respects:

1. The aim of minimizing investors' unwanted transition risk is better served by grandfathering than delay. From a risk mitigation standpoint, using delay instead of grandfathering "wastes" some of the accommodation provided on post-enactment decisions that were made after the new rule's enactment.

2. A second problem with delay is its continuing post-enactment effect on the timing of taxpayer behavior. The enactment of a schedule for delayed implementation of a newly adopted rule means that, even without future enactments (which would face the burden of inertia), the applicable rule will change over time in a predictable direction. Taxpayers therefore have a distortionary intertemporal incentive to shift activities to years in which these activities are treated more favorably. Thus, suppose that initially the cost of a building can be expensed but then a new rule is enacted, to take effect in 5 years, under which the deduction is reduced to the present-value equivalent of 30-year, straight-line depreciation. Taxpayers now have an incentive to rush buildings into service in the next five years, even if from a nontax standpoint this is too soon. This incentive would be reversed, in the direction of inducing delay, if the tax change were in the other direction.

Now suppose that the new rule is ratably phased in over a five-year period. That is, it applies to 20 percent of building cost the first year, 40 percent the second year, and so on. Although one day's delay will now never matter as much as it would if the implementation percentage went immediately from 0 to 100 percent at the end of the five years (thus reducing distortion in some cases), tax consequences have now been attached to timing within the five-year period (thus increasing distortion in other cases).

Grandfathering avoids such intertemporal distortion so far as the post-enactment period is concerned. Yet it cannot avoid the creation of such incentives for the preenactment prior to the effective date, reflecting the fact that to bar nominal retroactivity is to require an element of delay. In addition, if grandfathering involves a single effective date rather than being itself phased in (in the sense of increasing the implementation percentage on specified dates within the year of enactment), then it creates particularly strong intertemporal distortion with respect to the effective date, on which the implementation percentage jumps from 0 to 100 percent.

In addition, grandfathering (in common with delay) can distort post-enactment behavior in additional ways if the tax rule that it causes to apply is one that induces ongoing distortion. In illustration, suppose that the realization requirement was revised to provide an interest adjustment to the tax consequences upon transfer, thus eliminating its current policy content of favoring the deferral of appreciated gain. If preenactment appreciation was grandfathered, thus remaining taxable upon sale without any interest adjustment, then assets with such appreciation would continue to have locked in gain during the post-enactment period.

A similar example arose in chapter 8, where we saw that retaining present law for old corporate equity upon the adoption of corporate integration for new equity would result in perpetuating the distortive distinction between dividend and nondividend distributions. In general, as discussed in chapter 8, the most direct solution (political economy problems aside) is to provide or extract compensation in lieu of grandfathering, with the amount of compensation depending on the expected value of the future tax consequences without regard to the future behavior that actually occurs.

Given these points, grandfathering is not necessarily superior to delay from the standpoint of reducing intertemporal distortion. It does, however, unambiguously reduce these problems post-enactment if the old rule that it retains does not induce ongoing distortion. Thus, it may be a superior instrument in cases where the timing elasticity of taxpayer behavior is lower preenactment than post-enactment.

3. A further consideration raised by the choice between grandfathering and delay goes to adjustment costs upon the promulgation of a new rule (or more specifically, new information indicating that this rule will be taking effect). The term "adjustment costs" usually refers to the costs of reallocating resources in the economy in response to a rule change (Zodrow 1985, 212–13). However, it can be extended to cover as well the costs to taxpayers of acquiring information about a new rule that is needed for compliance, and to the government of learning whether the rule works as expected. In general, a variety of cases exist where adjustment costs may increase the appeal of delay relative to grandfathering and compensation.

George Zodrow (1985, 225) shows that, if marginal adjustment costs are convex (that is, increase disproportionately with the scale of the adjustment), it is possible, in a case of surprise, for delay to be the optimal transition instrument. Intuitively, the argument is that, under convexity and surprise, delay reduces adjustment costs by making the change smaller in present value terms. However, Zodrow's is a one-shot rather than a repeated-play analysis. If taxpayers observe that, in a given set of cases, surprise is met with delayed implementation, their incentive not to be surprised the next time is reduced. Since anticipation is desirable, all else equal, under convex marginal adjustment costs, the case for delay compared to full implementation may not be strengthened by Zodrow's analysis. Nonetheless, his model does suggest that delay may be the optimal transition instrument given convexity and surprise if one holds the level of accommodation constant.

Louis Kaplow (1986, 592 n. 254) notes another circumstance in which adjustment costs may make delay relatively appealing amongst transition instruments. Suppose that the allocative response to a new rule is slow in the case of surprise because adjustment costs are high. Again under a one-shot analysis, delay up to a point may do little to reduce the new rule's allocative effects, since even under immediate implementation they would have taken time. Thus, a given timetable for delayed implementation turns out to be less accommodating in its allocative effects than if adjustment costs were low. If one prefers that transition policy be unaccommodating, this reduces the harm that is done by any given delay timetable. Accordingly, from the anti–transition relief perspective, high adjustment costs may increase the appeal of a specific delay proposal relative to a specific grandfathering or compensation proposal. Nonetheless, from that perspective, high adjustment costs do not reduce the fundamental objection to accommodation, since if they are relied upon to increase the delay in implementation that is permitted in cases of surprise, they reduce taxpayers' incentives to avoid being surprised.

Turning to taxpayers' need to adjust to a new rule in the sense of acquiring information that will assist them in up-front compliance, even Kaplow, while generally a staunch opponent of accommodation when desirable policy changes are enacted, notes that it may support delay for a "limited time period" (591 n. 251). His assertion that this period should be limited seems to reflect the assumption that not much time is needed to read a new tax rule (or at least hire an expert who has done so), along with the general case against accommodation. However, one could imagine the needed period to learn about a new rule being somewhat longer, as when a new statute is sketchy and requires regulatory amplification. More generally, the prior analysis of convex and high resource-allocative adjustment costs may apply here as well, suggesting once again that in some cases adjustment costs may increase delay's appeal relative to grandfathering or compensation.

Finally, consider a case where policymakers are uncertain about the merits of a new rule because some aspects of its operation are hard to predict. For example, they might be uncertain about labor supply elasticities that would determine whether a tax rate increase was desirable on balance. Or they might be concerned that a complicated set of proposed new income tax rules has a hidden design flaw that would permit clever tax planners to exploit it in undesired ways. One way to gain further information about these issues would be to enact a small-scale pilot program first. This is essentially delay with a phase-in element (to the extent of the pilot program), and under some circumstances it would have advantages not attainable through grandfathering.

In sum, the argument for using delay rather than grandfathering is strengthened by the existence of special cases where adjustment costs make it a superior instrument. Even if these cases cannot be reliably identified in practice, they have broader implications given the lack of cases where adjustment costs make grandfathering the superior instrument. This suggests that the choice between delay and grandfathering, in the case of a policy change retroactive tax, should turn on the tradeoff between any adjustment cost advantages to delay, and any advantages to grandfathering with respect to risk mitigation and reducing distortion of post-enactment behavior.

C. Choosing between Grandfathering and Delay to Address Accounting Change Retroactive Taxes

The considerations governing the optimal choice of transition instrument are considerably different when we turn to accounting change retroactive taxes. Here, the question is not one of determining the relative range of application of two successive policies, with transitional adjustment serving to accommodate the old policy. Rather, the question is whether to impose a putatively one-time positive or negative tax on taxpayers who are somehow caught in the middle when the accounting change occurs, or instead to eliminate this tax, which reflects neither the old nor the new steady-state policy.

Thus, suppose that on December 31, 2001, I buy raw land for $100. Under the current income tax, raw land is nondepreciable, but its basis is generally recovered upon a taxable sale or exchange, implying a future deduction with the same present value as some immediate deduction—say, of $90. On January 1, 2002, Congress enacts a consumed income tax, under which all business outlays are expensed. Thus, the accounting change question is whether to wipe out my $100 basis, and the policy change question is whether this basis (assuming its survival) should generate a present-value-equivalent deduction of $90 or $100.

The delay options that Congress may consider are not easily disaggregated to treat the policy and accounting change elements distinctively. Suppose, for example, that the consumption tax might be phased in over five years rather than implemented immediately. This is one-size-fits-all transition. By contrast, Congress's grandfathering options can easily be disaggregated. For the accounting change, grandfathering would mean that *some* cost recovery would be permitted for my $100 outlay, while for the policy change it would keep the present-value-equivalent deduction at $90 rather than increasing it to $100.

Neither grandfathering nor delay addresses the policy change question in a particularly distinctive way. Under either one, the observed policy over time (bridging the two tax regimes) will provide a $90 present-value-equivalent deduction in some cases and $100 in others. Accordingly, no matter which transition instrument is expected, taxpayers may keep both outcomes in mind when they make investment decisions at different times, with their estimates presumably reflecting the particulars of its accommodation.

By contrast, grandfathering has distinctive incentive effects on the accounting change question. It would result in taxpayers' never being denied cost recovery by reason of a shift to front-end accounting. They therefore could disregard this prospect at all times if they anticipated grandfathering against accounting changes. Delay, by contrast, merely discounts the present value of the expected loss from an accounting change, leaving a retroactive tax with a positive expected value unless the expected delay is infinite.

With respect to accounting changes, therefore, grandfathering takes direct aim at the problem, which after all results from having preenactment items straddle two tax regimes. In addition, it permits disaggregation between the treatment of policy and accounting changes, as in the case where income tax basis is grandfathered but not the value of remaining income tax cost recovery. Delay, by contrast, does not directly address accounting changes and cannot separate any mitigation of their impact from the level of accommodation granted to the old policy. Grandfathering thus appears to be the clearly superior instrument for addressing accounting change retroactive taxes.

D. Partial Immediate Implementation versus Delay

Partial immediate implementation is generally closer to delay than to grand-fathering. Like delay, it makes no distinction between preenactment and post-enactment decisions, and it does not directly respond to accounting change problems. Thus, it generally is inferior to grandfathering where delay is inferior, and is best regarded as an alternative to delay where grandfathering is the inferior instrument or has been ruled out for political or administrative reasons.

The big difference between partial immediate implementation and delay goes to how they allocate their accommodation over time. Partial immediate implementation falls short of full immediate implementation in a manner that remains constant over time, while delay falls short only in the initial post-enactment period. Thus, if the two instruments are equally accommodating overall, partial immediate implementation must trade off being less accommodating initially for being more so later on.

This tradeoff's main effects on the two instruments' relative merits are as follows:

1. Ignoring the prospect of further enactments in the future, partial imme-diate implementation avoids delay's continuing post-enactment effects on the timing of taxpayer behavior. One does not benefit or lose by waiting for the final rule that has been enacted to take effect if it is already fully in place. This factor therefore tends to favor partial immediate implementation.

2. The two instruments may differ in the ratio of social benefit to social cost that results from their falling short of full immediate implementation. Suppose that the new government rule provides a particular item that, as its supply increases, is subject to declining marginal benefit and increasing marginal cost. (This is the typical structure of a supply-demand curve for a market commodity, but the same could hold, say, for providing increasing levels of progressive redistribution.) Permanently reducing the scope of the policy, and thus the amount supplied, affects the "last" cases in which it would otherwise have been supplied—by definition, the cases, amongst those within full implementation, in which marginal benefit was lowest and marginal cost highest. Thus, partial immediate implementation is relatively

benign, in that it reduces the policy's total marginal cost disproportionately to its total marginal benefit. Delay, by contrast, may tend to reduce benefit and cost proportionately, thus making it the inferior instrument insofar as marginal benefit declines and marginal cost increases with supply (Zodrow 1981, 406).[2]

Since partial implementation resembles grandfathering, rather than delay, in the sense of not increasing the degree of implementation in the course of the post-enactment period, adjustment costs can in some circumstances make it an inferior instrument to delay (Zodrow 1985, 229–30). The analysis here resembles that set forth above for the effect of adjustment costs on choosing between grandfathering and delay.

TWELVE

CONCLUSION

A change in government rules often has retroactive effects on people who made decisions before its adoption, subject to adjustment through transition policy. There is no uniform or simple answer to the question of how the government should burden or benefit people retroactively, just as there is no such answer prospectively. Indeed, retroactive and preannounced policy have more in common than has generally been recognized, the main difference simply being one of risk or variance. Retroactivity implies risk because future government decisions are hard to predict. However, eliminating the risk of change to a particular government rule that is in place when one makes decisions—or more precisely, reallocating this risk from a given economic actor to voters or taxpayers generally—need not be desirable given people's varying risk preferences, their ability to allocate risks through their own transactions, and the incentive effects of risk bearing.

Transition policy's incentive effects have typically been ignored, at least in the legal and economic literature on taxation, based on the mistaken view that all of the affected private decisions lie in the past when a positive or negative retroactive tax is imposed. This view ignores the fact that retroactive government decisions recur repeatedly and are likely to be observed, thus affecting people's expectations concerning future policy. A better view starts from the understanding that risk or variance as such does not imply any systematic direction of rule change, or of error in anticipating and observing it, and thus that there is no inherent reason why retroactive rules should affect incentives over the long run any less than preannounced rules. Accordingly, in general, the best way to analyze a given retroactive tax (risk problems aside) is to ask what would have been its incentive and distributional effects had it been accurately anticipated—although this is shorthand for actual *ex ante* anticipation plus *ex post* observation.

The importance of anticipation over the long run and the distinction between mere variance and systematic direction in comparing likely future to known current policy (what I call the transition risk and retroactive tax elements of the analysis) are two of the main economic insights that this book suggests should henceforth play a prominent role in analyzing transition policy. A third insight has both a general component and a particular application to changes in the tax laws. The general component is that there is no uniform relationship between the desirability of a given retroactive tax and of the steady-state rule change that gives rise to it. I use the term "policy change retroactive tax" to describe cases where the desirability of anticipation *does* turn on whether a newly adopted policy is good or bad. An example is repealing the municipal bond preference, thus making municipal bonds less attractive than otherwise even before repeal occurs if bondholders do not anticipate grandfathering.

In other cases, the desirability of a retroactive tax is unrelated to the steady-state merits of the rule change that gave rise to it. For example, consider compensating income tax practitioners for the loss of their livelihood if Congress repealed the current income tax. This would likely be undesirable without regard to the merits of the repeal, since it would tend to increase adjustment costs by encouraging overinvestment in acquiring income tax expertise when repeal was a real possibility.

In the area of tax law changes (but also in other areas, such as the issuance of pollution permits), an important application of the distinction between policy change and other retroactive taxes springs from the distinction between what I call a rule's policy and accounting content. A tax rule's steady-state policy content describes how, at equilibrium, the burden that it imposes is allocated between economic activities and distributed between individuals. Its accounting content describes how, when, and from whom the taxes that give rise to these burdens are actually collected. Here the main variables are nominal incidence as distinct from economic incidence, and timing as distinct from time value. As an example of merely nominal incidence, most economists agree that payroll taxes would mainly be borne by workers whether the nominal liability was assigned fully to them, fully to employers, or split evenly between the two, as is actually the case. As an example of merely nominal timing, the steady-state policy content of the current income tax would generally be unaffected by replacing, say, multiyear depreciation with immediate cost recovery that had the same present value.

Rule changes often combine policy change with accounting change, even if the latter is incidental and little noticed in public debate. The retroactive tax consequences of a tax rule change often turn at least in part on the accounting element, as in the case where shifting from the current income tax to a consumption tax that used expensing might cause a one-time denial of cost recovery through the disappearance of income tax basis. Where a tax rule change would result in a positive or negative accounting change retroactive tax in the absence of transitional adjustment, the incentive and distributional features of that retroactive tax are distinct from those of the accompanying policy change, and thus should be evaluated separately.

In evaluating retroactive policy, long-term considerations of political economy are important, no less than those of incentive and distributional effects under the more static assumption of full anticipation. The political economy implications of permitting burdens to be imposed or benefits provided retroactively rather than through preannouncement vary with the policy area, turning in particular on problems of organization (such as interest group politics) and information (such as fiscal illusion), as mediated by institutional design. As an example, despite the prediction of interest group theory that concentrated burden will evoke fiercer resistance than diffuse burden, it is plausible that, under certain conditions, administrative agencies will tend to be discouraged from taking private property by a compensation requirement. Considerations of political economy can suggest the promulgation of constitutional norms governing transition practice in a given area, whether these are explicit and enforceable legal rules or simply general principles that command sufficient prestige to influence political decisions at the margin.

With respect to tax rule changes, this book proposes two main constitutional norms. The first is that policy change retroactive taxes generally not be mitigated through transitional adjustment. One possible ground for this norm—which I consider false but others may accept—is the belief that policy changes in the tax law are mainly for the good, suggesting that anticipation is generally desirable. My own reason for proposing this norm is the belief that, within the realistic limits of its possible acceptance and exertion of influence, it would tend to reduce the prevailing asymmetry in favor of providing greater transitional adjustment when income tax preferences that worsen resource allocation are curtailed than when they are expanded. My second proposed constitutional norm is that accounting change retroactive taxes within the income tax generally be mitigated through grandfathering. Here the argument is that the random (from a policy standpoint) way they arise results in their generally being bad policy. Thus, in the income to consumption tax example, no one would seriously advocate denying cost recovery for a limited and arbitrarily selected set of business outlays, except under what is likely the delusive view that one can, in effect, hide the resulting capital levy despite its occurring in broad daylight, or persuade people that it will not recur notwithstanding its deliberate adoption.

These constitutional and case-specific policy judgments reflect particular premises about tax policy and politics that not all readers will share. Nonetheless, even if readers' views on these matters differ from mine, I hope they will recognize the value of this book's analytical structure in evaluating transition problems, and apply it in reaching their own conclusions. Transition policy has long been an area in which fundamental premises remain disputed and "not many results are available" (Rosen 1995, 347). This need not continue to be the case. While universal consensus may be unattainable and even undesirable, at least a common language and understanding of the relevant tradeoffs should now be within reach.

1. Despite their similar conclusions, the legal "new view" and its counterpart in economics rest on opposite behavioral assumptions: the occurrence of desirable anticipation under the former, and the nonoccurrence of undesirable anticipation under the latter. Thus, the lawyers, unlike the economists, use a standard economic framework with rational actors who respond to new information by adjusting their expectations.

2. Auerbach and Kotlikoff (1983) argue that owners of old assets generally enjoy windfall gains when the tax treatment of competing new assets becomes less favorable than previously, and incur losses when such treatment becomes more favorable. In chapter 7, I show that this requires unexplained systematic underanticipation of policy change. Auerbach and Kotlikoff (1987) model the purported efficiency gains from the capital levy component of a "cold turkey" replacement of the income tax with a consumption tax, based on assuming that investors will neither anticipate the capital levy nor expect it to recur.

3. All three of these contributions are anticipated in Kaplow (1986), but I express them more generally and develop them more systematically.

4. While the tax lawyers are not being retroactively deprived of specific tax items such as inclusions and deductions, their case may be more sympathetic than that of the bondholders from the standpoint of risk mitigation. Investment portfolios are generally easier to diversify than human capital.

5. The "Cary Brown equivalence theorem" holds that, under certain conditions, the tax savings from expensing an investment equal those from excluding the investment returns from income (Brown 1943).

1. At a price of $112.50, a taxable corporate bond that offered a 10 percent return that was taxable at 20 percent would pay $11.25, leaving the investor with $9 after tax.

1. If the borrower can prepay the loan without penalty, then she presumably will do so (transaction costs permitting) if the interest rate goes down. Thus, the lender will "win" only in the sense of not losing as she would have had interest rates gone up. One would

expect the overall terms of the arrangement to compensate the lender for granting the borrower this one-way option to terminate the loan prematurely.

2. Over time, such problems may conceivably addressed by new financial instruments—for example, permitting homeowners to hedge against general real estate risk (Shaviro 1995, 666).

3. This is simply the Coase Theorem at work. While Coase favored addressing externalities by assigning property rights rather than imposing Pigovian taxes and subsidies, within my terminology he was merely debating the choice of tax instrument.

4. Consider the problems posed by people's bets or deliberate gambles, as where X and Y have equal opportunities and indeed equal material wealth, except that they use financial instruments to bet on whether interest rates will go up or down. *Ex post,* the winner is wealthier and better off than the loser. Nonetheless, one could argue against progressive redistribution to re-equalize X and Y, since this would amount to forbidding them to bet, and thus make both worse off *ex ante,* assuming consumer sovereignty. But the problem is harder if X tends to win these bets with Y due to greater ability as a bettor. This may suggest that X has greater opportunities than Y *ex ante* after all, possibly for reasons of endowment that have nothing to do with choice, and that Y may be foolish to bet. Cf. Kaplow (1991).

5. But see Sanchirico (1997), arguing that supplemental redistribution through the tort system can be optimal if, say, care or accident levels are correlated with how well-off one is, and thus can function, like income or wealth levels, as a signal of relative endowment.

6. I omit the fourth case implied by having two variables: that where the retroactive tax is good only if the rule change is bad.

7. The root of this problem lies in the compensation scheme. I also should be deterred from building the house by the prospect that General Motors will want to buy my land without the improvements. In the ordinary course, however, I can be expected to take this prospect into account. Since General Motors' willingness to pay should be unaffected by an improvement that it does not value, I am likely to bear the cost of wasted construction in the event of a sale. In the government case, the problem is that the government pays me fair market value (which reflects my investment decisions) rather than the property's value to the government. This, in turn, reflects its takings power—a response to the holdout problem, which arises when property owners strategically refuse to sell, even at prices they would otherwise deem acceptable, because each hopes to extract a large share of the transactional surplus. Solving the private incentive problem here requires not that the government pay zero compensation for taking my property but, rather, that the compensation be independent of my land use decisions. Paying zero compensation is one special case of this general principle (Blume, Rubinfeld, and Shapiro 1984, 72).

8. The proposed Omnibus Property Rights Act of 1995 would have required compensation when certain regulatory mandates, including under the ESA, reduced property values by more than a threshold percentage. This legislation seems dead for now, but several states have adopted similar statutes for their own regulators. A percentage threshold for compensation can distort incentives by inducing landowners to increase the loss from regulatory issuance so that they will qualify for compensation (Ellickson 1996, 75).

9. Inflation is a lesser case of currency cancellation. However, we may welcome a decision to increase inflation by more conventional means, such as monetary policy, if this reduces cyclical unemployment. This argument could conceivably apply to currency cancellation, but seems far-fetched in practice.

10. A more familiar example would be getting married or having children to avoid the draft, but there one would face more difficult questions as to whether the "draft exemption subsidy" for such actions was independently desirable.

11. In practice, a tax bearing either label may fail to accomplish this. Thus, suppose we have a consumption tax with annual reporting and progressive marginal rates, in which consumption is included in the year when it takes place (a mere accounting feature). Under this tax, the saver may bear a higher tax burden than the immediate consumer by reason of being pushed into a higher marginal rate bracket by the extra consumption that the return to investment makes possible.

12. Repeal of the municipal bond interest exemption keeps accounting constant because it continues the current timing element of applying a constant tax rate across the period when the bond accrues income.

13. Since I define "policy" as necessarily time consistent, one could not, within my terminology, describe the basis wipeout as applying a new policy of denying cost recovery solely for preenactment expenditures.

CHAPTER FOUR

1. It might matter if error in one direction had especially bad consequences—for example, if overspending merely wasted a small percentage of national wealth while underspending invited foreign conquest.

2. To be sure, ingenious supporters of tax preferences can address natural scaling limits. An example is the investment tax credit (ITC), provided intermittently between 1962 and 1986 for certain depreciable assets, and at times contributing to an overall result more favorable than expensing, without literally permitting the taxpayer to deduct more than 100 percent of asset cost. The ITC, however, proved less politically resilient than accelerated depreciation, reflecting that it is an income tax preference on its face, whereas accelerated depreciation is such only relative to the perhaps obscure course of economic depreciation.

3. Kaplow (1986, 570) argues that agencies following the commonly assumed bureaucratic aim of budget maximization (Niskanen 1971) might welcome a compensation requirement that led the legislature to increase their budgets. However, empire building in the sense that Niskanen posited is not advanced by having to pay more for a constant set of inputs that yield a constant set of outputs. It is advanced by having *more* inputs and outputs—for example, building more roads, rather than paying more for the same or fewer roads (Niskanen 1971, 38; De Alessi 1967, 18). Paying more compensation to build the same number of roads might not benefit such an agency unless, say, a new bureaucracy arose to administer the payment of compensation.

4. In effect, the argument that one should buy off the beneficiaries of an inefficient subsidy by compensating them for repeal is similar to the argument for a one-time tax amnesty that increases current revenue but may induce people to anticipate its repetition, thus dissipating any overall societal or revenue gain. The tax amnesty problem is discussed, for example, by Baird, Gertner, and Picker (1994, 76–77).

5. Similarly, if Pigovian pollution taxes were enacted, the transition question would involve deciding whether current polluters should be compensated, such as through a payment or credit approximating the present value of expected future pollution taxes.

6. Lowi's other two categories are "regulatory" politics, where well-organized groups such as competing industries battle to shape policy, and "redistributive" politics, where large social classes, such as the rich and poor or business and labor, compete (689). Policy

in both of these categories avoids the pathology of distributive politics because there is greater competition between competing represented interests.

7. An example of transition losses permitting explicit tax rates to be lower is the Hall-Rabushka "flat tax" plan, which offers a 19 percent rate that would have to be increased to 20.1 percent if Congress chose to honor unused depreciation deductions from the preenactment period (Hall and Rabushka 1995, 78–79). An example of transition (and other) gains requiring politically unpalatable tax increases in other respects is corporate integration (Sheppard 1990, 1168).

CHAPTER FIVE

1. Prominent expressions of the comprehensive income tax norm include Simons (1938), Musgrave (1967), Pechman (1967), and Surrey (1973). A noted dissenting view appears in Bittker (1967).

2. However, I will make no effort to define the CTB, in either its income or consumption tax version. An immense literature shows that it cannot be fully defined. For example, does it allow medical and charitable deductions? (Compare Andrews 1972; Kelman 1979; and Griffith 1989.) To what extent should it respond indirectly to violations of its premises, such as by denying home mortgage interest deductions as a substitute for taxing the imputed rental value of owning one's home (Shaviro 1989a), or allowing accelerated depreciation in lieu of indexing for inflation? How, if at all, should it address the bias against market work, compared to leisure and housework, that is built into the very definitions of taxable income and consumption? Difficult though these questions are, it is sufficient for my purposes that the CTB often is reasonably well defined. Thus, an income tax CTB clearly would tax imputed rent and municipal bond interest, use economic depreciation or its present-value equivalent, and adjust for inflation. Even when the CTB answer is unclear, a CTB norm would tend to influence the relevant arguments. I thus generally assume that the CTB is sufficiently well defined to have meaning as a "constitutional" norm.

3. If alternative bad policies are not in competition, then eliminating one should result in overall policy improvement. Its elimination will have no marginal effect on the adoption of other bad policies.

4. Suppose, for example, that current consumption was a leisure substitute and that deferred consumption was a leisure complement, taking account of future as well as current work-leisure choices. There would now be an efficiency argument for the income tax over the consumption tax.

5. While the assumptions of flat rate taxes with full loss refundability are counterfactual, this only goes to show that these specific features may matter under either tax.

6. Admittedly, if the return to waiting is lower than most tax commentators have supposed, then the degree of inter-asset distortion caused by deferral preferences in the income tax preferences has been exaggerated. Note, however, that unrealized appreciation permanently escapes the current income tax base at death (IRC section 1014), that tax arbitrage transactions can be used to enhance the impact of timing inconsistencies within the income tax rules, and that the failure to adjust for inflation further accentuates the current significance of such inconsistencies.

7. There are, of course, periods during which movements towards or away from the CTB may predominate. Witte (1985, 288–98) shows that tax preferences generally expanded from about 1970 through 1981—perhaps reflecting the decentralization of legislative power

during this period, along with automatic tax increases through the mechanism of inflation (which effectively increased marginal tax rates, since rate brackets were not then indexed). Pressure then built for movement in the opposite direction, leading to base-broadening legislation in 1982, 1984, and 1986. The pendulum has mainly swung back away from the CTB since then, but this, too, may be subject to reversal at some point.

8. Compare Fallon and Meltzer (1991, 1810–11), noting that the specific warning against self-incrimination that the Supreme Court required in *Miranda v. Arizona* (384 U.S. 436 (1966)) was not given retroactive application, because the disruption to past and pending prosecutions was unjustifiable when "only a clairvoyant could have . . . predicted the precise set of safeguards that Miranda announced."

9. This provision was initially enacted to clarify that, notwithstanding the Blackstonean view that mere interpretations of the law should apply to the past without limitation, the Treasury had the discretion to grant transition relief when it amended its regulatory position (*Helvering v. Griffiths*, 318 U.S. 371 (1943), 398 n. 49).

CHAPTER SIX

1. This hypothetical assumes away not only measurement problems but also liquidity problems. If one can avoid the endowment tax by having no assets with which to pay it, then it is not truly a lump-sum tax.

2. A standard public finance maxim holds that the distortion caused by a tax rises with the square of the tax rate, thus increasing overall distortion if, say, it is alternately doubled and halved.

3. For rate changes, the administrative convenience of applying a single rate structure to the entire year may induce Congress to instead apply a single "blended rate" to the year of enactment. This adds an element of delayed implementation, a transition instrument that I discuss in chapter 11.

CHAPTER SEVEN

1. "Proxy taxation" is used in some cases, such as the partial denial of business meal and entertainment deductions incurred on behalf of others, presumably responding to the untaxed consumption value to those individuals rather than the payer. Yet the scope of proxy taxation is fairly limited.

2. In a narrow set of cases, pertaining to timeshares and residential lots, interest is charged on the deferral from using the installment method (IRCode section 453(l)(2)(B))—thus causing use of the method to affect only accounting, not policy, if the interest rate is correct.

3. An additional method for increasing the present value of cost recovery is to provide an up-front credit, such as the investment tax credit for various depreciable assets that was repealed in 1986. This, however, shares with accelerated depreciation the accounting linkage between swifter and more valuable cost recovery.

4. The initial Treasury I tax reform plan that ultimately helped engender the Tax Reform Act of 1986 only proposed a delayed effective date (1988), rather than grandfathering, to "mitigate the effects of [indexing] . . . on existing loans" (U.S. Treasury Department 1984, 197). The Treasury's willingness to provide less than full transition relief for existing loans may have reflected the fact that borrowers, the parties adversely affected by indexing, typically have the power to repay old loans, refinancing if necessary, and thus to mitigate any adverse transition impact.

5. The application of the passive-loss rules was phased in over several years, but its retroactive effect on preenactment shelters was nonetheless substantial, and contributed importantly to the estimated revenue and distributional neutrality of the Tax Reform Act of 1986 compared to prior law.

6. To be sure, this rule serves administrative convenience, since taxing capital gain at the rate that applied when it accrued would require a valuation method for allocating gain between periods with different capital gains rates. However, this could conceivably be done by assuming that gain accrued ratably like fixed-rate interest, thus eliminating any need to observe its actual accrual.

7. The main transaction cost impediment to purchasing private insurance against the risk that one's home will lose value is moral hazard, given the possibility of unobservable decisions by the insured regarding both home upkeep and price strategy when selling one's home.

8. Tax rate changes involve similar bets. For example, by entering a high-wage career such as medicine, one implicitly bets that other prospective entrants are unduly pessimistic about future tax rates on wages.

9. Although preexisting assets may qualify for new law tax benefits if they are sold to a new owner, this may trigger depreciation recapture by the prior owner, thus reducing the tax benefit from switching to new law treatment (Auerbach and Kotlikoff 1983, 131).

CHAPTER EIGHT

1. The Andrews ALI study is self-described as an alternative to integration, rather than an implementation of it. However, this reflects its transition policy towards existing corporate equity, rather than a distinctive prospective vision. (See American Law Institute 1989, 49–53.)

2. A corporate distribution has no net tax consequences under the Andrews ALI plan if corporate and shareholder tax rates are the same. However, the Warren ALI plan relies on realization to tax shareholders on the difference between applying their tax rates and the corporate tax rate to corporate earnings. The Treasury integration study discusses taxing shareholder realizations that relate to income that has been shielded from tax at the corporate level by the use of preferences (U.S. Treasury Department 1992, 64–65).

3. One possible problem with using earnings and profits, not noted by Auerbach, is that it does not include unrealized appreciation that, under present law, is taxable to the company upon distribution. Another problem is that many corporations may fail to keep earnings and profits accounts, and determining the amount in such accounts now would potentially require reviewing transactions going back many decades.

4. The Treasury integration study instead describes the new view as hypothesizing that "dividend payments offer no nontax benefits to shareholders relative to retentions" (116). Such a view would make a contestable empirical claim rather than a rigorous logical one. I define the new view in terms of the effects of a uniform distributions tax because that definition, unlike the one posed by the Treasury, is pertinent to assessing the extent to which the corporate tax law creates an incentive not to distribute corporate earnings.

5. The Treasury integration study's other main argument against limiting integration's benefits to new equity is that asset value "changes have typically been ignored in connection with rate changes that raise similar concerns" (90). Again, however, this book has repeatedly shown that transition issues do not pose a one-time, all-or-nothing proposition.

6. The effective date would have to be early enough to minimize "under-the-wire" contributions to corporate equity. This is a standard transition problem of intertemporal distortion. Note that contributing corporate equity too early would tend to increase one's liability under the Auerbach earnings and profits tax.

7. The scope of the subsidy arguably should be limited to reversing the Auerbach tax's effect on distortions 1 and 2, on the political economy ground that one-time compensation is best limited to substituting for what one could readily have done by more conventional means.

CHAPTER NINE

1. Auerbach and Kotlikoff note (1987, 80) that a wage tax concentrates its distortive effects on one margin of choice (work versus leisure), rather than spreading them over two (by also distorting the choice between current consumption versus saving). Yet the income tax's distortion of saving decisions does not imply any mitigation of the work distortion. Even if income tax rates are lower than wage tax rates that raise the same revenue, the reduced burden if one works to finance current consumption is offset by the increased burden if one works to finance future consumption. Thus, work distortion is not inherently reduced, although the ultimate efficiency playout "depend[s] on the particular structure of preferences."

2. Historically, capital income has occasionally faced a negative tax rate—for example, in the immediate aftermath of the 1981 tax act given the combined effect of accelerated depreciation and investment tax credits in the face of reduced inflation. Or consider tax benefits for retirement saving that allow one not only to avoid any tax burden on investment return but also to pay tax on withdrawals at the low marginal rate of one's retirement years rather than the high marginal rate of one's working years.

3. Proposals to make such use of a VAT have been made from time to time in the United States as well, both in Congress and by academics such as Michael Graetz (1997, 264–66).

4. In ignoring the possibility of *ex post* overanticipation of future wealth taxes, Auerbach and Kotlikoff repeat the error, discussed in chapter 7, of assuming that people's expectations regarding how a given investment will be taxed in the future are bounded to a range between myopically assuming the retention of present law and perfect foresight, rather than including possible overestimation of the extent to which the law will change.

5. A business-level consumption tax might disregard all transactions involving financial assets. If so, then cost recovery for such assets' remaining basis should be denied at the transition.

6. This is akin to the hypothetical suggestion at the end of chapter 8 concerning simultaneous adoption of a one-time tax on earnings and profits and an offsetting subsidy to old corporate equity generally. Once again, allowing a one-time subsidy to reverse past distortions would tend to undermine the ANR norm (since it has no obvious built-in limits) and thus raise serious political economy concerns.

7. Somewhat analogously, recent proposals by Alan Auerbach (1991) and David Bradford (1995) would modify the current income tax to subject the deferral of unrealized gain to an interest charge, to be collected at the time of sale but under assumptions about how the gain had accrued. My hypothetical proposal would apply assumptions about when the gain had accrued solely for purposes of determining applicable tax rates, rather than to levy an interest charge that reflects the income tax policy of including the return to waiting.

CHAPTER TEN

1. The Social Security tax is usually described as 12.4 percent of an overall 15.3 percent payroll tax (including the employer's share) on wages up to a threshold that, for 1998, stood at $68,400. However, these figures disregard the exclusion from the payroll tax base of the employer's share of the tax. Thus, to state the tax structure correctly in terms of the entire before-tax wage, one must divide stated marginal tax rates by 1.0765, and multiply stated dollar bracket amounts by 1.0765. Similar adjustments should be made in describing other taxes that exclude the employer share of payroll taxes. (See Shaviro 1999.)

2. The only sensible way to address such questions would be to ask what relationship we want between particular taxes and benefit payments, presumably given the overall tax-transfer picture. Feldstein and Samwick (1998, 221 n. 8), however, seem to think that the corporate and property tax revenues from investing Social Security funds would somehow really belong to the system, at least under their reform.

3. Advocates of considering Trust Fund investment in the stock market argue that the fund managers' investment decisions could be shielded from the political process. (See Advisory Council on Social Security 1997, 26). Others are skeptical (Advisory Council on Social Security 1997, 126–27, 155).

4. At a workshop on Social Security that was held at the National Bureau of Economic Research Summer Institute on August 5, 1998, Feldstein verbally defended his view of saving by noting the "tax wedge" between the social and private return to investment, and the externality implied by future generations' benefit from current saving. Yet the former of these cannot explain the entire claimed spread between real returns and discount rates, and the latter argument is not self-evidently correct. As I have discussed elsewhere (Shaviro 1997, 151–85), one could just as well argue that current generations are consuming too little relative to future generations and thus should save less, as that they are consuming too much and should save more.

5. One wonders why the proponents of the MB plan did not go a step further and purport to restore system balance by urging that benefits be tripled and that the shortfall be financed by a one-time head tax, say, in the year 2500.

6. One possible argument in favor of using a retirement system like Social Security in distribution policy is that it can reflect lifetime earnings and thus more easily achieve income averaging than can an annual system. Obviously, however, the fact that it only provides retirement benefits limits its distributional efficacy if one cannot easily borrow against expected future benefits.

CHAPTER ELEVEN

1. Given the political economy of reliance, this consideration may underlie Graetz's (1977) stated preference, as a general foe of transition relief, for providing any such relief through delay rather than grandfathering.

2. Zodrow emphasizes the special case where full immediate implementation happens to be optimal, in the sense of supplying the item at issue right up to the point where marginal benefit equals marginal cost, but the point holds more broadly.

REFERENCES

Ackerman, Bruce A. 1977. *Private property and the constitution.* New Haven, Conn.: Yale University Press.

Advisory Council on Social Security. 1997. *Report of the 1994–1996 Advisory Council on Social Security.* Baltimore, Md.: Social Security Administration.

American Law Institute. 1989. *Federal income tax project, reporter's study draft—subchapter c (supplemental study) distributions—William D. Andrews, reporter.* Philadelphia: American Law Institute.

American Law Institute. 1993. *Federal income tax project, integration of the individual and corporate income taxes, reporter's study of corporate integration—Alvin C. Warren, Jr., reporter.* Philadelphia: American Law Institute.

Andrews, William D. 1972. Personal deductions in an ideal income tax. *Harvard Law Review* 86:309–85.

————. 1974. A consumption-type or cash flow personal income tax. *Harvard Law Review* 87:1113–88.

Arrow, Kenneth J. 1963. *Social choice and individual values.* New York: Yale University Press.

Auerbach, Alan J. 1990. Debt, equity, and the taxation of corporate cash flows. In *Debt, taxes, and corporate restructuring,* ed. John B. Shoven and Joel Waldfogel. Washington, D.C.: Brookings Institution.

————. 1991. Retrospective capital gains taxation. *American Economic Review* 81 (1): 167–90.

Auerbach, Alan J., and Dale Jorgenson. 1980. Inflation-proof depreciation of assets. *Harvard Business Review* 158:113–25.

Auerbach, Alan J., and Laurence J. Kotlikoff. 1983. Investment versus savings incentives: The size of the bang for the buck and the potential for self-financing business tax cuts. In *The economic consequences of government deficits,* ed. Laurence Meyer. Boston: Kluwer-Nisoff Publishing.

————. 1987. *Dynamic fiscal policy.* New York: Cambridge University Press.

————. 1995. *Macroeconomics: An integrated approach.* Cincinnati: South-Western College Publishing.

Ayres, Ian, and Robert Gertner. 1994. Filling gaps in incomplete contracts. In *Foundations of contract law,* ed. Richard Craswell and Alan Schwartz. Oxford: Oxford University Press.

Baird, Douglas G., Robert H. Gertner, and Randal C. Picker. 1994. *Game theory and the law.* Cambridge, Mass.: Harvard University Press.

Bankman, Joseph, and Barbara H. Fried. 1998. Winners and losers under the shift to a consumption tax. *Georgetown Law Journal* 86:539–68.

Bankman, Joseph, and Thomas D. Griffith. 1993. Is the debate between an income tax and a consumption tax a debate about risk? Does it matter? *Tax Law Review* 47:377–406.

Barro, Robert J. 1996. *Getting it right: Markets and choices in a free society.* Cambridge, Mass.: MIT Press.

Birnbaum, Jeffrey H., and Alan S. Murray. 1987. *Showdown at Gucci gulch: Lawmakers, lobbyists, and the unlikely triumph of tax reform.* New York: Random House.

Bittker, Boris I. 1967. A "comprehensive tax base" as a goal of income tax reform. *Harvard Law Review* 80:925–85.

———. 1989. *Collected legal essays.* Littleton, Conn.: Fred B. Rothman & Co.

Bittker, Boris I., and Lawrence Lokken. 1989. *Federal taxation of income, estates, and gifts.* 2d ed. Boston: Warren, Gorham, & Lamont.

Blume, Lawrence, and Daniel L. Rubinfeld. 1984. Compensation for takings: An economic analysis. *California Law Review* 72:569–628.

Blume, Lawrence, Daniel L. Rubinfeld, and Perry Shapiro. 1984. The taking of land: When should compensation be paid? *Quarterly Journal of Economics* 99:71–92.

Bradford, David F. 1981. The incidence and allocation effects of a tax on corporate distributions. *Journal of Public Economics* 15:1–22.

———. 1986. *Untangling the income tax.* Cambridge, Mass.: Harvard University Press.

———. 1988. What are consumption taxes and who pays them? *Tax Notes* 39:383–96.

———. 1995. Fixing capital gains: Symmetry, consistency, and correctness in the taxation of financial instruments. *Tax Law Review* 50:731–85.

———. 1996. Consumption taxes: Some fundamental transition issues. In *Frontiers of tax reform,* ed. Michael J. Boskin. Stanford, Calif.: Hoover Institution Press.

———. 1998. Transition to and tax rate flexibility in a cash-flow type tax. In *Tax policy and the economy,* ed. James M. Poterba. Cambridge, Mass.: MIT Press.

Bradford, David F., and the U.S. Treasury Tax Policy Staff. 1984. *Blueprints for basic tax reform.* 2d ed. Stanford, Calif.: Hoover Institution Press.

E. Cary Brown. 1943. Business-income taxation and investment incentives. In *Income, employment, and public policy: Essays in honor of Alvin H. Hansen,* ed. Lloyd A. Metzler. New York: W. W. Norton.

Bruce, Donald, and Douglas Holtz-Eakin. 1998. Will consumption tax reform kill the housing market? Conference paper, Seminar Series in Tax Policy, American Enterprise Institute.

Buchanan, James M. 1967. *Public finance in democratic process: Fiscal institutions and individual choice.* Chapel Hill, N.C.: University of North Carolina Press.

Buchanan, James M., and Gordon Tullock. 1962. *The calculus of consent: Logical foundations of constitutional democracy.* Ann Arbor, Mich.: University of Michigan Press.

Buchanan, James M., and Richard E. Wagner. 1977. *Democracy in deficit: The political legacy of Lord Keynes.* San Diego, Calif.: Academic Press, Inc.

Bulow, Jeremy, and Kenneth Rogoff. 1989. Sovereign debt: Is to forgive to forget? *American Economic Review* 79:43–50.

Camp, Bryan T. 1987. The retroactivity of treasury regulations: Paths to finding abuse of discretion. *Virginia Tax Review* 7:509–53.

Clotfelter, Charles T. 1992. The impact of tax reform on charitable giving: A 1989 perspective. In *Do taxes matter: The impact of the tax reform act of 1986*, ed. Joel Slemrod. Cambridge, Mass.: MIT Press.

Coase, Ronald H. 1988. *The firm, the market, and the law*. Chicago: University of Chicago Press.

Conlan, Timothy J., Margaret T. Wrightson, and David R. Beam. 1990. *Taxing choices: The politics of tax reform*. Washington, D.C.: Congressional Quarterly, Inc.

Cramton, Peter, and Suzi Kerr. 1998. Tradeable carbon permit auctions: How and why to auction not grandfather. Resources for the Future Discussion Paper 98–34.

Cunningham, Noel B. 1996. The taxation of capital income and the choice of tax base. *Tax Law Review* 52:17–44.

Davies, David G. 1986. *United States taxes and tax policy*. Cambridge: Cambridge University Press.

De Alessi, Louis. 1969. Implications of property rights for government investment choices. *American Economic Review* 59:13–24.

Dixit, Avinash. 1996. *The making of economic policy: A transaction-cost politics perspective*. Cambridge, Mass.: MIT Press.

Downs, Anthony. 1957. *An economic theory of democracy*. New York: Harper Collins.

Easterbrook, Frank H. 1987. Statutes' domains. *University of Chicago Law Review* 50:533–52.

Ellickson, Robert C. 1996. Takings legislation: A comment. *Harvard Journal of Law and Public Policy* 20:75–84.

Eskridge, William N. 1988. Politics without romance: Implications of public choice theory for statutory interpretation. *Virginia Law Review* 74:275–338.

Fallon, Richard H., and Daniel J. Meltzer. 1991. New law, non-retroactivity, and constitutional remedies. *Harvard Law Review* 104:1731–1833.

Farber, Daniel A. 1992. Public choice and just compensation. *Constitutional Commentary* 9:279–308.

Farber, Daniel A., and Philip P. Frickey. 1991. *Law and public choice: A critical introduction*. Chicago: University of Chicago Press.

Feldstein, Martin. 1974. Social security, induced retirement, and aggregate capital accumulation. *Journal of Political Economy* 82:905–25.

———. 1976. On the theory of tax reform. *Journal of Public Economics* 6:77–104.

———. 1981. The tax cut: Why the market dropped. *Wall Street Journal*, 11 November, 26.

———. 1998. Introduction. In *Privatizing Social Security*, ed. Martin Feldstein. Chicago: University of Chicago Press.

Feldstein, Martin, and Andrew Samwick. 1992. Social Security rules and marginal tax rates. *National Tax Journal* 45:1–22.

———. 1998. The transition path in privatizing Social Security. In *Privatizing Social Security*, ed. Martin Feldstein. Chicago: University of Chicago Press.

Fisch, Jill E. 1997. Retroactivity and legal change: An equilibrium approach. *Harvard Law Review* 110:1055–123.

Fischel, William A. 1995. *Regulatory takings: Law, economics, and politics*. Cambridge, Mass.: Harvard University Press.

Fischel, William A., and Perry Shapiro. 1988. Takings, insurance, and Michelman: Comments on economic interpretations of "just compensation" law. *Journal of Legal Studies* 17:269–93.

Gale, William G. 1998. An evaluation of a national retail sales tax. In *Building a better tax system*, ed. Henry J. Aaron and William G. Gale. Washington, D.C.: Brookings Institution.

Gentry, William M., and R. Glenn Hubbard. 1996. Distributional implications of introducing a broad-based consumption tax. NBER Working Paper no. 5832. Cambridge, Mass.: National Bureau of Economic Research.

———. 1998. Fundamental tax reform and corporate financial policy. NBER Working Paper no. W6433. Cambridge, Mass.: National Bureau of Economic Research.

Goetz, Charles J., and Robert E. Scott. 1994. The mitigation principle. In *Foundations of contract law*, ed. Richard Craswell and Alan Schwartz. Oxford: Oxford University Press.

Goldberg, Daniel S. 1994. Tax subsidies: One-time v. periodic, an economic analysis of the tax policy alternatives. *Tax Law Review* 49:305–47.

Graetz, Michael J. 1977. Legal transitions: The case of retroactivity in income tax revision. *University of Pennsylvania Law Review* 126:47–87.

———. 1979. Implementing a progressive consumption tax. *Harvard Law Review* 92:1575–661.

———. 1985. Retroactivity revisited. *Harvard Law Review* 98:1820–41.

———. 1997. *The decline (and fall?) of the income tax*. New York: W. W. Norton & Co.

Green, Franklin L. 1997. The folly of long-term planning: A comment on the instability of the tax law. *Tax Notes* 74:481–98.

Griffith, Thomas D. 1989. Theories of personal deductions in the income tax. *Hastings Law Journal* 40:343–95.

Hall, Robert E., and Alvin Rabushka. 1995. *The flat tax*. Stanford, Calif.: Hoover Institution Press.

Hayes, Michael T. 1981. *Lobbyists and legislators: A theory of political markets*. New Brunswick, N.J.: Rutgers University Press.

Hoffman, Paul Gordon. 1976. Limits on retroactive decision making by the internal revenue service: Redefining abuse of discretion under section 7805(b). *UCLA Law Review* 23:529–48.

Joint Committee on Taxation. 1981. *General explanation of the economic recovery tax act of 1981*. Washington, D.C.: U.S. Government Printing Office.

———. 1985. *General explanation of the revenue provisions of the deficit reduction act of 1984*. Washington, D.C.: U.S. Government Printing Office.

———. 1987. *General explanation of the tax reform act of 1986*. Washington, D.C.: U.S. Government Printing Office.

Jones, Pat. 1988. The controversy over rifle-shot transition rules. *Tax Notes* 39:543–45.

Joskow, Paul L., and Richard Schmalensee. 1997. The political economy of market-based environmental policy: The U.S. acid rain program. *Journal of Law and Economics* 41:37–83.

Kahneman, Daniel, and Amos Tversky. 1973. On the psychology of prediction. *Psychological Review* 80:237–51.

———. 1979. Prospect theory: An analysis of decision under risk. *Econometrica* 47:263.

Kaldor, Nicholas. 1958. *An expenditure tax*. Hampshire, England: George Allen & Unwin, Ltd.

Kaplow, Louis. 1986. An economic analysis of legal transitions. *Harvard Law Review* 99:509–617.

———. 1990. Horizontal equity: Measures in search of a principle. *National Tax Journal* 42:139–54.

———. 1991. The income tax as insurance: The casualty loss and medical expense deductions and the exclusion of medical insurance premiums. *California Law Review* 79:1485–510.

———. 1995. Recovery of pre-enactment basis under a consumption tax: The USA tax system. *Tax Notes* 69:1109–18.

Kaplow, Louis, and Steven Shavell. 1994. Why the legal system is less efficient than the income tax in redistributing income. *Journal of Legal Studies* 23:667–81.

Kelman, Mark G. 1979. Personal deductions revisited: Why they fit poorly in an "ideal" income tax and why they fit worse in a far from ideal world. *Stanford Law Review* 31:831–83.

Kotlikoff, Laurence J. 1992. *Generational accounting: Knowing who pays, and when, for what we spend.* New York: Free Press.

———. 1998. Simulating the privatization of Social Security. In *Privatizing Social Security,* ed. Martin Feldstein. Chicago: University of Chicago Press.

Krent, Harold J. 1996. The puzzling boundary between criminal and civil retroactive lawmaking. *Georgetown Law Journal* 84:2143–84.

Kydland, Finn E., and Edward C. Prescott. 1977. Rules rather than discretion: The inconsistency of optimal plans. *Journal of Political Economy* 85:473–91.

Lerner, Abba P. 1964. The burden of the national debt. In *Public debt and future generations,* ed. James M. Ferguson. Chapel Hill, N.C.: University of North Carolina Press.

Levmore, Saul. 1993. The case for retroactive taxation. *Journal of Legal Studies* 22:265–307.

Charles Lindblom. 1965. *The intelligence of democracy: Decision making through mutual adjustment.* New York: Free Press.

Lipsey, R. G., and Kelvin Lancaster. 1956. The general theory of second best. *Review of Economic Studies* 24:11–33.

Litan, Robert E. 1996. Comment on Fischel's "Political economy of just compensation." *Harvard Journal of Law and Public Policy* 20:65–73.

Logue, Kyle D. 1996. Tax transitions, opportunistic retroactivity, and the benefits of government precommitment. *Michigan Law Review* 94:1129–96.

Lowi, Theodore. 1964. American business, public policy, case-studies, and political theory. *World Politics* 16:677–715.

Lyon, Andrew B. 1989a. The effect of the investment tax credit on the value of the firm. *Journal of Public Economics* 38:227–47.

———. 1989b. Did ACRS really cause stock prices to fall? NBER Working Paper no. 2990. Cambridge, Mass.: National Bureau of Economic Research.

Lyon, Andrew B., and Peter R. Merrill. 1998. Asset price effects of fundamental tax reform. Conference paper, Seminar Series in Tax Policy, American Enterprise Institute.

Malkiel, Burton G. 1989. Efficient market hypothesis. In *The new Palgrave: Finance,* ed. John Eatwell, Murray Milgate, and Peter Newman. New York: W. W. Norton.

Manley, John. 1970. *The politics of finance.* Boston: Little Brown.

Manning, Robert. 195. Tax bill: Congressional taxwriters set to turn back clock on capital gains. *Tax Notes* 69:397–98.

McChesney, Fred C. 1987. Rent extraction and rent creation in the economic theory of regulation. *Journal of Legal Studies* 16:101–18.

Munzer, Stephen R. 1982. A theory of retroactive legislation. *Texas Law Review* 61:425–80.

Musgrave, Richard A. 1959. *The theory of public finance.* New York: McGraw-Hill, Inc.

———. 1967. In defense of an income concept. *Harvard Law Review* 81:44–62.

Muth, John. 1961. Rational expectations and the theory of price movements. *Econometrica* 29:315–35.

Niskanen, William A. 1971. *Bureaucracy and representative government.* Chicago: Aldin Publishing Co.

Nolan, John S., and Victor Thuronyi. 1983. Retroactive application of changes in IRS or treasury department position. *Taxes* 61:777–87.

Noll, Roger G., and James E. Krier. 1990. Some implications of cognitive psychology for risk regulation. *Journal of Legal Studies* 19 (2): 747–79.

Nozick, Robert. 1974. *Anarchy, state, and utopia.* New York: Basic Books, Inc.

Olson, Mancur. 1965. *The logic of collective action: public goods and the theory of groups.* Cambridge, Mass.: Harvard University Press.

Pechman, Joseph. 1967. Comprehensive income taxation: A comment. *Harvard Law Review* 81:63–67.

Peltzman, Sam. 1976. Toward a more general theory of regulation. *Journal of Law and Economics* 19:211–40.

Ramseyer, Mark J., and Minoru Nakazato. 1989. Tax transitions and the protection racket: A reply to professors Graetz and Kaplow. *Virginia Law Review* 75:1155–75.

Robinson, Toni. 1987. Retroactivity: The case for better regulation of federal tax regulators. *Ohio State Law Journal* 48:773–813.

Rock, Cecily W., and Daniel N. Shaviro. 1987. Passive losses and the improvement of net income measurement. *Virginia Tax Review* 7:1–55.

Rosen, Harvey S. 1995. *Public finance.* 4th ed. Burr Ridge, Ill.: Richard D. Irwin, Inc.

Sanchirico, Chris William. 1997. Taxes versus legal rules as instruments for equity: A more equitable view. Columbia University Law School, New York.

Sansing, Richard, and Peter M. VanDoren. 1994. Escaping the transitional gains trap. *Journal of Policy Analysis and Management* 13:565–70.

Schattschneider, Emil. 1935. *Politics, pressures, and the tariff.* Englewood Cliffs, N.J.: Prentice-Hall.

———. 1960. *The semi-sovereign people: A realist's view of democracy in America.* New York: Holt, Rinehart and Winston.

Sen, Amartya. 1982. *Choices, welfare and measurement.* Oxford: Basil Blackwell.

Shachar, Avishai. 1984. From income to consumption tax: Criteria for rules of transition. *Harvard Law Review* 97:1581–609.

Shaviro, Daniel N. 1989a. Selective limitations on tax benefits. *University of Chicago Law Review* 56:1189–260.

———. 1989b. Risk and accrual: The tax treatment of nonrecourse debt. *Tax Law Review* 44:401–57.

———. 1990. Beyond public choice and public interest: A study of the legislative process as illustrated by tax legislation in the 1980s. *University of Pennsylvania Law Review* 139:1–123.

———. 1992. An efficiency analysis of realization and recognition rules under the federal income tax. *Tax Law Review* 48:1–68.

———. 1995. Risk-based rules and the taxation of capital income. *Tax Law Review* 50:643–724.

———. 1997. *Do deficits matter?* Chicago: University of Chicago Press.

———. 1999. Effective marginal tax rates on low-income households. Employment Policies Institute, Washington, D.C.

Sheppard, Lee A. 1990. The obstacles to corporate integration. *Tax Notes* 47:1168.

Shiller, Robert J. 1981. Do stock prices move too much to be justified by subsequent changes in dividends. *American Economic Review* 71:421–35.

———. 1998. Social Security and institutions for intergenerational, intragenerational, and international risk sharing. Paper presented at Carnegie-Rochester Public Policy Conference, Rochester, N.Y., April 24–25.

Simon, Herbert. 1957. *Models of man*. New York: Wiley.

Simons, Henry C. 1938. *Personal income taxation: The definition of income as a problem of fiscal policy*. Chicago: University of Chicago Press.

Slawson, W. David. 1960. Constitutional and legislative considerations in retroactive lawmaking. *California Law Review* 48:216–51.

Stavins, Robert N. 1995. Transactions costs and tradeable permits. *Journal of Environmental Economics and Management* 29:133–48.

Strnad, Jeff. 1991. Tax depreciation and risk. California Institute of Technology Social Science Working Paper 765. Los Angeles: California Institute of Technology.

Sunstein, Cass R. 1997. *Free markets and social justice*. New York: Oxford University Press.

Surrey, Stanley S. 1957. The Congress and the tax lobbyist—how special tax provisions get enacted. *Harvard Law Review* 70:1145–82.

———. 1973. *Pathways to tax reform*. Cambridge, Mass.: Harvard University Press.

Thaler, Richard H. 1991. *Quasi-rational economics*. New York: Russell Sage Foundation.

Thompson, Barton H. 1997. The endangered species act: A case study in takings and incentives. *Stanford Law Review* 49:305–80.

Tribe, Laurence H. 1988. *American constitutional law*. Mineola, N. Y.: Foundation Press.

Truman, David. 1951. *The governmental process: Political interests and public opinion*. New York: Alfred A. Knopf.

Tullock, Gordon. 1959. Problems of majority voting. *Journal of Political Economy* 67:571–79.

———. 1975. The transitional gains trap. *Bell Journal of Economics* 6:671–78.

———. 1989. *The economics of special privilege and rent seeking*. Boston: Kluwer Academic Publishers.

———. 1993. *Rent seeking*. Brookfield, Vt.: Edward Elgar Publishers.

Tversky, Amos, and Daniel Kahneman. 1973. Availability: A heuristic for judging frequency and probability. *Cognitive Psychology* 5:207–32.

———. 1974. Judgment under uncertainty: Heuristics and biases. *Science* 185:1124–31.

U.S. Treasury Department. 1984. *Tax reform for fairness, simplicity, and economic growth*. Washington, D.C.: U. S. Government Printing Office.

———. 1985. *The president's tax reform proposals to the Congress for fairness, growth, and simplicity*. Washington, D.C.: U. S. Government Printing Office.

———. 1992. *Report on integration of the individual and corporate tax systems: Taxing business income once*. Washington, D.C.: U. S. Government Printing Office.

Warren, Alvin C. 1981. The relation and integration of individual and corporate income taxes. *Harvard Law Review* 94:717–800.

———. 1993. Commentary—financial contract innovation and income tax policy. *Harvard Law Review* 107:460–92.

———. 1996. How much capital income taxed under an income tax is exempt under a cash-flow tax? *Tax Law Review* 52:1–16.

Weinstein, Neil. 1980. Unrealistic optimism about future life events. *Journal of Personality and Social Psychology* 38:806–21.

Witte, John F. 1985. *The politics and development of the federal income tax.* Madison, Wisc.: University of Wisconsin Press.

Zelenak, Lawrence. 1989. Are rifle shot transition rules and other ad hoc tax legislation constitutional? *Tax Law Review* 44:563–625.

Zodrow, George R. 1981. Implementing tax reform. *National Tax Journal* 34:401–18.

———. 1985. Optimal tax reform in the presence of adjustment costs. *Journal of Public Economics* 27:211–30.

———. 1991. On the "traditional" and "new" views of dividend taxation. *National Tax Journal* 44:497–509.